Certain People

Books by Stephen Birmingham

YOUNG MR. KEEFE

BARBARA GREER

THE TOWERS OF LOVE

THOSE HARPER WOMEN

FAST START, FAST FINISH

"OUR CROWD"

THE RIGHT PEOPLE

HEART TROUBLES

THE GRANDEES

THE LATE JOHN MARQUAND

THE RIGHT PLACES

CERTAIN PEOPLE

Certain People

America's Black Elite

Stephen Birmingham

Little, Brown and Company — Boston — Toronto

COPYRIGHT © 1977 BY STEPHEN BIRMINGHAM
ALL RIGHTS RESERVED. NO PART OF THIS BOOK MAY BE REPRODUCED
IN ANY FORM OR BY ANY ELECTRONIC OR MECHANICAL MEANS IN-
CLUDING INFORMATION STORAGE AND RETRIEVAL SYSTEMS WITHOUT
PERMISSION IN WRITING FROM THE PUBLISHER, EXCEPT BY A RE-
VIEWER WHO MAY QUOTE BRIEF PASSAGES IN A REVIEW.

FIRST EDITION
T 05/77

LIBRARY OF CONGRESS CATALOGING IN PUBLICATION DATA
Birmingham, Stephen.
    Certain people.

    Includes index.
    1. Afro-Americans—Biography. 2. Upper classes—
United States. I. Title.
E185.96.B48   301.45′19′6073022   [B]   76–56221
ISBN 0–316–09642–3

Designed by Susan Windheim

*Published simultaneously in Canada
by Little, Brown & Company (Canada) Limited*

PRINTED IN THE UNITED STATES OF AMERICA

For

C. E. L.

"You have to live with yourself and so . . ."
— CHARLOTTE HAWKINS BROWN

"Oh, they're the upper crust all right. They ought to call themselves the National Association for the Advancement of *Certain* People!"
— A cabdriver in Atlanta

Foreword

A BOOK GROWS FROM MANY SOURCES — FROM PEOPLE, OF course, but in a variety of ways. Some books are painful to research, others pleasant. Some seem almost to research themselves.

When I first mentioned to friends (white) that I (also white) planned to write a book about the black upper crust in the United States, the first reaction of my friends was, inevitably, "But won't you have trouble getting to them? How will you get to know them? How will you get them to talk? After all, you're white. They're black."

What happened was that they got to know me.

Along the curiously convoluted but powerful grapevine that keeps the black aristocracy of America informed, from city to city, of what is going on, word spread very quickly that I was interested in the lives and histories of these "certain people." Letters arrived from people who had heard of this project — people offering to help, inviting me to their cities, their homes, and offering to share with me their experiences, feelings, and memories. Other people telephoned. All were enthusiastic. The feeling seemed to be that enough — perhaps too much — had been written about "problem" blacks, and blacks with problems. There was a feeling that ghetto blacks have been overexposed, even glamorized, and that the time had come for blacks of social achievement, education, and economic success — and who, in many cases, belong to families who had been achievers for many generations — to put aside their traditional reticence and step forward, and do a little boasting.

It would be impossible here to list all the people who stepped forward in this way and volunteered their lives and stories to this book, nor was it possible to use every life and every story that I got to know. But there are a number of people who deserve special thanks. First, I am enormously indebted to Mr. David Grafton of Chicago, who, hearing that I was writing this book, spent an extraordinary amount of time setting up appointments, arranging interviews, seeing to it that I overlooked few of his city's black elite, and pushing the news along the national grapevine. In Chicago, I also owe a large debt to Mr. and Mrs. John H. Johnson, to Mrs. Gertrude Johnson Williams, to Mr. Basil Phillips, and to other editors and officers of the Johnson Publishing Company, who not only supplied me with valuable personal and corporate information but also gave me generous access to the *Ebony* photo library. Nor should I overlook other Chicago Johnsons — none of whom are related to each other — such as Mr. and Mrs. George Johnson, Mr. Al Johnson, and Mr. Bob Johnson, all of whom deserve words of thanks. Not everyone in Chicago is named Johnson, and I am also grateful to Mrs. Etta Mouton Barnett, Mr. Bill Berry, Mr. Alvin Boutte, Dr. Margaret Burroughs, Dr. William C. Clake, Mr. George Coleman, Mr. and Mrs. Eugene Dibble III and their children, the late Dr. T. R. M. Howard, Mrs. Jewel Lafontant, Mrs. Barbara Proctor, Mrs. Bettie Pullen-Walker, and Dr. and Mrs. Lowell Zollar.

In Atlanta, my old friend Dr. Charles Turner was especially helpful. In that city, I would also like to thank Mr. Owen Funderburg, Mr. and Mrs. Henry Cooke Hamilton,

Mrs. Freddye Henderson, Mr. Donald Hollowell, Mrs. Edward Miller, and Dr. and Mrs. Asa G. Yancey. In Memphis, I must thank Mr. Ronald Anderson Walter, who, throughout the two years it took to prepare this book, maintained a lively interest in the project and a lively correspondence with its author. I would also like to thank Mrs. Lois Conyers, Mrs. Dorothy Dobbins, Mr. and Mrs. John W. Fleming, and Mrs. Margaret Hough — all of Cincinnati.

In Washington, D.C., for their help and interest I would like to thank the Hon. Henry E. Catto, Jr., Mrs. Beverly Gasner, Mrs. Mary Gibson Hundley, Mr. Warren Robbins, Mr. and Mrs. John W. Syphax, Mr. William T. Syphax, and Mrs. Anne Teabeau.

In New York City, a number of people were particularly helpful, including Dr. George Cannon, Mr. Christopher Edley, Mrs. Josephine Premice Fales, Mr. Butler Henderson, Miss Gerri Major, Mr. and Mrs. Henry Lee Moon, Mr. Guichard Parris, Miss Frances Sanders-Bisagna, Mr. Bobby Short, Mrs. Jane White Viazzi, and Mr. Carl Younger.

I would also like to acknowledge the pleasure it has been to work editorially with Mr. Ned Bradford of Little, Brown, and to remember the early help and support of another brilliant editor, the late Mr. Harry Sions. As always, I am indebted to my friend and agent, Mrs. Carol Brandt, for her coolheaded guidance of the project from the outset.

While all the above people contributed greatly to the book, I alone must be held responsible for any of its omissions, errors, or shortcomings.

S. B.

Contents

List of Illustrations and Credits

I

The Gentry

Polish

FOR NEARLY FIFTY YEARS, DURING THE FIRST HALF OF THE twentieth century, one of the most dominant, though comparatively little known, forces in Negro life in America (before the term "black" became fashionable) existed in the person of a doughty little dark-skinned woman named Charlotte Hawkins Brown, the founder and headmistress of a school called the Palmer Memorial Institute in Sedalia, North Carolina, not far from Greensboro. Mrs. Brown, who — since she had received a number of honorary degrees — preferred to be addressed as "Doctor Brown," was originally from Boston, and Palmer Memorial Institute was named after her late friend, also a Bostonian, Mrs. Alice Freeman Palmer.

Most Palmer graduates assumed that Alice Freeman Palmer was also black. She was, in fact, white, and was the second president of Wellesley College, from 1881 to 1887. When Alice Freeman Palmer and Charlotte Hawkins Brown met, they became friends, and both shared a concern for the quality of education that was then being offered to young Negroes in the South (Wellesley was one of the earliest women's colleges to admit blacks, and Booker T. Washington's daughter attended Wellesley). And, with Mrs.

Palmer's help, Charlotte Hawkins Brown had been able to get financial backing from certain wealthy New Englanders, and was able to open the doors of her school in Sedalia in 1902, the year that Alice Freeman Palmer died.

It had been Alice Freeman Palmer's idea that Palmer Institute should be a school for needy black children in North Carolina. But Dr. Brown had not exactly followed her late friend's wishes to the letter. The school that she founded was not at all a school for impoverished local Negroes. It was, instead, an exclusive preparatory school for the wealthiest and best-born black children in the United States. There were only a handful of day students from Sedalia and Greensboro. The rest, who were boarders, arrived by Pullman and in chauffeur-driven limousines. "We accept," Dr. Brown used to say, "only the *crème de la crème*. Anybody who is anybody sends their children to Palmer. They come to us, and we polish off any rough edges." Palmer Institute was, in other words, the first and only private black coeducational finishing school in America.

It was quite a thing to go to Palmer, and Dr. Brown never let her students forget it. The enrollment was small — between two and three hundred boys and girls. The tuition, though somewhat lower than that of the great New England prep schools, was high enough to make a Palmer education available only to the moneyed. Correct speech, manners, decorum, and deportment were stressed. So were neatness and cleanliness. At Palmer, if you arrived with a "colored accent," you were expected, by graduation, to have got rid of it, and to have learned to emulate Dr. Brown's own precise New England speech. Dr. Brown had a fetish about posture and another about table manners. There were no slouchers in the classroom or at the dinner table, and girls were taught to sit with their knees together and boys, when they crossed their legs, could do so only at the knee. At Palmer, you were taught never to blow on your soup to cool it, never to spoon it toward you, and never to slurp when swallowing it. Everyone had to study French. Everyone was required to learn piano, plus one other instrument, and there was a piano in every dormitory. Tennis was also emphasized. There were uniforms — three sets for the girls: gingham dresses for spring, navy blue skirts, blouses, and ties for fall and winter, and dress uniforms, which consisted of white, formal-length gowns and white gloves. The boys wore Palmer blazers, and there were formal dinners once a week for which the boys were required to wear tuxedos. There were also regular formal teas, where the boys wore cutaway coats, stiff collars, white shirts, black ties, and black shoes.

What the legendary "Miss Charlotte" Noland was to her exclusive, all-white Foxcroft School in Virginia, Charlotte Hawkins Brown was to the blacks who attended Palmer. Of matronly bearing, she had short hair and wore tiny round spectacles. Being from Boston, she wore her skirts unfashionably long and always wore sensible black oxford shoes. She was always gloved, and always hatted. She had two favorite coats — a mink with a matching hat, and a Persian lamb with a matching mink-trimmed toque. She also had — or had had — a husband, who was something of a mystery. He was never mentioned, and had obviously vanished from her life long before she founded Palmer.

She was an unabashed snob. It was better, she taught, to be an Episcopalian than to be a Baptist. Her niece, Marie, had married Nat "King" Cole, of whom she thoroughly disapproved, since she had little use for Negroes who went into sports or show business. But when Nat Cole visited Palmer, and played the piano for an informal gathering of students, the students loved him, and finally convinced Dr. Brown that her nephew-in-law might actually be a legitimate person, even a gentleman. Her two "best friends," she liked to say, were Mary McLeod Bethune, who founded Bethune-

Cookman College, and Mrs. Eleanor Roosevelt. Her conversation was sprinkled with references to "dear Mary" and "dear Eleanor." In reality, this was not quite the case. Her relationship with Mrs. Roosevelt was cordial, but hardly intimate; the two women did not even call each other by their first names. And, on Mrs. Roosevelt's part, it involved a certain amount of condescension. Charlotte Hawkins Brown was one of those whom Eleanor Roosevelt often referred to as "our good colored people." In the case of Mrs. Bethune, the two women were actually archrivals. Dr. Brown regarded Mrs. Bethune as her chief competitor in the field of Negro education. Mrs. Bethune was also on good terms with Mrs. Roosevelt, and the two black women vied fiercely for the First Lady's attention. Whenever Mrs. Bethune was handed a new honorary degree, Dr. Brown struggled for one of her own to match it and to even the score.

Charlotte Hawkins Brown was, needless to say, a strict disciplinarian. Everyone at Palmer had to learn to recite the school's credo, a verse that Charlotte Hawkins Brown had composed:

> *I have to live with myself and so*
> *I want to be fit for myself to know.*
> *I want to be able as days go by*
> *Always to look myself straight in the eye.*
> *I don't want to stand with the setting sun*
> *And hate myself for the things I've done.*

Dr. Brown stood daily at the door of Palmer's chapel with a box of Kleenex in one hand. Whenever a girl appeared with rouge on her lips, Dr. Brown would say firmly, "Palmer girls *do not* wear lipstick," and, with her Kleenex, she would just as firmly wipe the offending lipstick off. When she was on the warpath, she signaled it by wearing purple. Once, a small infraction of the school rules had been committed, and the students decided to stick together; no one would name the person who had committed the misdeed. So, in purple, Dr. Brown expelled the entire student body, and presented each boy and girl with a ticket home. One young man, who was from San Francisco, was quite sure that, in time, Dr. Brown would relent and invite her students back. So, instead of going to San Francisco, he went only as far as Chicago, where he had an uncle he could visit, and cashed in the balance of his ticket. Sure enough, after a few weeks Dr. Brown told her students that they could come back to school. But when the San Francisco boy returned, and Dr. Brown discovered what he had done, she sent him to San Francisco all over again — for dishonesty and not doing what he was told.

Dr. Brown never used the term "black." To her generation, to call someone black was to call him a dirty name. She occasionally used the word "Negro," and, less occasionally, "colored," or "people of color." Most often she would say "one of us," or "our kind," or "our sort." But when she asked, "Is he one of us?" or, "Is she our kind?" she was not asking simply whether the person was a Negro. These expressions had special connotations. A person who was "our kind" was, first of all, an educated person. He was also a person from a good, and educated, family. He was a person who was well-spoken. He was also, in most cases, a person with light skin and white features, whose nose didn't spread and whose hair didn't kink. Even though white features were an indication of illegitimacy somewhere back in the family tree, it was Dr. Brown's unspoken belief that it was probably a good thing to have good white ancestors as well as good black ones.

Though Dr. Brown liked to say that her school contained not only "the best Negroes," but also offered "the best in Negro education," not all of her students agreed with her.

"I thought, if this is the best, then God help the rest," recalls one alumna of Palmer, who was particularly struck by the fact that, for all the emphasis on politeness, gentility, and good manners, Palmer students often behaved very badly. "They were snobby, rude to the help, acted as though they owned the world, and did terrible things to each other," she says. Once a group of older boys invited a group of newly arrived freshmen to go "snipe-hunting" with them. The newcomers innocently accepted the invitation, and discovered that snipe-hunting involved a fairly brutal initiation ritual, at the end of which the younger boys were left hung by the waist from their belts in the branches of trees.

Still, everybody who was anybody in the black world, as Dr. Brown put it, sent their children to Palmer. Madame C. J. Walker of Indianapolis, a lady tycoon who became, with a hair-straightening device, the first black woman millionaire, sent her children and grandchildren there, as did Madame Sarah Spencer Washington, whose Apex Hair Company made her rich in New Jersey. Paul Robeson's nieces went to Palmer, as did the daughter of Mantan Moreland — the big-eyed black comic character actor of early Hollywood films. The wealthy banking, real estate, and professional families from Atlanta — the Partees, the Yanceys, the Alexanders — many of whom have been rich for three or four generations — all sent their sons and daughters to Dr. Brown's school. Concert singer Carol Brice (whose father was the school's chaplain) is a Palmer alumna, as is Muriel Gassett, whose mother was a Dobbs, of the distinguished Atlanta family. Then there were Funderburgs, an illustrious family from Monticello, Georgia, and numerous sons and daughters of successful professional men — doctors, lawyers, educators, clergymen, and the like — all members in good standing of the black upper crust, or Establishment.

And the school was, in many ways, innovative. In order that her students might have a taste of what was being offered to the sons and daughters of upper-class whites, Dr. Brown instituted a program under which Palmer students spent several weeks each year at a New England prep school — usually Northfield and Mount Hermon Academies in Massachusetts. Dr. Brown was one of the first educators to offer "Negro History" as a regular, required course. She was also determined that her students be exposed to culture — to art, literature, and music — and, once a year, at Christmastime, the entire student body was required to perform Handel's *Messiah*. No Palmer student, however, ever learned a Negro spiritual. Spirituals, after all, were from the lower classes, the men who lifted the bales, toted the barges, and stooped to pick cotton in the fields.

But for all this the main emphasis at Palmer was on acquiring good breeding, social poise, and polish, and on imitating the ways, deportment, and social values of the white world. In 1941, Charlotte Hawkins Brown wrote and published a slender book of black etiquette called *The Correct Thing — To Do, To Say, To Wear*, with a subheading describing the contents as "A Ready Reference for The School Administrator, The Busy Teacher, The Office Girl, The Society Matron, The Discriminating Person." Dedicated to "The Youth of America," *The Correct Thing* became required reading at Palmer and is, in many ways, an interesting volume. On the surface, the book seems merely a rewording, if not a copy, of the rules of behavior delineated by Emily Post, and Dr. Brown fully acknowledges her debt to Mrs. Post in a bibliography. But, when examined closely, it is something else again. Under familiar headings such as "Table Service," "Grooming," "The Earmarks of a Lady," "Invitations, Etc.," "Travel," "Introductions," "How to Behave," one discovers that, though this is intended as an etiquette book for black ladies and gentlemen, never once is any mention made of the single most important factor that sets blacks apart — the color of their skin. In fact, the only reference to blackness or black people is in an oblique, almost shyly tentative sentence in the "Grooming" chapter, in which Dr. Brown selects a WASP, a Scandinavian, and a black to make her point:

> The arrangement of one's hair adds to or detracts from one's general appearance as it increases or decreases one's power of personality. Study the contour of your face carefully. What makes Katherine Hepburn or Greta Garbo or Marian Anderson *personality plus* may make you *personality minus.*

Black hair has, of course, always been a problem, as has been the black's alleged fondness for gaudy, ostentatious styles of dress. Dr. Brown's little book makes several allusions to this but, again, they are so oblique as to pass almost unnoticed. For example, in a section on how to behave "At the Dance," she advises, "Avoid being bizarre in dress or make-up. Do not be too conspicuous in an unbecoming hair dress. You will attract attention, but those whom you will attract will mark you as an ill-advised, poorly bred, unartistic creature."

In Emily Post's *Etiquette,* Mrs. Post uses quaintly fictionalized names of characters to illustrate her bits of advice — "Mrs. Wellbred" and "Mrs. Goodblood" always do the right thing in *Etiquette.* In *The Correct Thing,* however, Dr. Brown tends to use the names of prominent American black families which, perhaps, only a black would recognize. Her sample letters and invitations go out to "Mr. and Mrs. Ernest Washington," "Mr. and Mrs. W. A. Dobson," and "Mr. John Thomas Jones," and Dr. Brown's informal notes go out to persons with the somewhat flowery, labial, and foreign-sounding names which mothers of Dr. Brown's generation often gave their daughters — to Dear Lula, Dear Arona, Dear Yvonne, Dear Vesta, Dear Cecie, Norvelle,

Raven, Ghretta, Olivia, Mamie Ella, Elise, Nadine, and Mayme.

If there is one underlying theme in *The Correct Thing*, it is Know Your Place — know your place in the white world, and in the black. The book abounds in references to "your status" and "your social equals," and "your station in life." In a section on "Calling," for instance, Dr. Brown suggests:

> Making people in your neighborhood feel comfortable with a call, whether or not they are one's social equals, is a gracious thing and has its own reward in the satisfaction usually sought by people who embrace Christianity as a source of ethics. This call may be supplemented by an invitation to visit "our Sunday School," or to hear "our minister" or to come to the lecture at "our Community Center." . . .

No one, needless to say, in Dr. Brown's book is invited to a function at a country club but, instead, to hotels, church social rooms, or college halls. "Don't go where you're not wanted," Dr. Brown reminds. "You, of course, cannot be invited to all of the parties in town, or out of town." And in a section on business etiquette, Dr. Brown outlines rules of classic black subservience to the white ruling class: "Don't argue with the employer. Assume at least that he is right. Answer promptly always. Don't be afraid of being too courteous. Go out of your way to serve your employer. He will remember the little kindnesses not included in the pay envelope in a larger way some day." Finally, in an extraordinary section titled "Doors," Dr. Brown says:

> If one must knock on the door of a room or office, it must be a gentle tapping. When bidden to enter, take firm hold on the knob, turn it gently, pull the door open at least two-thirds of the way so as not to touch either the

door or door jamb, pause for just a second to recognize the person who may be looking your way, and as gently close the door as you opened it. Do not make the mistake of letting a self-closing door push you into the room, for it will embarrass you and prevent you from presenting your best appearance. Your doom may be sealed before you speak a word.

From Palmer Institute, Charlotte Hawkins Brown did her best to get her graduates into the best Eastern colleges — Wellesley, Vassar, Smith for the girls, and Yale or Harvard for the boys. Failing this, she tried to get them entered in the various emerging black colleges and universities in the South, particularly the "fashionable" ones, such as Talladega College in Alabama. A number of Palmer alumni are also graduates of Talladega. At Talladega, a girl was expected to join one of the "good" black sororities — Alpha Kappa Alpha or Delta Sigma Theta. Sigma Gamma Rho and Zeta Phi Beta were considered sororities for lower-class blacks. Fraternities were somewhat less important for the men, but a Palmer graduate was also expected to join a good one like Alpha *Phi* Alpha.

In 1950, when Charlotte Hawkins Brown was sixty-six, a fire badly damaged Palmer Memorial Institute. The school quietly went out of business not long after that and became a part of Bennett College in Greensboro. There was, after all, at that point no real need for an elite black prep school, since prep schools in New England and elsewhere in the country were by then clamoring to take in black students. Upper-class black boys and girls now go to Hotchkiss, Groton, Middlesex, and St. Marks. Still, the Palmer influence lingers on, and it is still considered "quite the thing" to have gone to Palmer.

Charlotte Hawkins Brown, of course, represents the thoughts and values of upper-class blacks in the thirties and forties, and to people in the 1970's her views and the way she ran her school might seem ridiculously antique. And yet, in a sense, she represented great progress toward a degree of black self-confidence and self-assurance. She had, for example, at least one predecessor in the black etiquette-book field. He was Edward S. Green of Washington, who, in 1920, published *The National Capital Code of Etiquette Dedicated to the Colored Race.* Mr. Green's is a much more fawning, self-effacing volume — virtually a textbook on Uncle Tomism — and reflects poignantly the much sadder state of affairs that existed then. In his book, Mr. Green advises, "Strive to please . . . be a good 'listener.' You will be amazed at the reputation you will presently gain for being intelligent, without having to express any opinions yourself." In his preface, he explains that "This volume has been prepared with the end in mind of properly fitting the young man or woman to occupy their proper place in society; to assist them in acquiring the poise and bearing that is absolutely essential for their future happiness and welfare." Say little, Mr. Green counsels; strive to be inconspicuous; wear dark colors, black stockings.

In a particularly touching chapter on "Correct Letter Writing," Mr. Green takes up the case of a fictional Edgar H. Wilkins, who is writing, humbly, to ask his friend, the equally fictional John H. Edwards, for a loan. The loan is for $15.00. Mr. Green offers an example of how Mr. Wilkins might compose his letter ("There are few of my friends to whom I should write for financial assistance, but I feel that you will understand and appreciate . . .") and how Mr. Edwards might turn him down ("I have not half the amount you desire now on deposit.") Next, the author considers the possibility that Edwards has given Wilkins his loan, but that Wilkins has failed to repay it. Less than three weeks have gone by, but the tone of the correspondence changes considerably — from "Dear Ed" to "My dear Wilkins" — as Edwards's reminder letter ("I should appreciate your courtesy in giving this your early attention") goes out to his friend. Still Wilkins does not respond and, by September 10, Edwards has had enough and writes as follows:

> Mr. Edgar H. Wilkins,
> 1440 Kennard St., City
> Dear Sir:
>   Over a month ago, I wrote you courteously concerning the $15.00 loaned you early in July. You are of course aware that this should have been paid long ago. Your failure to meet your obligation and your continued silence concerning the matter, if persisted in, will eventually destroy the respect and confidence I have always held for you.
>   My patience is becoming exhausted and I shall expect a satisfactory reply from you by return mail.
> Yours very respectfully,
JOHN H. EDWARDS

The reader of *The Capital Code of Etiquette* is left in suspense as to the final outcome of the Wilkins-Edwards affair.

Reaching her stride nearly a generation after the publication of Mr. Green's little volume, Charlotte Hawkins Brown was an advocate of much more pride on the part of blacks, even though, along with pride, she advised a certain amount of caution. Today, it might be easy to assume that what Charlotte Hawkins Brown stood for has disappeared entirely. It is true that many blacks would now label Dr. Brown an "Aunt Tom," or an "Oreo" — referring to the cookie that is black on the outside, but white within. Many blacks would ridicule her attitudes and pronouncements. It is because of people like Charlotte Hawkins Brown that the National Association for the Advancement of Colored People — the backbone of which was formed by many of her

former elite-minded students — has been sneeringly labeled
(by less affluent blacks) "The National Association for the
Advancement of *Certain* People." There was no doubt in
Charlotte Hawkins Brown's mind that *certain* people were
better than other people, and more "fit" for themselves to
know. What Dr. Brown stood for were the subtle but nonetheless powerful forces that differentiate social classes. She
separated the black *haves* from the white *haves,* and she also
separated the black *haves* from the black *have-nots.* Even
more important, she separated the old-line black families
and their children from a newer generation of blacks who
were struggling out of poverty and, in one way or another,
managing to achieve a certain degree of affluence. Self-made
blacks she considered the gauche *nouveau riche.* They were
simply not in the same class as her *crème de la crème.* One
might suppose that, in this day and age, the distinctions of
class that she drew, and the differences she represented, no
longer pertain to the black community. Alas, that is not
quite the case — not yet.

The Bootstrappers

2

"How I Got Over"

AN OLD NEGRO GOSPEL SONG IS CALLED "HOW I GOT OVER," and it celebrates "getting over" to Jesus. But the phrase also has a more general, secular meaning in the black world, which, in the modern idiom, could be translated to mean "how I made it" — in a business sense — from next to nothing at all to huge success and riches. A small, wizened, very black lady of eighty-five sits today in a large, carpeted office behind a big desk, high above Chicago's bustling Michigan Avenue, with an imposing view of the lake beyond, and talks, in a richly Southern accent, of "how I got over." She owns the modern eleven-story tower of steel and glass in which her office sits, and much more — including an AM radio station, part of a cosmetics business, and the big house in East Drexel Square in which she lives. She is Mrs. Gertrude Johnson Williams — "Miz Gert" to her friends — vice president of the Johnson Publishing Company, which publishes *Ebony* and several other magazines, of which her son, John H. Johnson, is president and chief executive officer. John Johnson is often called the wealthiest black man in America, but his mother, Mrs. Williams, takes full and unabashed credit for her son's success. "That's right, I did it!" she says cheerfully. "I'm the woman behind the man! I put everything I had into him. I had strength, and I had health, and I had determination. I had faith in myself and in the Lord, and now" — she makes a sweeping gesture — "just you look and see how it's all come back to us. Every day, I look around, at this beautiful building and all we've done, and I just sit back and look at how I got over, and I thank the Lord." Mrs. Williams has never heard of Charlotte Hawkins Brown, nor of the Palmer Memorial Institute, and if she had she would be unimpressed. On the other hand, she likes to remind visitors that not long ago, when she visited Atlanta, she was invited to dinner by the governor of Georgia at the Executive Mansion, and that the leading citizens of the town gave her a surprise birthday party. "The Lord brought me over," she says. "And now, it's like an old saying the old folks had in the South — all I have to do now is sit back and spit in the ashes!"

A conducted tour of high school students, exclusively black, who are being shown around the offices of Johnson Publishing, pauses outside Mrs. Williams's office door, and the tour guide says, in hushed tones, "This is the office of Mrs. Gertrude Johnson Williams, Mr. John Johnson's mother, who got him started with a loan of five hundred dollars and put her furniture up for collateral." "That's right, honey!" Mrs. Williams calls out. "I'm the one, I'm the one that did it! I'm the mother, and with the Lord's help I got us over."

Though Mrs. Williams gives a major share of credit to the Lord, a certain amount of mortal business acumen must not be ruled out, nor should a good deal of restless ambition and a certain vision. In the little town of Arkansas City, Arkansas, where Gertrude Johnson Williams grew up (Williams was her second husband; John Johnson's father was killed in a sawmill accident when John was six years old) there was not much to offer her only son. There was not even a local high school that blacks could attend. And Mr.

Williams was not much help. "Oh, he always made money — he always *worked*," Gertrude Williams says. "But the trouble was, Williams just couldn't *hold on* to any money. He spent the whole of it on drink and gambling." In order to scrape together tuition money to send young John to high school in a nearby city, his mother went to work, running a field kitchen for a dredging company crew, where the boss was kind enough to let her take home food to feed her family, "tote privileges," as it was called in the South. At one point, when things looked particularly dark, Gertrude Williams's mother offered to take the boy. The proposition was placed before young John, who had also fallen into the habit of calling his mother "Miz Gert," and he said firmly, "I want to stay with Miz Gert." His grandmother was indignant, and said, "Who *is* this Miz Gert?" He replied, "Miz Gert is my mother." It was at this point that Gertrude Williams began to realize that her son might possess spunk and determination to match her own.

Still, when John graduated from the eighth grade in Arkansas City, there was not enough money for the high school tuition the following year. So his mother made him go back to grade school in the fall and take the eighth grade all over again — much to his displeasure.

In 1933, Gertrude Williams was fed up — both with Arkansas City and with Mr. Williams. She was in her early forties and her son was fifteen, and she saw no future for either of them where they were. "I had a friend in Chicago," Mrs. Williams says, "and she wrote me and said that things were better for colored folks up there. So I said to Williams, 'I'm going. You can come too if you like, but if you don't like I'm going anyway. You can't stop me, and nobody can stop me.' He said he was staying, so I said goodbye, and Johnny and me got us on the bus." In Chicago, despite the Depression, she got a job "working days for a white lady," worked evenings as a seamstress, and rented a tiny flat. Six months later, Mr. Williams showed up. "I told him he could stay if he wanted, but he wasn't going to tell *me* what to do, and I told him, 'I'm not going to be *responsible* for you. You can stay on my terms, but if you don't like my terms, out you go, 'cause it's *my* name that's on this lease!' " He stayed, and on her terms.

Chicago in the twenties and thirties had become a Mecca for upwardly mobile blacks. In those days, Chicago was the railroad capital of America, and railroad lines fanned out from Chicago like filaments of a spider's web. The railroads, with their demand for conductors, brakemen, and Pullman car porters, had attracted blacks to the city, and there was already a large black community that was stable, prospering, and displaying many of the attributes of a solid middle class. (To be a Pullman car porter in those days was a mark of great status for a black man; to work the Pullman cars, a man had to be trustworthy, a "gentleman," the work was steady and the pay, with tips, was good; similarly, it was a mark of status to work for the Post Office, and the Post Office in those days relied primarily on the railroads.) In Chicago, before it happened significantly elsewhere, many black families already owned their own homes, had automobiles, and were sending their children to college. The hopes of Chicago's blacks were high.

Gertrude Williams already knew her son was smart. When he was three she had taught him the alphabet, and he could read before he entered the first grade. At Chicago's black DuSable High School, still pushed and encouraged by the relentless Gertrude, young John was an honor student. He became president of his class, then president of the student council, editor of the school newspaper, and editor of the senior class yearbook. (For many years, since he never graduated from college — though he has received a number of honorary degrees — John Johnson listed these achievements in his paragraph in *Who's Who*.) At John Johnson's high school commencement, the speaker was one Earl B. Dickerson, an executive of the Supreme Life Insurance Company of America, one of the largest black-owned insurance companies in the country. Dickerson was impressed with the young student body president, and hired him as an office boy for $6 a week. That was in 1936, when jobs of any sort, for young men of any color, were not easy to get.

Part of Johnson's job at Supreme Life was to comb through magazines and newspapers for black news items, and to compile a summary of these for the company president. He was also, as a result of his high school newspaper experience, placed in charge of putting out the company house organ. As he collected news items on blacks, he noticed a significant fact. Whenever a black made an important achievement, or outdid a white man, that made news. Similarly, it was news whenever a black man committed a crime. But no national publication devoted itself to the day-to-day existences, and problems, of normal black people who led routine, unheralded lives. He discussed this with friends, who agreed that there appeared to be a need for a black news digest. Moonlighting after hours at Supreme Life, and quietly "borrowing" the use of the company's printing equipment, Johnson began putting together a dummy issue of the kind of publication he had in mind. To seek subscribers, he decided he would have to send out direct-mail fliers, but that would require money. It is still not easy for a black to borrow money, and it was much harder in 1942. After several unfruitful visits to loan companies, he went to his mother.

"I didn't have any money," Gertrude Williams says, "but I said, 'I'll pray on it.'" Typically, her husband was unwilling to help. "He just wasn't interested," she says. "I told John the only thing I owned was my furniture." Would she be willing to sell some of her furniture? "I'll have to pray on that," she told him. A week or so later, he came to her again. He had learned of a man who would loan him the money if the furniture were put up as collateral. Again, she said she would first have to pray. When he came to her a third time, she agreed to let the man come to appraise her furniture. He came, and told her that $500 was the most money he could offer her, and, with that, every bit of property Gertrude Williams owned was mortgaged.

The $500 worth of advertising fliers, however, quickly yielded $6,000 worth of subscription orders. John Johnson's monthly *Negro Digest,* as he called it, was on its way, and the Johnson Publishing Company was born. Still, in the first months, the sledding was not always easy. At one point, $100 was desperately needed and John Johnson and his mother went to a well-to-do black friend and asked to borrow the money. They were refused, and so Gertrude Williams went to her white employer, who loaned her the money. "She trusted me, she knew I was reliable." (Later on, when the same black friend saw that Johnson Publishing was beginning to be successful, "He tried to get on the bandwagon," Gertrude Williams says, "and I told him, 'You wouldn't give us money when we needed it. Now we don't need your money.' ") Today, the Johnson Publishing Company, conservatively estimated to be worth between $50,000,000 and $60,000,000, is solely owned by John Johnson, his mother, and his wife, Eunice. When John Johnson's stepfather also tried to get on the bandwagon, he was given a job as a building superintendent.

Gertrude Williams does not speak in the polished, cultivated accents of a Charlotte Hawkins Brown. In fact, she considers emphasis on such matters sheer frippery. "I'm the same woman I always was," she says. "Folks used to say to me, Miz Gert, what you got on your *mind?* I said, just one thing — that little boy. It's the same today. My duties now are to see over everything. I fill his place when he's away. I can sign any check he can sign. I'm there whenever he's honored. I got so many plaques and awards I can't count 'em! It's because I believed the Lord was going to bring us out. Nobody gets between my son and me, not even his wife. If it's a question of her or me, it's me he listens to. I'm his mother, and I'm his best friend, because he always trusted me to be a Christian and a mother. I taught him to wait and pray, and he saw how I suffered and how I sacrificed to bring him on up. During the early days, he worked, and I worked. I took in sewing night and day. I helped him buy an old second-handed car when he needed it, and he worked nights with a chauffeur service for college students. Now I spend Christmas and New Year's in Palm Springs, California. I've been to Hawaii, Mexico, and Canada, but I haven't changed. I still help everybody — we have to help each other — and if I'm not at Emanuel Baptist Church every Sunday morning, a dozen people call to ask me where I'm at. I've got some nieces and nephews and cousins in the South — they write and ask for help, and I help them. I send them something every Christmas, and I don't just send *stuff*. I send *money*. And I send money to friends, too, that needs help. I say, 'The Lord knew what he was doing when he didn't give me more children, just my son. It was the Lord that brought us *both* over.' I've got nothing against anybody, I've got love in my heart, and my love of my son is like my love of the Lord. A girl friend once asked me, 'Miz Gert, would you take *money* for him?' I just laughed and said, 'Honey, there isn't that much money in the whole wide world!' "

~ 3 ~

Apartment Hunting

THE TALL BUILDINGS OF STEEL AND STONE AND GLASS THAT line Chicago's North Lake Shore Drive array themselves in a wide arc along the shore of Lake Michigan, a glittering symbol of the city's wealth and power. These proud apartment houses, curving northward in a seemingly endless procession of canopied entrances and uniformed doormen, address the morning sun and the shimmer of the lake in an attitude of limitless self-satisfaction. The buildings are, of course, a magnificent facade, a screen that hides a somewhat different situation because just a few short blocks to the west of Lake Shore Drive the city shrugs its shoulders and collapses into an appalling slum of cheap rooming houses and dingy bars, weed-filled vacant lots and cracked sidewalks where it is dangerous to walk at night, an area that has become predominantly black. Still, North Lake Shore Drive — the "Gold Coast," as it is called — remains Chicago's most prestigious address. Here, in vast floor-through apartments and a few remaining private city mansions, live Chicago's rich.

Along Lake Shore Drive are not only the homes of Chicago's Old Guard — Swifts, McCormicks, Wrigleys, Swearingens, Seeburgs, Paepckes, and Palmers — but also the newrick *arrivistes.* Anyone who has prospered mightily in the city is expected to move to Lake Shore. Still, there was more than the usual stir caused in 1970 when Mr. and Mrs. John H. Johnson moved into not one, but two, huge apartments at the Carlyle, at 1040 North Lake Shore, one of the most opulent buildings on that opulent street. It was not just that Mr. and Mrs. Johnson were black, but the alleged means by which the Johnsons got their double apartment was the talk of the town.

The Johnsons, so the story went, wanted to buy an apartment on the Carlyle's twenty-fourth floor. But a neighbor in an adjoining apartment objected. And so John Johnson, who is known in the rich black community affectionately as "The Godfather," made the neighbor an offer he couldn't refuse — and asked the neighbor to name his price for the apartment. The neighbor named the price, Johnson wrote out a check, and bought the second apartment. The Johnsons knocked down walls, threw the two dwellings together, and created what is now considered to be one of the largest — and is certainly one of the most spectacular — apartments in town.

What actually happened was something a little different. The Johnsons had already owned, for several years previous to their dramatic move, an apartment on the eighteenth floor of the Carlyle. But they had been looking for a larger place — higher up, with a better view. And Eunice Johnson, a stylish, bubbly, throaty-voiced woman, had been toying with the idea of putting two apartments together. When an apartment on the twenty-fourth floor became available, the only problem was to persuade the owner of the second apartment on the floor to sell. Prejudice was not the issue, and the woman who owned the second apartment had no objection to living next door to blacks. But she had just redecorated her apartment, and was reluctant to give it up. John and Eunice Johnson not only made her a handsome offer for her place, but also sweetened it with $15,000 extra for the woman to redecorate the Johnsons' old apartment on the eighteenth floor. And so the trade was amicably arranged. "She was very nice about it," Eunice Johnson says. "When she finished her redecorating on the eighteenth floor, she wrote me a note saying that she hadn't spent the entire fifteen thousand, and enclosed a check for me for six hundred dollars' change."

And so the Johnsons have their double apartment. They turned decorators Arthur Elrod and William Raiser loose on the place, and, some $250,000 later, the apartment was all done in colors of honey, beige, gold, caramel, and earth brown. "We wanted colors that would match our skin tones," says Eunice Johnson, a fashion-conscious lady who is also a talented interior designer. The walls of the huge double living room are composed of unfinished strips of barn siding, alternating with panels of beige marble. A large coffee table is made of alternating strips of zebrawood and mahogany, with strips of burnished brass at the edges. The thick woven-to-size rug is of custard-colored beige, and the floors are of petrified wood. A room that serves as an office-den has walls covered with leather. Opening off the long central foyer are two marbled and gold-fitted powder rooms, one for ladies and one for gentlemen. Both Eunice and John Johnson have private bed-sitting room suites in the apartment, as do their children, John, Jr., and Linda, and their bathrooms are equipped with bidets and sunken Jacuzzi whirlpool baths. Beds operate electrically, and closet and dressing room doors swing out to reveal countless built-in compartments with Lucite trays for gloves, hose, lingerie, purses, an entire closet for shoes, another for dresses, another for furs. Library walls are covered with real leather, and closet walls are upholstered with imitation fur. Most spectacular, perhaps, is the Johnson kitchen, which, again, is a double affair, with two complete cooking-serving areas, four refrigerator-freezers, two stoves, an electronic oven, a charcoal pit for barbecuing, six sinks, a double pantry, three dishwashers. Though the Johnsons employ a cook and butler, Eunice Johnson is not above going into her kitchen to whip up a pound cake for a special guest. She loves to show off her apartment, pointing to a large Picasso that dominates the dining room, to the two fully plumbed bars, to sliding room dividers that disappear into walls. At Eunice Johnson's dinner table, glasses are of the heaviest crystal, tableware is of the heaviest silver, the coffee cups are of the thinnest Limoges, and the napkins are of the heaviest damask. And yet, for all the luxury that surrounds her, Eunice Johnson is able to view her circumstances with a certain humor. Showing a photograph of herself chatting with Marc Chagall, she says, "When I first met him at the White House—" and then breaks off with a laugh. "Listen to me," she says. "Listen to me saying, 'When I met him at the White House'!"

Eunice Walker Johnson, whom John Johnson married in 1941, is also from a small town in Arkansas, but comes from a very different sort of background. Along with her considerably lighter skin, straight hair, and what blacks call "nice white looks," she is also of good family. Though she did not attend Palmer, she is very much the "Palmer type." She graduated from fashionable Talladega College and, in fact, her maternal grandfather, William H. McAlpine, founded Talladega, which was originally established as a school for Baptist ministers. Grandpa McAlpine was a close friend of Booker T. Washington's. At Talladega, Eunice Walker was properly a member of Alpha Kappa Alpha and, after college, she went on to get a master's degree at Loyola University. Her father's father was a property owner in Alabama and, though far from rich, the Walkers had been comfortably off for some time, and were a far cry from the abject poverty in which John Johnson grew up. Eunice's father was a physician, and her mother was principal of the local high school. Two of her brothers are also medical doctors, and her sister is a Ph.D. For John Johnson, marrying Eunice was a distinct move upward in the black social scale, and for Eunice, her marriage to John Johnson was also considered a "catch," since by 1941 he was already a young man whose star was visibly on the rise.

John Johnson also gives his mother full credit for his share in his success. "She pushed me all the way," he says. "For a long time, I never even knew that fathers were necessary. We were poor, we were sharecroppers, and there was never enough money to pay the boss man, but it was a wonderful, happy childhood." He is more casual about attributing success to prayer and the Lord, however, and thinks that his own inventiveness as a salesman was a major factor. In the beginning, there was resistance on the part of distributors and news dealers against placing *Negro Digest* on newsstands. It wouldn't sell, they claimed, and "Negroes don't buy magazines." To overcome this attitude, Johnson got on the telephone and spent days telephoning news dealers, in variously disguised voices, and asking, "Do you have the new issue of *Negro Digest?* You don't? Can you tell me where I can find it?" The little ploy worked, and dealers began placing orders. And the magazine did sell. Today, renamed *Black World,* and devoted largely to black literary matters, the magazine has a monthly circulation of over 50,000. "I'm often asked when *Negro Digest* first became successful," Johnson says, "and I say that it was with the first issue. It had to be, or there'd never have been a second issue."

Three years later, he was ready for a much more ambitious undertaking — a big, slick-paper picture magazine to be called *Ebony,* which was to be in size, appearance, and format an unabashed imitation of *Life,* which was then the giant of white American weeklies. When he was accused of trying to ape the white man's *Life,* Johnson shrugged off the criticism, saying that this was precisely his intention — just as *Newsweek,* in the beginning, had imitated *Time. Ebony* was to be the *Life* for black people, and the chief difference between the two magazines would be that the faces in the photographs in *Ebony* would be for the most part black. The first issue of *Ebony,* with a press run of 25,000 copies, appeared in 1945.

Ebony was an immediate success with readers. But, within a year of its appearance, the magazine was in deep financial trouble. It could not seem to attract national advertisers and, without national advertisers, it did not appear that it could survive. Despite Johnson's sales efforts to convince space buyers that blacks bought cars and smoked cigarettes as well as whites, Detroit and the tobacco industry — and other national advertisers — remained unimpressed. Then Johnson had an idea. Many of the black people he knew, including his mother, owned Zenith radios. He is still not sure why, but Zenith is a popular brand name with blacks. Johnson wrote to Zenith's president, Eugene McDonald, and asked for an appointment to discuss advertising. McDonald's response, at first, was chilly; advertising was not his department, he said. But Johnson, not to be put down, wrote to McDonald again, and asked to see him about Zenith's business *policy.* This got him an appointment, and a toe in the door. Before going to see McDonald, however, Johnson did a bit of homework on the man. McDonald, he learned, had once accompanied Admiral Peary on an expedition to the North Pole. So had a black explorer named Mathew Hensen, who had written a book on the experience. To his meeting with Eugene McDonald, John Johnson brought an autographed copy of Hensen's book, which he presented to the president. He got his ad. Following Zenith's lead, other national advertisers began following suit.

Still, the going was not always easy for the young publisher and his publications. In 1949, when Johnson was ready to acquire his first office building, he found a suitable one that was for sale on the South Side. It belonged to a white undertaker who, because the neighborhood was becoming integrated, was eager to move elsewhere. But the mortician was unwilling to sell to a black, and turned down Johnson's offer of $60,000. More cunning was required and, to trick the undertaker, Johnson deployed a white lawyer to act as his agent. The lawyer succeeded in buying the building for Johnson for only $52,000, but first asked if he could send a maintenance man over to inspect the premises. The mortician agreed, and John Johnson, disguised as a maintenance man, wearing white overalls, a cap, and carrying a flashlight, came to inspect his new purchase. "There's no use getting angry at a white man like that," Johnson says today. "All you've got to do is try to outsmart him."

Most successful black men would agree with Johnson. Most of their business lives have been spent not trying to integrate with the white establishment, but to outsmart it at its own game.

Today, *Life* is dead, and *Ebony* flourishes, with a circulation of over 1,300,000 copies, its pages crammed with national advertising. *Ebony,* furthermore, is one of the few remaining "big" magazines that has not, for reasons of economy, been forced to reduce its page size — though *Ebony*'s bulky weight costs the Johnson Publishing Company well over a million dollars a year in postage. The Johnson Publishing Company now publishes five different magazines — *Ebony Jr.!, Black Stars, Jet, Black World,* and its flagship, *Ebony.* The company is now in the book publishing business too, owns an AM radio station in Chicago, and has moved out of the South Side into the new eleven-story building on Michigan Avenue, as prestigious a business address as Lake Shore Drive is a residential one. The Johnson Building, also sumptuously decorated and furnished, contains a quarter-million-dollar collection of paintings and sculpture by black artists and a top-floor executive suite that is very nearly as spectacular as the Johnson apartment. The company's annual sales are in the neighborhood of forty million dollars, and the little empire has also extended into real estate, insurance, and banks. John Johnson today sits on the board of Zenith, as well as a number of other companies, including Bell & Howell, Greyhound, and Twentieth Century–Fox. He is also chairman of the board and largest single stockholder of the Supreme Life Insurance Company of America, the company that first hired him as an office boy, and where he feels that his services have compensated for the early borrowed use of the company's printing presses.

John Johnson is a stocky, compactly built man with close-cropped hair and a narrow moustache, whose face bears a strong resemblance to that of the late Martin Luther King. Moving about his office or apartment, smiling easily and talking with his big, easy voice, he seems a bundle of tightly compressed energy. He gestures with his hands, fidgets in his chair, jumps up and down, seems unable to sit in one place for longer than a moment. To relax, he has taken up golf. In business, he had adopted the philosophy of the late Marcus Goldman, founder of Goldman, Sachs & Company: "Always say no," he says. "If you say no *first,* you can always change your mind later on and say yes." He insists he bears no bitter feelings about the hardships of the old days, or those that accompanied his upward climb — no hard feelings about what he and many other blacks feel is a conscious conspiracy among whites to keep blacks down, and in their place. Yet when he talks about such things, his big fists clench, and his eyes cloud over and focus on some inner space. He turns, mid-sentence, and gazes out the window.

His wife is outwardly more easygoing. Dressed by designers such as Dior, Givenchy, and St. Laurent, she seems more comfortable in her surroundings, both at home and in the office. She is *Ebony*'s fashion editor, and also directs the *Ebony* Fashion Fair — an annual traveling fashion show that tours American cities and raises hundreds of thousands of dollars yearly for black charities. Twice a year, she goes to Europe to select the fashions for the show and, while she is there, her husband, who also follows fashion, badgers her by trans-Atlantic telephone with suggestions, tips, ideas. Eunice Johnson personally hand-picks — though, again, with her husband barraging her with suggestions — all the models for her shows, as well as those who are used in *Ebony*'s fashion pages, and has been responsible for developing the modeling talents of such black models as Naomi Sims. In winters, Eunice Johnson vacations alone in the family's Palm Springs house, while her husband stays behind and works. (When Johnson bought the Palm Springs house, with its heated swimming pool, he realized that, though he was over fifty, he had never learned to swim; there had never been enough time.) In many ways, Eunice Johnson is just as driven as her husband and, when there are white guests at her dinner table, and her black cook produces dinner rolls that are — to Eunice's way of thinking — not sufficiently heated, she becomes visibly perturbed. Though John Johnson has managed to lose all traces of a Southern, or Negro, accent, Eunice Johnson — oddly, in spite of her educated background — has not. When Northerners, or whites, fail to understand her, she also becomes upset, and her eyes turn inward.

It would be easy to suppose — easy, particularly, for a white person to suppose — that John Johnson's meteoric rise, his Horatio Alger rags-to-riches success story, would have made him the cynosure of all eyes among blacks, that black parents from the ghettos as well as from the middle class would point to his photograph when he dines at the

White House, and say to their children, "See what that man did? You can do it too!" It would be simple to guess that, particularly among the many black rich, and more particularly among the many black rich in Chicago, John Johnson and his wife would be regarded as contemporary heroes, and that they would be sought after universally by those in black society and by anyone who had attained, or wanted to attain, a modicum of success in the business world. It would be nice to think that all this is what has happened. But, alas, it is not quite the case. Though the Johnsons have frequent public functions to attend, they have few private friends. Public functions seldom take place on weekends. When the Johnsons are alone on a Saturday in their enormous apartment overlooking the huge silver lake, their telephone seldom rings and, as the sunset turns the tall stone and glass facade of Lake Shore Drive to gold, John and Eunice Johnson prepare for a quiet evening at home.

4

Johnson vs. Johnson

ONE FREQUENTLY FINDS, IN THE MARRIAGES OF SUCCESSFUL black families, a situation like that of the John Johnsons — where a dark-skinned man is married to a relatively light-skinned woman. In fact, it is only rarely the other way around. Also noticeable is the fact that the wife is often better educated, and from a "better," older established family, than her husband. There are several reasons for this, some of them quite complex.

One reason is psychological. An ambitious black man, eager to rid himself of the shackles of poverty, often considers it both a business and social asset to marry, as one man puts it, "one of these light-skinned beauties." Light-skinned black women are quite aware of this and know, when it comes to marriage, that they can take their pick, and will often choose, among various suitors, the man who is the most successful, or who shows the greatest promise. Despite such slogans as "Black is Beautiful," white looks are still the American standard, and the Lena Hornes of the black world — who are not only light-skinned but also have no visible "black features" — have by far the best time of it.

There is also an historical factor. In the days of slavery, there was a distinct difference between the house slave and the field slave, and an important caste system developed among the slaves themselves, one which continues to exist today. It is not uncommon to hear a black person say, with more than a touch of pride, "My ancestors were *all* house slaves." The house slaves were at the top of slavery's pecking order, and their descendants know this. In the South, house slaves were selected for their intelligence, their cleanliness, their reliability and honesty — and their looks. If a house slave failed to demonstrate these qualities, he or she was banished to the fields. Field slaves were selected for their strength and health, and not much else — their ability to work hard, long hours in the out-of-doors in the chill of winter and the steaming heat of summer. From the earliest days of slavery there was little commingling between the house servants and the field hands, whom the house servants regarded as "trash."

In the houses of Southern planters, the house slaves were better treated. In a real sense, they had to be, for they were entrusted with caring for children, preparing meals, running the house, caring for guests. In many households, slaves were treated almost as members of the family and, working as maids, cooks, nurses, and laundresses, the house slaves were predominantly women. In the house, these women learned the ways and manners of Southern gentlefolk — how to set a table properly, how to arrange flowers, how to keep silver gleamingly polished, how to treat good furniture (and how to distinguish it from bad), and otherwise how to run a manor house. Because, in many wealthy Southern families, the children were taught by tutors, with the children's nurses in charge of seeing to it that they did their lessons, many of these women became self-educated — learned, at least, to read and write, which their fellow slaves in the fields had no real opportunity to do. These women learned to behave and talk, and also to think, like members of the Southern white aristocracy.

There were, of course, throughout the long years of slavery, many liaisons between the female house slaves and the male plantation owners or their sons. The lighter-skinned offspring of these unions were frequently acknowledged by their fathers, especially the girls, and especially the "pretty" little girls. The boys were needed for work in the fields, and were usually dispatched there as soon as they were old enough, but the pampered little girls were frequently sent to the North, or even to Europe, to be educated. The descendants of these light-skinned, well-educated little girls are the *grandes dames* of black society today.

After slavery was abolished, the same sort of situation prevailed. If there was education in a Southern black family, it was usually on the mother's side. In the next generation, if there was sufficient money to educate children, it was the daughters who benefited from it. This was a matter of sheer practicality, at first; the boys were needed at home, to work on the little farms. Later, it became almost a tradition that, if anyone in the family were to be highly educated, it should be the women. Of course, when these women returned home from their schools and colleges, they often found only less well educated, and in many cases darker-skinned, black men to marry. It is one reason for the dominance of the mother's role in black family life.

In Chicago, George Johnson's background — and success — are very similar to John Johnson's, though the men are in no way related. Perhaps this is why they do not get on. John Johnson laughs off the talk about long-standing friction between the two Johnsons, and says, "Sure, we've had our differences from time to time — but it was never anything serious. Eunice and I were invited to George's son's wedding, weren't we?" George Johnson is more guarded, and says, "I'd rather not talk about it," and adds, "Nobody will ever change Johnny." Part of the trouble may boil down to simple business rivalry, for George and John Johnson are the two richest black men in the city, and possibly in the country, and it is nip and tuck from day to day which Johnson is richer than the other. With the same name, people are forever mixing the two men up, giving one Johnson the credit for something the other Johnson has done, and this has been a galling situation on both sides. Also, George Johnson is nearly ten years younger than John Johnson, and, to some people, appears to have achieved his success more rapidly.

A reservoir of envy between the two men, which had developed over the years, was supplied afresh not long ago when — or so it seemed to George Johnson — John Johnson overstepped himself and moved into George's territory. George Johnson's fortune has been made through his Johnson Products Company, which manufactures a wide range of black cosmetics such as Ultra-Sheen and Afro-Sheen. Johnson Products Company had long advertised in Johnson Publications, particularly *Ebony*. Then, all at once, Johnson Publications announced that it, too, was going into the cosmetics business. George Johnson was, quite understandably, less than happy with this development, which he considered unduly competitive. To add insult to injury, *John* Johnson's cosmetics line, called Fashion Fair, was designed for a better-heeled market, and would be sold in such elegant specialty stores as Neiman-Marcus in Dallas, and Bloomingdale's in New York. *George* Johnson's wares had always been sold in drugstore and supermarket chains, and were much less expensively priced. Not only did it seem to George that John was invading his cosmetics business, but also that John was, in some ways, saying that his were the finer products.

Naturally, John Johnson advertised his fledgling cosmetics line in *Ebony*. Naturally, George Johnson scrutinized his rival's advertising campaign closely. It began to seem to George Johnson that John Johnson was giving himself preferential treatment in terms of where in the magazine Fashion Fair's advertisements were being placed. George Johnson complained to John about this, and, when his complaints seemed to be being ignored, George Johnson grew bitter. Finally, George Johnson angrily withdrew all Johnson Products advertising from all Johnson publications. For many months, both Johnsons sulked in their respective tents. Eventually, the two men patched things up somewhat, and George Johnson returned to *Ebony* with his advertising. But relations between the two have remained notably cool. When George Johnson was invited to be on a television panel to discuss the situation of blacks in Chicago, he declined when he learned that John Johnson would also be on the panel.

To people who know and admire both men, it seems a pity that the two most successful blacks in Chicago do not get on. And yet it is perhaps inevitable that there should be a certain amount of professional jealousy between two men who have worked so hard and long against what seemed a common adversary — the white Establishment. Like John Johnson's, George Johnson's battle began when he was very young and, like John Johnson, he also had an ambitious mother. Johnson was born in 1927 in the little town of Richton, Mississippi, where his father worked in a lumber mill. Like many rural black girls, George Johnson's mother married young and started having children right away. She had given birth to three sons when her brother and sister in Chicago wrote to her of better conditions there, "and that great lady," as George Johnson puts it, "decided to pack us all up and move us north." Priscilla Johnson and her three little boys boarded a bus and arrived in Chicago on a Saturday. The following Monday morning, she started working at Michael Reese Hospital. She was a little over seventeen years old.

Growing up in Chicago, the Johnson boys attended public grammar schools and high school, shined shoes together as a team, and divided a paper route. After high school, George's older brother went to work for the Fuller Products Company, a manufacturer of black cosmetics, whose president, S. B. Fuller, has been credited with helping a number of young blacks get their start in business, though Mr. Fuller's own business later fell upon hard times. When George Johnson graduated from high school, he too was able to get a job at Fuller Products, and eventually the boys managed to get their mother a job there too, working in the labeling division. By the early 1950's, George Johnson had been made a production manager at Fuller.

In 1950, Johnson married Joan Henderson, a tall, slender, and beautiful light-skinned girl two years younger than he who had been his high school sweetheart. At the time, Joan had had a year and a half of college. It looked as though their future would be reasonably secure, but their first son was born with a deformed foot, which required a series of expensive operations and therapy. To help pay the mounting medical bills, Joan Johnson went to work — a thing that proud black men, like Old World husbands, consider a mark of shame. George Johnson himself took a second job as a busboy, working fifteen hours a day, and on weekends he worked as a door-to-door salesman and ran a car-wash rack. Most of those early years, Johnson remembers feeling that he might momentarily collapse from physical exhaustion.

Then, by chance one day he stepped onto an elevator at Fuller, where he noticed that his fellow passenger was a black man with "a disgusted look on his face," and Johnson fell to talking with the man. The man, it seemed, was a barber on Chicago's South Side, who had come for help to a black company and had been turned down. George Johnson listened sympathetically, and the man invited him to come down to his barbershop. Though the shop was outwardly unprepossessing, when he entered the door George Johnson was impressed to see signed photographs of such men as Duke Ellington and Nat "King" Cole. All the stars of the black entertainment world, it seemed, came to Orville Nelson's barbershop when they were in Chicago to have their hair "processed," or straightened.

Essentially, all hair straighteners consist of sodium hydroxide, but Johnson immediately saw that Orville Nelson's straightener was a crude product. It was burningly painful to apply to the scalp, and there were often other, more unpleasant, side effects — broken or falling hair, or an itching rash. What was needed, Johnson saw, was an emulsifier — lanolin, mineral oil, or some other oil or combination of substances — to make Mr. Nelson's straightener a product that would be smooth, creamy, painless, and safe to use. At Fuller, George Johnson had learned a bit about emulsifiers. He had also heard tales about people like Madame C. J. Walker of Indianapolis, a manufacturer of black cosmetics who had become the first woman in America to earn a million dollars, and who had died leaving her daughter a huge fortune. (Madame Walker adopted the title "Madame" because it was something of a tradition in the cosmetics industry; the late Helena Rubinstein, for example, liked to call herself "Madame Rubinstein." The formula for Madame Walker's first hair straightener for "wayward, wrinkled hair" came to her, she said, in a dream.) Johnson took some of Mr. Nelson's hair straightener away with him and, in his lunch hours, began experimenting with various emulsifiers. He also had a friend named Herbert A. Martini, a German chemist, who had a small laboratory. Martini became interested in the problem, and offered to help Johnson try to solve it. When George Johnson was not working during his

Fuller lunch hour or at Martini's lab, he mixed and stirred ingredients over his kitchen stove and sink.

After about six months, Johnson and Martini had arrived at a formula that satisfied them, and brought the result to Orville Nelson. Nelson tried it on his customers, who were immediately so ecstatic that Nelson suggested that he and Johnson form a partnership and go into business together. Nelson, with all his celebrity contacts, would be in charge of sales and promotion. Johnson would be in charge of manufacturing.

When George Johnson presented this idea to his mother, she told him he was crazy. It would mean giving up his good job at Fuller Products. But Johnson, arguing that nothing ventured was nothing gained, insisted that he be allowed at least to try, and his wife, Joan, supported him, believing that it was worth the gamble. And so, in 1954, George Johnson left Fuller Products, his wife took another job, with the criminal court, and the hair straightener called Ultra Wave Hair Culture was officially launched. Johnson and Nelson had figured it would take about $500 to get their new business underway. When George Johnson approached a white loan company for his $250 share, explaining that he wanted the money to start his own business, the loan manager piously explained that blacks did not do well in business. "He told me that he was going to do me a favor, and not give me the money," Johnson says. Undaunted, he went down the street to another branch office of the same loan company. This time, however, he said that he wanted the money to take his wife on a vacation to California. For this purpose, he was quickly given his $250. In its first day of operations, Johnson's little company was down to exactly one dollar in the bank.

The trouble was that Ultra Wave Hair Culture was *too* good a product. Almost overnight, Orville Nelson's barbershop was doing a round-the-clock business in hair straightening, with customers lined up outside the door. To keep up with his trade, Nelson had no time to do the selling job he had agreed to do, and George Johnson found himself doing all the manufacturing *and* the selling of Ultra Wave. Within two weeks, Johnson realized that his sales potential — black barbershops all over Chicago were snapping up Ultra Wave as fast as he could turn it out and as fast as he could peddle and deliver it to them from door to door — should have been at least $100,000. But, as a one-man operation, it had sales far lower than that. Furthermore, Orville Nelson was getting Ultra Wave at cost, as part of their agreement, and so Nelson was not even a profitable customer. When it became clear that Nelson either could not or would not pull his share of the weight of the business, Johnson sued Nelson, and their partnership was dissolved. Nelson, of course, had in the meantime learned enough about the formula of Ultra Wave to make it himself (cosmetics formulas are not patentable), and so, with the breakup of the partnership, Nelson became Johnson's chief competitor. Johnson's slight edge over Nelson lay in the fact that Johnson now owned the Ultra Wave name — and it was a name that blacks were beginning to ask for in barbershops. It still rankles with George Johnson that Orville Nelson got his picture on the cover of *Ebony* before he did.

In 1955, George Johnson brought his wife into the business to help him out. Joan Johnson had had bookkeeping training, and so she handled the orders and accounts. She also helped put up the merchandise, label the jars, and load the trucks. The Johnsons took turns stirring up vats of Ultra Wave with long sticks. As the mixture cooled, it thickened to the density of a heavy paste, and stirring was backbreaking work. Still, in 1954, George Johnson did $18,000 worth of business. A year later, he did $75,000. That year he leased his first space — in the back of a beauty supply company on Chicago's 63rd Street. Soon more space

was needed, and the Johnsons moved again, into a Lithu-
anian neighborhood, where no blacks were wanted and
where their windows were periodically broken and where,
once, they were bombed. In 1958, the company moved
again to a three-story building out of which, that year, the
Johnsons did $250,000 worth of business. They were, it be-
gan to seem, on their way.

Up to that point, George Johnson had been selling his
product exclusively to barbershops. But his old boss, Mr.
S. B. Fuller, with whom he had remained friendly and whom
he still regarded as his mentor, kept reminding him, "Barbers are the worst payers." And so, in 1958, Johnson decided
to move away from barbershops with a women's line, called
Ultra Sheen, for beauty parlors. There were a few hair
straighteners for women already on the market, but these
"relaxers," as they were called, all required a two-part ap-
plication — first the cream base, then the actual straightener. For women, hair straightening was a reasonably costly
and time-consuming operation, and most women were still
straightening their hair with Madame C. J. Walker's
straightening formulas and hot comb. Johnson's Ultra
Sheen was the first no-base relaxer, and to teach beauticians
how to apply it Johnson set up educational clinics — first in
Chicago and then in other cities across the country. It took
about three years to establish Ultra Sheen in the women's
market. Then, in 1966, Johnson was ready to introduce
Ultra Sheen to the consumer at the retail level, and
launched an extensive national advertising campaign in
such black magazines as *Ebony* and *Essence,* on black radio
stations and in black newspapers. He also introduced a
shampoo and a cream rinse.

In 1967, however, hurrying in the wake of the Civil
Rights movement, the natural, or "Afro," look in black hair
came suddenly into vogue, catching George Johnson somewhat off guard. Suddenly black men and women turned

away from hair straighteners and were letting their hair grow out and curl at will. Quickly, Johnson came out with Afro Sheen, a product that added highlights to hair done in the Afro style. For the full, bubbly "Blow Out" style, he offered a Blow-Out Kit, which contained a mild relaxer that prevented hair breakage, made it softer and easier to manage. Within a year, Johnson's Afro Sheen products were number one in the marketplace.

In 1969, the Johnson Products Company went public, with an offering on the American Stock Exchange, and by 1974 the company's sales on all its toiletries products were between sixty and seventy million dollars a year. Johnson's company had become known as "the black Procter & Gamble," and, despite the 1974 recession and stock market slump, Johnson Products stock was still being traded ahead of the original offering price. George Johnson likes to point out that all of his various cosmetic and hair products can be used by white people, and that the make-up requirements of a black woman are no different from those of a white woman just back from a week on a Florida beach. His research has revealed that he has many white customers. Still, he prefers to concentrate his sales and advertising efforts on the black consumer market, "because that's the market I know." At the moment, Johnson is experimenting with fragrances — particularly a men's cologne — having discovered that black men are bigger users of cologne than black women.

Not surprisingly, not long after George Johnson launched his men's fragrances, John Johnson came out with a shaving lotion and cologne of his own. The scent is called "Mr. J." And, naturally, "Mr. J." is a more expensive item, and is sold only through select department and specialty stores.

George Johnson has been accused, of course, of getting rich "off his own kind," and of capitalizing, Uncle-Tom-like, on blacks' insecurities and inner needs to achieve "nice white looks," and to have "good" hair. "What's wrong with that?" he asks. "The need was always there. With my products, I set about fulfilling it. Many black women wish their skins were lighter, wish their hair were straighter. Our makeup lightens their skins, our relaxers straighten their hair, and make these women happier with themselves."

George Johnson — a burly, easygoing man who seems inwardly much more relaxed than his like-named rival — has also, in the less than twenty years that it took him to rise from relative poverty to the status of a multimillionaire, managed to surround himself more enthusiastically with the trappings of a very rich man. Clearly, no one enjoys having money more than George Johnson. His company headquarters are now housed in a spanking new and lavishly decorated building on Chicago's South Side. With 450 employees, this building is already inadequate, and there are plans afoot for a big new annex in an adjacent vacant lot. For the past five years, George and Joan Johnson and their four children have lived in a sprawling California ranch-style house in the fashionable Chicago suburb of Glencoe, surrounded by manicured gardens, a swimming pool, and pool house. Though they are the only black family on the street or in the immediate neighborhood, they have encountered no racial prejudice. "If a black man has enough money, he can live anywhere," Johnson says. The Johnsons also have a spectacular sixteen-room winter retreat in the hills above Runaway Bay, Jamaica, where they belong to the adjacent country club. Joan Johnson, still slender and beautiful, with straight, fine hair — "My hair is too fine for the Afro style" — which she wears in a long bob, just touching her shoulders, dresses with the understated expensiveness of a well-to-do suburban matron, favoring sweaters and skirts and Gucci shoes. She has become something of a legend among her friends for her organizational ability and efficiency. In a single day's shopping in Miami, she completely furnished the Jamaica house. She had to hurry; the Jamaican government was about to impose a ban on imports from the United States.

"It's very simple. When I shop, I buy everything in quadruplicate," she says. Because, in addition to the houses in Glencoe and Runaway Bay, the Johnsons also have a weekend retreat — on a six-hundred-acre farm in McHenry, Illinois, where George Johnson runs a cattle-feeding operation with a stock of 1,800 head of cattle. Johnson also owns two more farms in Mississippi — "because that's where I was born, and the property is cheap. Mississippi is a state that has only one way to go — up." The two Mississippi places comprise 5,000 acres all told, with 1,500 head of cattle on each farm. The larger of the two farms has eleven buildings, including two houses — one for George Johnson and one for his mother. His mother also has the forty-second floor of Chicago's McClurg Court, a building in which her son has a major interest. George Johnson's brother John also has an apartment in the building. The Johnsons' Glencoe house requires a staff of three, and all the other houses are staffed with caretakers. George Johnson flies his own single-engine Beechcraft, and has a seventy-five-foot yacht, *The African Queen*, which sleeps twelve, plus crew, and regularly cruises from Lake Michigan through the St. Lawrence Seaway to Fort Lauderdale, and on into the Caribbean.

In addition to his presidency of Johnson Products, George Johnson is also Chairman of the Board of Chicago's Independence Bank, is on the boards of Commonwealth Edison, the Urban League, Northwestern Memorial Hospital, the Chicago Area Boy Scouts, and the Chicago Lyric Opera. For good measure, the Johnsons are members of the exclusive Tres Vidas Country Club in Acapulco.

George Johnson has brought his two brothers into his company. Brother John is vice president in charge of sales, and brother Robert is traffic manager. Johnson admits that, since he has become rich, a great many relatives whom he had never heard of before "came out of the woodwork," asking for jobs or, in some cases, money. "I try to help them out," he says, "but I don't believe in too much nepotism." And yet the possession of which he is proudest is his oldest son Eric, who is twenty-five. Eric Johnson graduated from Babson Institute, then worked for a while for Procter & Gamble, learning the white side of the toiletries industry. "Then I brought him into my company for a while, for training," Johnson says. "Right now, he's in the Graduate School of Business at the University of Chicago. I have a plan on him. Yes, I have a real overall plan on him. He'll get his master's degree in business — that will take him less than two years. Then he'll go to work for us in marketing. In five years, Eric will be an officer in my company. That's my five-year plan on Eric. Eric is very success-oriented."

George Johnson smiles contentedly at this thought, and accepts a cup of coffee that his black butler offers him on a silver tray. George Johnson continues smiling and with, perhaps, more than just a trace of smugness adds, "Johnny Johnson's son was a high school dropout."

Meanwhile, as the Johnsons bicker and jockey for position, another dissatisfied voice has been heard from in Chicago — this time from a woman. She is Mrs. Bettie Pullen-Walker, an animated auburn-haired lady in her middle thirties, who edits and publishes *MsTique* magazine, which she calls "the very first magazine to be published anywhere that gives a consistently positive view of the black female." With fiction and articles on such subjects as "Are You a Sex Symbol," "When the Affair Is Over," "Unmasking the (Married) Players," and "Living In or Shacking Up," *MsTique* is clearly intended as a black answer to *Cosmopolitan,* and Bettie Pullen-Walker has been referred to as a black Helen Gurley Brown. Mrs. Pullen-Walker, whose maiden name was Thompson (her hyphenated name combines the names of two previous husbands), is both a member of the black Old Guard and of the new achievers. She traces her ancestry back to Columbia, South Carolina, where, in the middle 1800's, her maternal great-grandmother inherited considerable property, which has remained in the family to this day. This great-grandmother married a man named Ben Frazier, a Muskogean Indian from Mississippi, and family legend has it that Ben Frazier's ancestors were early Indian activists — moving across the plains attempting to frustrate the white man's efforts to relocate all Indians to reservations and to induce them to give up all their tribal ties. Ben Frazier himself made a tidy fortune as a fur trader.

Most of Bettie Pullen-Walker's family have been educators, and it was as a teacher that she started out after graduating as a psychology major from Roosevelt University in 1964. In 1973, as a woman of some means, Mrs. Pullen-Walker decided to branch out, and *MsTique* was launched — complete with a *Cosmopolitan*-like cover girl and centerfold (though not nude). It is probably too early to say how successful *MsTique* will eventually be, and it is still not running completely in the black. Mrs. Pullen-Walker blames this on advertiser — and advertising agency — indifference to "approximately fifteen million black females in this land," and she complains of being "shoved around" by agency representatives. She says, "I have never experienced a more circular pattern of referrals, unkept promises, requests for marketing material that are not ever acknowledged, unreturned telephone calls, and a whole range of disrespectful and unbusinesslike behavior as I have had from agency representatives."

Her new venture, she points out, has been more than adequately publicized in the news media in general. But she claims that *MsTique* has been largely ignored by the black press because of the fierce competition for advertising. She also blames sexism. "Sexism is also rampant among black males, who dominate the black press," she says.

From this, one assumes she is talking about men like John Johnson.

III

The Old Guard

5

Family Trees

GEORGE JOHNSON INSISTS THAT HIS PERSONAL PHILOSOPHY IS based on two principles. "First, I believe in the Golden Rule," he says. "It really works. It's a great formula for success. Second, a man has got to believe in casting bread upon the waters. I'm more concerned with what I give than with what I receive." To put this theory to work, Johnson has established two foundations. One of these busies itself contributing funds to 290 different charitable organizations — black, nonblack, "and even Jewish" — on an annual basis. The second is dedicated to minority youth, primarily black, who want an education. "We have a hundred and twenty kids in school right now that we're supporting," Johnson says.

Education has always provided the principal avenue out of the ghettos for all minority groups. But, Johnson feels, too many educated blacks have gone into teaching, or the clergy, or have become doctors or lawyers — where the opportunities to make money are limited. "There haven't been too many blacks venturing into *business*," he says. "And that's what my foundation's for — poor black kids who can handle responsibilities and who want to make it in *business*. Because that's the only way they're going to make it — in business." This is one reason why, he says, he put his new office building where it is — in the predominantly black South Side and not, as John Johnson did, on fashionable Michigan Avenue. "School buses with black kids go back and forth in front of my building every day," he says. "They see it, and maybe they say to themselves, 'There's a black man who's got a big business. Maybe I can start a business like that someday.'" Tours of his factory are conducted regularly for black schoolchildren in the area, and the message offered by the tour guides in always the same: "If there's going to be improvement and progress among our people, it's going to come about through more black *business.*"

Not all the members of America's black elite would agree with George Johnson's emphasis on business education — nor, for that matter, would many upper-class blacks agree that either George or John Johnson qualifies as spokesman for either the upper class or for blacks in general. "After all, who *are* the Johnsons, anyway?" sniffs one black woman from Chicago, whose family *hubris* has been pronounced for several generations. "I knew that I was of the elite when I was born. We were the family that other blacks looked up to. Nobody really looks up to those Johnsons. Oh, of course they've gotten very fancy, with their big houses, their yachts and Cadillacs. We have an expression for people like that — 'nigger rich.'"

There is more to black improvement and progress, many people feel, than simply making large sums of money — much more. It is a question of breeding, manners, speech, family background, and a way of "doing things." Seemliness and probity count for more than property or possessions, and many Old Guard blacks regard such families as the Johnsons as vulgar upstarts, *nouveaux riches* who, with their ostentatious ways, are little more than an embarrassment and, as a result, do their race more harm than good. It is very much like the way Old Guard Jewish families regard the Jews who show up at Miami Beach hotels and wear mink stoles and diamonds with their swimsuits, or the way the Old Line Irish mocked their new-rich countrymen who hung lace curtains at their windows. It is the classic battle between the established family and the newcomer. If you've got it, the Old Guard feel, you *don't* flaunt it.

Mr. and Mrs. John W. Fleming live on a winding, tree-lined street called Iris Avenue in Cincinnati. Iris Avenue is a street of private homes in the $40,000 to $75,000 range and, because the street dead-ends, it is quiet with very little traffic. It is in an area called Kennedy Heights, which is not only expensive but also integrated. Though Lina Fleming says, "White people don't like you if you look too much like them," she gets along well with her white neighbors. Most of her friends, however, are black or, like herself, the color of coffee with lots of cream.

Lina Fleming, in her middle fifties, is a woman of promptly revealed opinions, who admits that many of her tartly expressed sentiments have ruffled feathers on both sides of the racial fence. "I don't think integration is the answer. I think the Negro schools did a great job." (Like many Old Guard blacks, she eschews the fashionable word "black" for the more traditional "Negro.") She also says, "I don't believe in busing. I don't think it's necessary." More than anything, she is infused with an overwhelming sense of family pride, and has outlined a book that she intends to write, to be called, simply, "The Family." Sample from Mrs. Fleming's outline: "Note their dress, their speech, and their habits of walking, greeting, etc. Note their table manners, manners of cleaning their houses, making and unmaking their beds, preparing their meals, especially specific kinds of food, etc." "We were *somebody*," she says. "We were people of status. We were of good stock." She also admits that her black-skinned husband is not of as good stock. "I'm an Episcopalian," she said. "My mother thought the Episcopalians were more liberal. He's a Baptist, and a member of the Bethel Baptist Church. Bethel Baptist is headed up by Reverend and Mrs. Harry Brown. She's the social arbiter of the church. He was a janitor and she was a beautician. But Brown went to the University, and took speech lessons, and they both went to a seminary and got degrees. Mrs. Brown puts on weddings. She puts on big banquets, with flaming baked Alaska. But some of those Baptists have never been outside the city, have never been to a hotel."

John Fleming's father was a minister from Somerville, Tennessee, who came to Cincinnati in 1915. But when John Fleming was ten, his father departed for somewhere in the South, never to be heard from again, and his mother was left with eight children to raise. John Fleming was the only one of his brothers and sisters to go to college, walking five miles from his home in downtown Cincinnati to the city university in the suburbs, and another five miles back each night, stopping to change the sheets of cardboard in his shoes three times along the way. Lina Fleming's background was much different.

She was taught, as a little girl, that there were two kinds of people — "people like us," and "those other people." If she brought a new friend home from school, her mother would ask, "Are they people like us?" If they were not, and were "those other people," her mother would see to it that the friendship was promptly terminated. Lina Fleming's grandmother was equally class-conscious. "Grandmother felt that being in sports or entertainment wasn't proper. I was horrified when I found out that I was related to Joe Louis! When I found out, I confronted Grandmother with it. She said, 'I know, I'm sorry. I hoped you'd never know.'"

On genealogical matters, Lina Fleming is almost dizzyingly well informed. "My father's grandfather came from Jamaica with two brothers and a sister. He worked his way across Virginia. I don't know if they were Negroes or Indians. One of my great-great-grandfathers was a white man named John Meadows, who had a lot of property. John Meadows had a mulatto daughter, and he didn't want her to marry just *anybody*. My great-grandfather was Elbert, and he worked for John Meadows, *not* as a slave, and Elbert took the name of Meadows, and married John Meadows's daughter. Elbert's brother was elected to the House of Representatives under Rutherford B. Hayes, and was lynched on his way to the House. Elbert's store, a blacksmith shop, was on the Meadows acreage — about five thousand acres, all told. Daddy's grandmother looked white. My father's mother was a Meadows, and the Meadowses supposedly had slaves of their own. She fell in love with a former slave boy named Wright, who shod her horses, and married him. It was considered a great *mésalliance*. Daddy went to Tuskegee where he met Mother. He was Nathan Wright.

"Mother was a Hickman. My mother's grandparents were custodians of the Eclectic Medical School, and my grandfather practiced medicine in Paris, Kentucky. He was on the board of Berea University, which was founded for the children of white men who had mulatto wives. My great grandmother laid the cornerstone of the Union Baptist Church. After Mother and Father were married, they lived in Louisiana. He worked in insurance. He taught the poor black farmers the importance of insurance, and made enemies among the whites. They were going to lynch him, but we were warned and my mother and I got on a train for Cincinnati, where Mother's family had property. For a long time, we didn't know where Daddy was."

The Hickman property was at Camp Denison, a former Army base just behind Indian Hill, Cincinnati's most expensive suburb. The large main house had been at one time a barracks, and was surrounded by extensive gardens. At Camp Denison, life was decorous and mannered. Since

Grandmother Hickman was very much a *grande dame,* other black women in the area came to her for advice on how to do things properly. Her house was meticulously kept, furnished with antiques, many of which Lina Fleming has inherited, and meals were served on the dot, on fine china, a table of gleaming mahogany, with silver napkin rings. Grandmother Hickman was famous for her food, and for her Sunday dinners there were often as many as thirty cars parked in the driveway. "We didn't *eat* what colored people ate," Lina Fleming says. "We ate mushrooms, asparagus, broccoli — I never heard of Soul Food until I went to work for the Welfare Department. Both my mother and my grandmother were recipe cooks. Grandmother Hickman reared us by the book. Our table manners had to be perfect. We had to say 'please' and 'thank you,' we had to say goodnight to everyone before we went to bed, and to say good morning when we came down for breakfast. We wore prescription shoes. We went to museums, the symphony, to plays. We read from Charles Lamb's Shakespeare. In those days, Negroes couldn't go to the Summer Opera, but Grandmother had been to New York, where she had season tickets to the opera, and heard Caruso. So we went to the park on opera nights, and sat outside on benches so we could hear the opera."

When Lina Fleming's father finally managed to join his family in Cincinnati, he was penniless, and had to go to work for a private white family — the Krogers, who own a supermarket chain — as a gardener. This was a terrible blow to Nathan Wright's pride, and it also pained him to have to live more or less off his wife's family. He did, however, become executive secretary of the N.A.A.C.P. Still, Lina Fleming says, "Grandmother Hickman always felt that Mother had married beneath her station."

Again, it was the women who seemed to carry the family.

"All the women on my grandmother's side were free women," Lina Fleming says with pride. "None of them ever worked for white people. My grandmother's sisters were black and tall, with lots of hair, but my grandmother was a light olive color. My cousin Ella is very, very white. She could pass for white if she wanted to. A lot of people pass, of course. They cross over, and are never heard from again. When I was a young girl, seeing all these light-skinned relatives gathering at family dinners, I once said to my grandmother, 'Didn't some of those white men get at them?' She gave me a look I'll never forget, and said to me, 'Don't you ever mention that again!'

"My grandmother's friends were an international group. Anybody who was anybody who came through Cincinnati stopped to see her. People came from London, Paris, Rome. Doctor King used to come to Sunday dinner, and used to tease her about all the food she gave away to the poor. At Christmas, we'd go around with baskets of food for the poorer families. Marian Anderson was a friend of the family, even though she was in entertainment. After all, she sang *opera*." When Lina, her sister and two brothers weren't being trained, they played, but even their games were educational. "We played math games, and read to each other from Proverbs and Aesop's Fables." From the time she was two years old, Lina's sister Lydia wanted to be a doctor, and would play with her grandfather's stethoscope. Brother Nathan wanted to be a minister. "Sometimes when Lydia was playing doctor, she would kill off her patients and let Nathan conduct the funeral." When Lydia, who is now a doctor as well as married to one, was doing her residency in Boston, there was no place for her to live except with a white family, where she had been asked to help out as a baby-sitter. Because this meant "working for whites," Lydia Wright wrote to Grandmother Hickman for advice. Her grandmother replied, "Any work, as long as it's honorable work, is all right — as long as it helps you go through school."

Lina, her sister, and two brothers all graduated from Walnut Hills High School, Cincinnati's public high school for gifted children. "My mother and grandmother always told us we were superior — we were the best, and the brightest. We had to be, and we *were.*" Even at Walnut Hills, though, the Wright family detected racial slights, either real or imagined — such as the fact that black children were assigned to use the swimming pool during the last period on Fridays, just before the pool was emptied for the weekend. Lina Fleming herself graduated from Fiske University, and her brothers and sister are all college graduates. "There are twenty-eight college degrees in my immediate family — and nine Ph.D.'s!"

"My family would compare with *any* upper-class family, white or Negro," she says. "And I'd have to say we'd come out better than most whites. My brother Nathan's first wife was a Cardoza — there's old Jewish blood there, the *best* Jewish blood. My brother Hickman was an executive with *Ebony,* but he couldn't get along with the first vice president. So he left, and went as an executive with Clairol. Later, the man who was first vice president left, and Hickman was asked back to *Ebony* to replace the man he couldn't get along with! Now Hickman is second in command! My brother Nathan was an Episcopal minister, but he left the church when he got his divorce. Now Nathan teaches at the State College of Albany — sociology and Black Studies. He's married again, to a white girl. We weren't too happy about that. She could have been hostile, but she was nice. When I met her, I said, 'Well, now you're in the family, I suppose we'll have to be friends.' We are, more or less. Her name was Carolyn May — she's related to that Mr. May who was married to Marjorie Merriweather Post. She's from an old Philadelphia family, related to Longfellow — she's a D.A.R. and in the *Social Register*. Let's see if they drop her for marrying Nathan! She's all right. They live in a big house in Selkirk, New York, with thirteen acres and eight acres of lawn — an old mansion they fixed up, full of antiques. They have a couple — a white couple — that keeps house for them. My daughter Diana went to St. Anne's Academy in Arlington, Massachusetts, and from there to Western College for Women, in Oxford, Ohio, which is now a part of Miami University. My niece, Debbie Wright, went to Yale, and was senior class orator in 1973. Another niece, Patty, speaks five languages. Another niece is in a training program at the Chase Manhattan Bank in New York. The other day, she had lunch with David Rockefeller. My sister Lydia is quite rich. She's probably the richest of us all. She made a lot of money in the stock market. She has a huge house in Buffalo, full of museum-quality antiques and beautiful paintings — but not *showy,* like some of those other, those trashy people. I mean, my family is *distinguished*. White people may not know it, but *we* know it — we're superior."

And yes, Lina Wright Fleming admits, she has her own firm set of prejudices. "I'm prejudiced against Catholics," she says, "and I'm prejudiced against WASPs, and I'm prejudiced against some of my fellow blacks. I mean Negroes. It's those people in the ghettoes who say 'black.' We say 'Negro' — people like us."

Roots

IN THE MIDDLE PART OF THE 1800'S, NEAR THE LITTLE TOWN of Effingham, Illinois, a small community of mulattos came into existence. There was a similar settlement near Lawrence, Kansas, and there were others scattered across the Middle West and Southwest. Behind these families was white money, for these people were all descendants of the white landed gentry — men who, unlike the common image of the cruel slave-owner, acknowledged their love-children, and maintained two, or in some cases more, families. These children were sent away to be educated at the finest schools and colleges in the United States and Europe. When they came back, they took positions in various corporations, and helped found the first black universities and churches, became the first black professionals as educators, lawyers, and physicians. Thus, even before the Emancipation, there was a black middle class in America.

Gradually, these families moved to the larger cities, where they lived so quietly as to be almost invisible — which was exactly the state of affairs they preferred. They could not be, and in most cases did not wish to be, assimilated into the white world, and at the same time they were envied and resented by the black have-nots for the simple reason that they had more. Their chief philanthropic endeavors centered around the activities of the National Association for the Advancement of Colored People. In its early years the N.A.A.C.P. operated as a kind of exclusive club.

In many cities, these families have been living quiet, comfortable, but isolated lives for as many as five generations. Proud, conservative and tradition-bound, they have placed the emphasis of their lives on refinement and good living — good silver, good linen, good antiques. In many cities, when integrated neighborhoods opened up, these families refused to move to them because they preferred to live near their friends and relatives. In Chicago, for example, families like the Gillespies, McGills, Abbotts, and George Cleveland Halls remained in their big houses on the South Side after it became unfashionable, where they kept chauffeurs and maintained summer homes on Cape Cod or Martha's Vineyard. Still, conspicuous consumption was frowned upon, and costly items were acquired only if they were also useful. When the father of Mr. Leonard Evans of Chicago was criticized, by a less-well-off black, for driving a Cadillac, he carefully explained why he needed a big car. When he drove his family to visit their relatives in the segregated South, the children could sleep in the car, and not suffer the indignities of "colored-only" motels.

These upper-class blacks, furthermore, have always carefully referred to themselves as "middle-class." The phrase "middle-class" has a special meaning to blacks. To whites, it is essentially an economic consideration. Any family with, say, an annual income in the $20,000 to $35,000 range would be considered middle-class. Archie Bunker would be considered middle-class; he owns his own home, has a steady job, and his wife does not need to work. But in black America, class is a question of dignity and, more important, stability. To own your own home, unmortgaged, and to own your own car, unfinanced, is class. To be in debt, or to drift from job to job, is not class. Divorce is anathema, and illegitimacy is worse. Upper-crust blacks routinely express pity for poor blacks on welfare, but along with this pity are great feelings of disdain. Upper-class blacks voice concern over "street blacks," and blacks who are drug-users, criminals, or pimps, but beneath this concern is something very close to contempt. Twenty years ago, a foreigner might have been puzzled by the patrician status accorded to Mr. A. Philip Randolph of Washington, D.C. It is true that Mr. Randolph had all the courtliness, dignity, and refined good manners of a Clifton Webb. But, after all, the Nashville-born labor leader was a sleeping car porter. Could he be upper-class? In black America he can indeed. In Denver, for many years, the women who were the leaders of black society were *all* the wives of Pullman porters. They owned their homes, had stable marriages, sent their children to college and, while their husbands traveled, formed their own exclusive little social circle, where, over teacups and silver services, they hemmed sheets for the needy. "To be middle-class among blacks is mainly a way of life," says one woman. And to say "we are middle-class" is merely a more genteel way of saying "we are upper-class."

To a white, black standards of class can be confusing. In Washington, for example, Dr. and Mrs. John Bulmer live in a strikingly modern house, designed for them, on the west, or white, and more fashionable, side of Rock Creek Park. Dr. Bulmer is a dentist, his wife is a social worker, and their joint income is comfortably above $50,000 a year. But more important than their earnings is the fact that both Bulmers are Old Line black, light-skinned, born with a sense of family roots and status. The Bulmers' house is decorated not only with good taste but with a proud sense of understatement. The light upholstery is kept stain-resistant not with plastic slipcovers but by a family that is simply careful not to stain it. The Bulmers' architect used much glass in his design, but there are no imposing cerise-shaded lamps to dominate their windows, and the Bulmers have resisted the temptation, noticeable among newer-rich black families, to cover their walls with African art or sculpture. They have a color television set, but it is not enormous and ensconced in a Chinese modern console; it is small, and can be rolled out of sight when not in use. To newer-rich black families, trips to Europe, Africa, Hawaii, and cruises in the Caribbean are a mark of status. The Bulmers vacation at an old farmhouse in upstate Vermont.

And yet, when they first moved into their new house, Mrs. Bulmer says, "My neighbor came around one morning, and we had coffee. She asked me where we came from, how much we'd had to pay for the house, and what my husband did. Can you *imagine* that?" A white person certainly could imagine, and would probably see nothing wrong with, such friendly curiosity. But the black upper-class are, by inbred tradition, much more reticent, and consider it poor taste to ask, on short acquaintance, such personal questions. After all, your new neighbor might have to answer that she was from a farm in rural Mississippi, and that her husband sorted mail for the Post Office — answers that might pain and embarrass her to divulge. In black society, such information is to be conveyed gradually, discreetly, indirectly, over a polite period of time. All this is a part of having "class."

In Chicago, Leonard Evans's antecedents came from the little mulatto community outside Effingham, Illinois. He himself, a tall, courtly, white-haired man, with very light skin, has the same sense of family past and deep roots in American history. One of Evans's great-grandfathers fought for the British in the American Revolution, thereby earning his freedom from slavery. At the time, blacks had a choice — they could remain as slaves or fight for the British, and Mr. Evans's ancestor chose to fight. After the war, he worked as a fur trapper on the Ohio River, and prospered. In the early 1840's, he went to Louisville, Kentucky, where — whether out of a sense of justice or not — he purchased the old slave auction house, turned it into a church, and became a minister. His son — Leonard Evans's grandfather — helped feed the Union soldiers who came through Louisville during the Civil War. Evans's father was born in Louisville in 1882, graduated from Fiske and Columbia School of Architecture and, after fighting in World War I, returned to Louisville and founded the architectural firm of Evans & Plato, which designed many of the city's churches and temples.

On his mother's side, one of his great-grandmothers was a slave who was sold in Charleston and ended up in Macon, Georgia, where she worked in the household of a wealthy banking and shipping family. She had nine children, five of whom were lost in the Civil War. A sixth child died from a spider bite, and two of her sons were kidnapped and never heard from again. Only one daughter survived. She married a man named James Claybrooks, who had fought with Teddy Roosevelt and who was a member of another old-line family. But when Leonard Evans's mother was born in 1882, she was rejected by her mother because she was the result of a rape by a white man. She was blue-eyed and blond and was raised by her great-grandmother. Her father, she has hinted, was a member of one of the greatest retailing families of the United States. But she has proudly refused ever to acknowledge them, or to say who they were. "A mixed-blood background has distinct advantages," Evans says. "But in families like ours, we are told never to admit having white blood. It's a fact, but it's never mentioned. To do so is considered to be in very bad taste."

Evans's mother was sent to Spelman, a private school in Atlanta, and then to Fiske, where she graduated *magna cum laude*. For a while she taught mathematics at Tuskegee under Booker T. Washington. At Fiske, she had met Evans's father. When she married him and moved to Louisville, Evanses had been in the city for over seventy years, and were definitely among the black Old Guard. Still, haunted by her illegitimacy, she was afraid she would have trouble establishing herself socially in Louisville. "So Mrs. Booker T. Washington wrote letters of introduction for her to all the Louisville elite. With those introductions, she was accepted," Evans says. "And of course Mother had been taught all the proper things." Later, when the senior Evanses moved to Hinsdale, Illinois, Mrs. Booker T. Washington did the same thing, and helped ease the Evanses smoothly into the upper class there. In Hinsdale, for example, Mrs. Washington wrote to Mrs. George Cleveland Hall, whose husband was a noted physician. "Mrs. Hall was *the* social leader in Hinsdale," Evans says. "This was around 1912, and all the old-line families have a similar background and history — Thurgood Marshall, the Bond family in Washington, the Tanner family in Philadelphia, and the Alexanders. This was a pattern. It reflected a quality of life, a quality of taste and refinement in art, literature, speech, manners. In families like these, the genes show."

Leonard Evans's wife's family is similarly rooted and well based. Though his wife's grandfather was illegitimate, his father was a Civil War general, who acknowledged him and had him prepared for admission to the United States Military Academy at West Point. He was accepted but, because of a slightly deformed hand, he was turned down when he arrived at the Academy. He returned to St. Louis, where he became a school teacher. One of Mrs. Evans's great-grandfathers was also a fur trapper and also prosperous, until he was drowned on the Mississippi River. His children were all well educated, and Mrs. Evans's father, a Chicago doctor, was medical director of the black Liberty Life Insurance Company. "In Chicago, both my wife's family and mine were part of the black Establishment," Evans says. "We were the Uncle Toms — intelligent, urban for several generations, very clannish, light-skinned but antiwhite. There were never any white people at our dances or coming-out parties. The trouble is, our group has no leadership. Black leadership is preoccupied with the poor, and the militants can't produce what they promise. There have always been poor people, and there always will be. Sixty percent of the urban blacks are in the middle class, but the rich get richer and the poor get poorer. Segregation would have worked, if they'd only segregated the money. But they segregated everything *but* the money. Ninety-eight percent of the money is still controlled by whites, and there's been a white gentlemen's agreement: Never give a contract to a Negro."

Still, Leonard Evans has done all right. Ten years ago, he launched *Tuesday,* a black supplement that now appears in twenty-three newspapers and twenty-five markets with a monthly circulation of nearly 5,000,000. Evans estimates the current worth of his company at between $10,000,000 and $12,000,000, and is currently planning to break into television. The Evanses have a large apartment in Chicago's Hancock Tower, and a winter home in Tucson. The Evanses have two grown sons, and the older, Leonard, Jr., is lighter-skinned than either of his parents. As a young teenager, he faced the crisis common to many light-skinned blacks — a crisis of Who Am I? Because of the color of his skin, he was rejected by both blacks and whites, and one day he came home from school and asked his father, "Dad, what are colored people?" His father replied, "We are." The boy thought a moment, and then said, "Well, maybe you are, but Mom and I aren't." For a while, to the distress of his parents, he went through a period of rebellion — with a Honda, leather jacket, boots, growing a beard and shoulder-length hair. "But eventually the genetic qualities began to emerge," says his father, and the older boy, now twenty-nine, is in charge of his father's television venture. The younger son, Midian, was sent to a white preparatory school in New England and then, for balance, to Howard University. Today, he is in charge of *Tuesday*'s financial operations. "I've tried to instill in both my sons a sense of pride, of deep family pride," Evans says. "It's a rich mixture that they come from, and I've tried to make them aware of it. Even if some of their ancestors were slaves, they can be proud of that, too. After all, it was the Negro slaves who developed the cotton industry, one of the greatest industries in the country."

But pride is not undiluted with a certain bitterness, and the one terrible blemish in his family's past haunts him, and is something, clearly, that he can never forgive or forget. "My mother is ninety-one now," he says, "and she's never told me who her father was. She knows, of course, because her mother told her. I suppose I'll never know. All she'll say was that it was a man 'from a great retailing family.' One of the Rosenwalds, do you suppose — the Sears, Roebuck family? They were German Jews. Were any of them blond, with blue eyes? It's a terrible thing when you have to tell your sons that their grandmother was illegitimate. At least I can tell them that I put out more magazines in a year than Sears, Roebuck puts out catalogues."

Rebel

IT IS CLEAR THAT IF THERE IS ONE THING THAT IS WANTING among the educated, prospering, and upwardly mobile black middle-to-upper class it is any sort of *consensus*. It is difficult to find two articulate blacks who agree on anything. In Chicago, some people take John Johnson's side in the Johnson-Johnson rivalry, and others take George Johnson's. Still others feel that their dispute — over such matters as the placement of advertising and variously priced cosmetic lines — is silly or, worse, self-destructive to both these talented men in its sheer pettiness. Some would agree with Leonard Evans on the value he places on the genetic enrichment of white blood. Others would consider Evans a snob of the worst sort, and point out that Evans's white-ancestor pride seems an odd contradiction to his apparent shame about his mother's illegitimacy. Still other blacks think that ancestor worship — or even ancestor talk — is foolish in the extreme. "How," asks one man, "can you be proud of circumstances over which you had no control?" In the black world, the whole problem of illegitimacy is a knotty one and produces, in some people, a kind of schizophrenia, and an inability to decide which identity to embrace. In Chicago, however, at least one black woman is fiercely proud of being illegitimate.

Barbara Proctor, still in her thirties, is a beautiful, mocha-colored woman, who, in a few short years, has risen from relatively little to the point where she is now president and sole owner of Proctor & Gardner Advertising, Inc., the largest black advertising agency in the world, with annual billings of over $4,000,000. ("I'm Proctor and I'm Gardner. My maiden name was Gardner. I had a less than admirable reason for naming my agency — I felt Procter & Gamble deserves a little inconvenience. Besides, I had had to change my name to get in the business.")

Among Chicago's successful blacks, Barbara Proctor is noted for her blunt outspokenness ("She's a terror!" says one black businessman), and has a reputation as a fire-brand, a stirrer-up of controversy, and as a rebel with a cause. The cause is herself and her son — fourteen-year-old Morgan — for the most part. "I'm a chronic embarrassment to my mother," she says. "My mother still lives in Washington, still works in the Pentagon. My younger sister goes to ballet school, does a little charity work — my mother thinks that's what *nice* little colored girls should do. Not start a business like mine. Not go to the office every day, and leave my son at home with sitters. Not be a mover and doer, like me. It's foolhardy to be a rebel and not be economically free. Without money, there is no survival, and without survival, there is no change. And those bottomless blacks can't help you. To succeed, you have to play footsie with the white Establishment."

Barbara Proctor is convinced that her illegitimacy gave her a head start in life. "I know a lot of dominating people," she says, "and many of them are illegitimate. My illegitimacy planted an aggressive determination in me that others didn't have. It gave me drive, and also a sense of balance. I had no great striving need to prove who I was in terms of family, which is such a waste of time, but I did learn that if I could do a white girl's homework for her, she would be my friend; I was clear on the realities." She adds, "Of course I believe in a cohesive family unit. I *had* one. I was reared by my grandmother. We were a very close-knit little family. That's a thing about blacks: we don't neglect our own. No one is ever homeless. We look out for each other. Like crazy old Miss Tillie down the street, who was always running away. Whenever Miss Tillie ran away, we'd just go out and look for her and bring her back. Another woman I used to know had a drug-addict son. She said, 'He may be a snake, but he's *my* snake.' "

Too many wealthy or upper class blacks, Barbara Proctor feels, "have adopted the negative aspects of elitism — the ostentatious things, the jewels, the big cars, the big apartments and houses." Recently Barbara Proctor read somewhere that there has been a marked increase in the number of black nursing homes. "Think of that," she says. "Black nursing homes! That would never have been the case when I was growing up. Even if we could afford it, we wouldn't *dream* of shoving our old people into nursing homes. Nursing homes are another negative part of this new elitism. I say to my black friends, 'Economically we move up, but morally we move down.' Needless to say, they don't like to hear that sort of thing."

Sitting in her large, ultramodern corner office high above Chicago, stylishly — but not ostentatiously — dressed in a silver pants suit from I. Magnin, Barbara Proctor likes to talk about how Proctor & Gardner Advertising, Inc., came into being. She has always been relentlessly ambitious, and managed, in four years, to graduate with three degrees — a bachelor's in education, English and sociology. For a while, she taught school, worked as a social worker and for a real estate agency. She had always wanted to be a writer, "But my writing needed discipline. I needed to learn to say what I had to say concisely, and briefly." So she went to work as a writer-producer in an agency. A jazz enthusiast, she worked also as a contributing editor for *Downbeat,* wrote a couple of television specials, produced a column for a South Side newspaper, and contributed to seven different books on jazz. "I sort of tumbled into advertising," she says. "Working with radio, I realized that our impression of America is projected through the media, and that advertising and merchandising control a great deal of what we think about." She also realized that all the media rating services were run by whites, that white researchers were afraid to go into black ghettos with their questionnaires, and that the questionnaires, usually prepared by whites, bore no relation to what blacks wanted, did, or thought about. "They'd send out a questionnaire that said, 'Do you, when you go out dancing, prefer to (a) waltz, (b) foxtrot, (c) jitterbug.' Black people don't dance any of those things!"

So she began to think in terms of a black advertising agency that would reach blacks in a way that related to their special needs. "I knew that the chances of a black agency surviving were remote," she says. "Others had tried it, and failed miserably. I was also told that it took at least a million dollars to start an agency, and I know that major credit is always nearly impossible to get. I started out trying to borrow two hundred thousand. I managed to get a loan of eighty thousand. Talk about black businesses being undercapitalized! Oddly enough, they never asked me whether I'd had any black advertising agency experience. I hadn't. Most black agencies start out with too many small accounts. I wanted just a few big ones, and started with four — Jewel Food Stores, a major chain, Sears of Chicago, and, nationally, Kraft Foods for the black community — products like

Parkay, Miracle Whip mayonnaise and Barbeque Sauce —
and Gillette, with portions of their Personal Care and
Paper Mate division."

The little company — consisting of Barbara Proctor, her
account man, her art director, and her media director —
started out in a third-floor walk-up. "From May 1970 to
February 1971, we existed on twenty-six thousand dollars,"
Barbara Proctor says. "It was life on a principle. We worked
nights and weekends. The problem was always what to do
until the check comes. We managed by revolving checks —
depositing one check to offset one we'd just written, then
writing another against the deposit. It worked, thank God,
for six months — the checks went in and out of banks so fast
that even the banks got confused." By April 1971, however,
Proctor & Gardner Advertising, Inc., was able to move into
its handsome new offices, and the staff now numbers twenty-
two. "The white agencies *tolerate* us," she says. "Much of
the power structure really doesn't want us to exist. You see,
we're dealing with whites who've never had to come to grips
with blacks before. We've had to be a half-jump ahead of
the white — and to get out of the way before the gun goes
off. White companies still take a wait-and-see, time-will-tell
attitude, even though we've been in business now for longer
than any other black agency has. We still have a severe
credit problem. Because we're black we have to pay *on the
nose.* If we don't, they'll go right to the accounts, personally,
an insult they would never impose on a white agency. I'm
under extreme pressure — the same pressure that's on all
black businesses."

Interestingly, many of Proctor & Gardner's creative staff
are white. "A black agency has to pay *more* for good black
talent," Barbara Proctor says. "That's because a talented
black can always get a good job in one of the big, prestige
shops. So we rely on agressive young white talent that wants
to start in advertising, and is willing to work for a lower

salary. We'll eventually lose these kids, of course, but we'll hope to fill their ranks with bright new faces fresh from college."

Barbara Proctor also says, "We have to work with other black businesses, of course; many of them are hostile. They are not eager for us to succeed, either. It's difficult to get blacks to cooperate in a venture because they don't trust each other. So many of the black middle class want to buy the things that are 'like the white folks'.' I want to guide people to *buy black.* Of course, if I wouldn't comment on the things I see going on around me — the hypocrisy, the snobbery, the suspicion — I might be doing even better than I am."

Barbara Proctor admits that her voracious striving for success has cost her a great deal in terms of her personal life. She has divorced her husband, a road manager for Sarah Vaughan. Their only son has little interest in this business. "I asked him if he would like to take over the business one day and he said 'Never!' It's because the business has taken so much family time. He'll never be an ordinary boy, just as I am not an ordinary woman. He paints well, and he wants to be an artist, and he seems to think that when he's ready he'll move right into the white world, but he'll find out soon enough that it's more difficult than talent and desire. Racism will become a reality."

People who know Barbara Proctor and who admire her ambition and drive, often wonder why, with no one who cares to leave her growing business to, she continues to work so hard, setting new, more elaborate goals for herself each year. "What's she trying to prove?" one friend asks. "She makes a lot of money, but she doesn't seem to enjoy it. I don't believe she's ever even taken a vacation."

Barbara Proctor smiles at this and says, "I suppose I could say that I'm doing what I do for *my people,* to build a foundation for my race. That may be part of it, but it's only one part. I wanted to succeed because I was born to succeed. There is a contribution I must make whether it makes my personal life comfortable or not. One really cannot defy a mission. The more you resist, and try to stay in the past, the more things never change, the longer we'll remain just another 'minority group.' But we never were a minority, you know. After all, two-thirds of the world is not white. The real minority group are the WASPs. Maybe *they're* the ones we should all be sorry for. Could a WASP with all my so-called disadvantages do as much as I've managed to do in four short years? Sometimes I frankly wonder."

IV

Getting Started

8

Memberships

CHARLOTTE HAWKINS BROWN'S PALMER MEMORIAL INSTITUTE may have been the most prestigious, but it was not the only fashionable private school for well-fixed blacks. There was also St. Frances Academy in Baltimore, a girls' boarding and day school run by the Oblate Sisters of Providence, a religious community of black nuns that was established as early as 1829. In Rock Castle, Virginia, St. Francis de Sales School is another Catholic girls' school, run by the Sisters of the Blessed Sacrament and affiliated with the Catholic University of America in Washington. At St. Francis, each school day begins with holy mass and, in addition to a regular college preparatory course, the school offers business and general courses. Like Palmer, both St. Francis and St. Frances are "uniform schools." Unlike Palmer, however, St. Francis de Sales does not make music instruction mandatory, but charges extra for it. St. Francis de Sales is the sister school of the first black military school in America, St. Emma Academy, also in Rock Castle. In addition to the military, St. Emma, with its surrounding 1,700 acres of farmland, offers a complete agricultural course and has a trade school that teaches students to be automobile mechanics, cabinetmakers, carpenters and such. The two schools share social events, and have joint commencement exercises.

There are elite primary schools for blacks as well, and one of the most selective of these is the Junior Academy of Brooklyn, which takes children — mostly from Brooklyn and Manhattan — from nursery school through junior high school. "To gain admittance, students must be recommended either by the parent of a child in the school or by a church or one of the recognized organizations, such as Jack and Jill of America or the Business and Professional Women," explains Mrs. Dorothy M. Bostic, who founded the Academy in the late 1940's. "Most of our students are the children of professionals. We always have a long waiting list for the earlier grades."

For many years, boys and girls who attended such schools as the Junior Academy or Palmer or St. Francis de Sales were sent away to summer camp at the equally elitist Camp Atwater in East Brookfield, Massachusetts. Like Palmer, Camp Atwater had vaguely religious origins and was run by the Springfield Urban League — supposedly for the children of underprivileged blacks in the Springfield area. In fact, it turned out to be something very different, and "underprivileged" children arrived at Camp Atwater in chauffeur-driven limousines from New York, New Jersey, Washington, and Philadelphia. The daughter of the president of Howard University was a camp counselor. Such families as the distinguished Dammonds from New York sent their children to Camp Atwater. (The Dammonds are descendents of Ellen Craft, a heroine from slave days; so fair was Ellen Craft's skin — she, the family claims, was a descendent of Thomas Jefferson — that she was able to disguise herself as a white man going north for medical treatment and to escape slavery in Georgia. Traveling with her was a "manservant" named William, who was actually Ellen Craft's husband. They traveled to Boston in first class accommodations, and arrived in time to take part in a mass meeting against slavery at Faneuil Hall.)

Atwater, under the surveillance of a Reverend and Mrs. DuBarry of Springfield, was strictly run. July was for the girl campers, and August was for the boys. "We all knew each other, and our parents all knew each other," recalls one alumna of many July summers at Atwater. "I remember one afternoon, coming home from a canoe trip, and seeing all the girls from my cabin in a huddle down by the side of the lake. There was obviously some sort of crisis. It turned that two little black-skinned girls from Springfield had arrived whom nobody knew. We didn't know who their parents were. They didn't look like us, dress like us, talk like us. We were sure they were covered with germs. We made them sleep in the center of the cabin, as far away from our bunks as we could get them."

Far more important than where an upper-class black goes to prep school or camp has been which fraternity or sorority he or she joins at college, or which club or fraternal order he or she joins afterward. In fact, black educators have often complained that, in terms of the Greek letter societies, upper-class black parents spend far more time and energy grooming and preparing their children for the social side of college life than they do for the academic side. On most college campuses, the most prestigious sorority is Alpha Kappa Alpha, followed by Delta Sigma Theta, both of which were founded at Howard University. The real reason why Delta Sigma Theta does not have the status of AKA is probably that AKA is smaller; Delta has nearly 250 chapters, while AKA has just over a hundred. To get into AKA on most campuses it is almost essential that one's mother have been an AKA also, and, preferably, one's grandmother. As for the Deltas, according to one AKA, "The Delta girls were never quite as *respectable.*" To counter allegations that they are snobbish and exclusive, the AKA's point out that their chapters and alumnae organizations raise thousands of dollars a year for scholarships, and to help to support such organizations as the N.A.A.C.P., the Urban League, and the United Negro College Fund. The Deltas, on the other hand, have been cited by the American Library Association for their bookmobile and library projects.

The oldest black college fraternity, Sigma Pi Phi, was organized in Philadelphia in 1904, and has now come to be known simply as *Boulé*. Although the original aim of this society was to bring together "an aristocracy of talent," *Boulé* quickly became a symbol of all that is snobbish, restrictive, and antiblack in American Negro education. Only the "best" black men were taken into *Boulé*, membership in each chapter was kept small, and the number of chapters was kept few. To belong to *Boulé* meant that a man had escaped from the working class, and had entered the bourgeoisie, if not the elite. Two years later, as an "answer" to *Boule*'s exclusiveness, Alpha Phi Alpha was founded by eight black students at Cornell. Since then, Alpha Phi Alpha has expanded to membership in the tens of thousands and, because of its size, it has somewhat eclipsed *Boulé* in social importance on American campuses and in the quality of black business and professional men it has produced. Alpha Phi Alpha likes to boast that it has produced over forty college presidents, dozens of judges, a number of bishops, and that more than half the alumni members in the Philadelphia and Greater New York chapters are doctors, dentists, pharmacists, and men who own their own businesses. ("Better and Bigger Negro Business" is one of the mottoes of the fraternity.)

Neither Alpha Phi Alpha nor Sigma Pi Phi, however, have had the impact on black businesses that the black fraternal orders have had. As early as 1865, there were black lodges of Elks, Odd Fellows, Masons, and True Reformers in every city in America that contained a significant black population. The oldest of these black societies is the Masonic Order, organized in Boston in 1775 and chartered twelve years later by the Grand Lodge of England under the name African Lodge Number 459. It was founded by Prince Hall, a West Indian, along with fourteen other blacks assigned to a British army regiment. The original purpose of the order was to provide members with mutual aid and protection in times of sickness and "distress."

Prior to the Civil War, there were at least two secret societies in existence set up by free blacks in the South — the Galilean Fishermen and the Nazarites. After Emancipation, a proliferation of others came into being, including the Knights and Daughters of Tabor, the Order of Good Samaritans, and the Colored Knights of Pythias. Each had its secret ritual and ceremony, an esoteric handshake and other signals and codes of ethics for its membership.

The social and political life of the black community revolved around the meetings, parties, conventions and other affairs that took place at these lodges. They were where banquets and wedding receptions were held, where card parties were organized. They were centers of community news and gossip and, it would seem, of interminable feuding among the members.

These lodges collected large sums of money. There was a seemingly endless variety of dues and assessments — local dues, grand lodge dues, supreme grand lodge dues, initiation fees, grand lodge fees, supreme grand lodge fees, and special fees, plus assessments for building funds, endowment funds, education funds, and special funds. Many fraternal orders also sold such paraphernalia as fraternal rings, pins, tie clips, cufflinks, sweetheart pins and other jewelry, as well as the costumes and other trappings that were put on for special meetings and occasions. It has been estimated that blacks contributed at least $168,000,000 to fraternal orders between 1870 and 1920. Many lodges also sold insurance and endowment policies to their members.

What the members got in return for their large outlays of cash is worth noting. Obviously, as the lodges and clubhouses quickly become repositories of large amounts of black capital, there were certain dangers, and there were many men who just as quickly lost sight of their orders' lofty goals, and were led into temptation. For a lodge treasurer to vanish with lodge funds was not unknown, and so it was essential that the man who supervised the coffers be a person of the highest probity and integrity. He had, in fact, to become the town's leading black citizen, topmost in the pecking order, the equivalent of the president of the town's biggest bank. Often, he was the town's leading physician or clergyman (black churches were also collecting large amounts of money).

The lodges were, in fact, the first black banks, and most of the black banks in America — as well as the black insurance companies — grew directly out of them. The lodges loaned money to their members, provided savings accounts and depositories for valuables, and offered mortgages. They were kindergartens and training schools in high finance. Because the lodges were, after all, private clubs, not only the treasurers but the general membership were learning how to handle and invest money. The monthly meeting when the treasurer's report was read was usually unanimously attended. Some lodges went directly into business. The Grand Lodge of Masons of Mississippi, for example, early in the twentieth century bought a thousand acres of timberland and went into the lumber business. During the same period, the True Reformers organized a bank, a chain of retail stores, a hotel, a newspaper, a nursing home for old people, and an all-black community called Browneville. The Independent Order of St. Luke, under the leadership of a forceful black woman named Maggie L. Walker, operated a printing plant, a bank, an office building, a restaurant and restaurant supply house, and a department store.

The argument, often given, that blacks have not attained a degree of wealth and success because of their "late entry" into the commercial world, is not valid. Between 1900 and 1910 there was an unprecedented black business and building boom, as the members of the various lodges within a city, or in other cities, strove to outdo each other for the good of themselves and the good of the order. In the process, of course, of building larger and larger buildings and acquiring larger and larger properties, many lodges overextended themselves, and many of their enterprises passed quickly into white hands. There was also the apparently insoluble problem of internecine bickering, jealousy, and squabbling. What seemed to be the major black business coup of this period was undertaken by the Odd Fellows of Georgia, under the leadership of a dynamic man named Benjamin T. Davis. In 1912, the Georgia Odd Fellows bought an entire block of land on Auburn Avenue in Atlanta, and constructed a five-story office building at a cost of $250,000. The following year, Davis and his group built an auditorium on the rest of the land for $180,000. At this point, however, when things seemed rosiest, the members of the order fell to wrangling. There were charges, countercharges, recriminations, and accusations of alleged mismanagement of funds. The disputes could not be settled, and the order went into receivership in 1916.

Feuding, mismanagement, lack of expertise, excessive and in some cases conspicuous spending (the earliest black banks went in heavily for costly marble facades, heavy chandeliers, carved pilasters, and ceilings decorated with gold leaf) all conspired to doom many early black enterprises — along with the eagerness with which white men moved in and took over the moment a black business began to founder. And yet the fraternal lodges, and the businesses they spawned and in some cases ruined, taught important lessons. The first black bank in America, the Freedmen's Savings and Trust Company, was chartered in 1865, on the initiative of missionary groups and the Freedmen's Bureau, by the United States government. It was ostensibly a philanthropic operation to help the freed slave enter the economic community, "organized and controlled by white friends of the Negro for his benefit." It was also designed to encourage black thrift and initiative and, to black men of the period, the creation of the Freedmen's Bank was as symbolic of their new freedom as the Emancipation Proclamation. No one expressed this better than Frederick Douglass, the wealthy black Washingtonian who became the bank's last president, when he said, "The history of civilization shows that no people can well rise to a high degree of mental or even moral excellence without wealth. . . . The mission of the Freedmen's Bank is to show our people the road to a share of the wealth and well being of the world." Douglass had been a slave who escaped and made his way to Canada, and then to England. In London, he had been taken up by Mayfair society, where he was something of a curiosity. No one could believe that this courtly, bearded gentleman had actually been a slave, and enough money was raised — $700 — to buy him his freedom. He returned to the United States, where he went on the lecture circuit as an eloquent and outspoken Abolitionist. From his lectures and, later, from his Rochester-based newspaper, the *North Star,* he became a rich man.

In addition to its supposedly lofty aims, it was generally assumed that funds deposited in the Freedmen's Bank were protected by the government. To bolster this misconception, the passbooks that were issued to depositors were emblazoned with the likenesses of President Lincoln, General Grant, General Howard, and others whom blacks had come to regard as their saviors, and the bank buildings themselves were draped and festooned with American flags. The bank's initial capitalization came from hundreds of thousands of dollars' worth of unclaimed deposits of black soldiers who had died or disappeared during the Civil War and left no survivors, and in its first year branches were opened in Louisville, Richmond, Nashville, Wilmington, Memphis, Mobile, and Vicksburg. By 1871, there were thirty-four branches, thirty-two of them in the South and, at its peak, the bank had seventy thousand depositors and deposits of $19,952,647.

The trouble was that, though the bank used black cashiers and tellers — who dressed in high collars, morning coats, and wore red-white-and-blue boutonnieres — and, in some branches, employed black "advisors," the board of directors of the Freedmen's Bank was a mixture of financially naïve, though well-meaning, white missionaries, and financially unscrupulous white entrepreneurs who were looking for *their* road "to a share of the wealth, etc." The $260,000 headquarters of the Freedmen's Bank in Washington had a particularly imposing facade of tall brownstone slabs, and was elegantly appointed and furnished within. But behind the closed doors of the directors' chamber, the schemers were at work — making illegal loans to one another, investing in overcapitalized and speculative ventures, or simply dipping their hands into the till. Later, it turned out that for most of its existence the Freedmen's Bank was actually controlled by the notorious New York financier Jay Cooke, and by 1872 the bank had been all but destroyed by fraud and embezzlement. As economic conditions got worse in 1873, and Cooke and his henchmen began to see the handwriting on the wall, the directors cast about for a black man to name as president. The most distinguished black of the day was Frederick Douglass, and so the honor was given to him. If worse came to worst, went the reasoning, the blame for the bank's collapse would fall on a black man.

Douglass should have known better than to accept the post or at least have done a bit of probing into the bank's financial situation. Later, he was to say sadly, "I inherited a corpse." But at the time, no doubt, the offer to be a bank president flattered his ego, and he clearly enjoyed it when, as he wrote, "I waked up one morning to find myself seated in a comfortable arm chair, with gold spectacles on my nose, and to hear myself addressed as President of the Freedmen's Bank. I could not help reflecting on the contrast between Frederick the slave boy, running about at Col. Lloyd's with only a tow linen shirt to cover him, and Frederick — President of a Bank — counting its assets by millions."

And worse did come to worst, just three months later, with the Panic of 1873. Douglass ordered desperate economies, and even invested $10,000 of his own money in hopes of saving the sinking institution. But it was much too late, and Douglass ordered the bank to close its doors. All across the country the news of the closing of the Freedmen's Bank struck the black community like a thunderbolt. Weeping and unbelieving, blacks whose savings had been inside lined the streets outside the banks' locked branches. W. E. B. Du-Bois said, "Not even ten additional years of slavery could have done so much to throttle the thrift of the freedmen as the mismanagement of the series of savings banks chartered by the Nation for their special aid." And the Nation, it seemed, had made no guarantee of depositors' accounts. In all, over a million dollars in savings were lost by the newly freed slaves.

It was not until fifteen years after the Freedmen's Bank debacle that, out of the fraternal orders, banks for blacks were tried again. In October, 1888, the Capital Savings Bank opened in Washington. That same year, organized by the Grand Fountain United Order of True Reformers, a savings bank by the same lengthy name was chartered, also in

Washington. Next came the Mutual Trust Company of Chattanooga, and, in 1890, the Alabama Penny Savings and Loan Company opened in Birmingham. Between 1899 and 1905, twenty-eight more banks were organized by blacks, most of them by fraternal lodges. Most of them, too, went under — through bad management, lack of skill (the president of Alabama Penny Savings, for example, was a clergyman, and the vice president was a bartender), or as a result of the periodic panics and depressions that characterized the era. Some black financial institutions, however, survived.

John Merrick, for example, was born a slave in Clinton, North Carolina, in 1859. He taught himself to read and write and went to work at the age of twelve in a Chapel Hill brickyard. He also shined shoes in a Raleigh barbershop, taught himself the barber's skill, and, in his spare time, studied high finance. In 1880, he moved to Durham where, twelve years later, he owned five barbershops and was the personal barber of the tobacco tycoon Washington Duke. Merrick was a frugal man and, at Mr. Duke's suggestion, he invested every penny he could in real estate. He also noticed the burgeoning business that was involved in the fraternal orders, and in 1883 he established the Royal Knights of King David. Fifteen years later, with a local physician, Dr. Aaron McDuffie Moore, he organized the North Carolina Mutual and Provident Association. The first few years of the insurance company were difficult, but John Merrick forged on, firing salesmen who were unproductive, hiring new ones that were. Before his death in 1919, Merrick's company, renamed North Carolina Mutual Life, had $16,096,722 worth of insurance in force. Merrick had organized, in the meantime, a number of satellite companies — the Bull City Drug Company, the Merrick-Moore-Spaulding Real Estate Company, the Durham Textile Mill, and the Mechanics and Farmers Bank. North Carolina Mutual is the largest black-owned insurance company in the United States today, followed by John Johnson's Supreme Life Insurance Company of America.

The other, Atlanta Life, was founded by Alonzo F. Herndon, who, like John Merrick, was also born in slavery in 1858, and — by coincidence — was also a barber. As a young freed man, he acquired several barber shops and, in 1882, Herndon moved to Atlanta, where he quickly became known as the best barber in town. In 1904, he opened a fancy establishment on Peachtree Street which was described at the time as "the most popular and most successful business of its kind in the country." Herndon got into the insurance business almost by accident. In 1905, the Georgia legislature passed a law requiring mutual aid societies to deposit $5,000 with state officials. Many — particularly those run by black churches — could not meet this requirement, and so Alonzo Herndon came to the rescue. He purchased several church associations, including two that he bought for $160. Atlanta Life was started in a one-room office in the Rucker Building on Auburn Avenue. Ten years later, capital stock of $25,000 was subscribed and sold — with Herndon buying most of the stock himself — and in 1922 the capital stock of the company was increased to $100,000, with Herndon again buying nearly all of it. By the time he died in 1927, Atlanta Life was a major institution in the black community, as it remains today.

While the fraternal orders were helping black business-men — or at least *some* black businessmen — get ahead in a money sense, the sororities and social clubs were helping women advance socially. Out of Alpha Kappa Alpha and Delta Sigma Theta have sprung such women's organizations as The Girl Friends, started in New York in 1927 by sixteen friends — girl friends, one supposes. The Girl Friends has expanded, and has several dozen chapters in as many cities. Though it is primarily a social club, The Girl Friends are active in community service. Then there is the small and exclusive Gay Northeasterners, known for its beautiful balls, and composed for the most part of New York and Connecticut ladies. In Memphis, the Memphis Dinner Club is so selective that it has only eight members. The Smart Set Club of Houston, founded in 1944 by the smartest of Houston's smart set, was originally composed of the five wives of the city's five leading doctors and dentists. Houston's black society reverberated with the news several years ago that The Smart Set was expanding its membership to twelve. In Philadelphia, there is the Cotillion Society, which, despite its name, has nothing to do with debutantes. It supports an opera company, and offers a showcase for young black singers, musicians, and other artists. To be "in" in Roanoke, Virginia, one would want to join the Altruist Club and, in Washington, there are a number of quaintly named clubs, including the What Good Are We, the Sappy Sues, and the Regular Buddies — all modeled more or less on The Girl Friends. One of the larger national women's clubs for the upper crust is known as The Moles (husbands of Moles are called The Mules), which has chapters in 24 Eastern cities, from as far south as Georgia and as far west as Illinois. In addition to purely social doings — teas, luncheons, and card parties — The Moles support a black scholarship program.

There are also elite clubs for both men and women, such as Jack and Jill of America. Jack and Jill members must be parents, and the organization runs a club for children called the Jack and Jill Juniors. One of the purposes of Jack and Jill is to see to it that proper young girls meet proper young boys. And the women's clubs are backed up by purely social men's clubs, where men gather at each others' homes or hotel suites just for camaraderie and good times — such as the Royal Coterie of Snakes in Chicago, the Me-Do-So Club in Baltimore, the Original Illinois Club in New Orleans, the Comus Club of New York and Brooklyn, the Bachelor-Benedicts in Washington, the Strikers in Mobile, and the Cotillion Club in Detroit. These clubs were originally founded by small groups of men from particular professions — doctors, dentists, pharmacists, lawyers. Sons and close friends of members are eligible for membership. They must be proposed, seconded, and passed by the entire group before they are taken in. Gerri Major, the former society editor of *Ebony,* has said, "Maneuvering to insure inclusion of a relative on one of these lists rivals the intrigue of foreign diplomats seeking American financial aid. Guest lists, too, are limited. An invitation is a royal command, thankfully acknowledged." In many cities, the men's social clubs sponsor the black debutante balls.

Then there are summer clubs, at resorts where affluent blacks vacation and have summer homes — at Highland Beach, Arundel-on-the-Bay, Columbia Beach, or Eagle Harbor, all on Chesapeake Bay, or on Martha's Vineyard at the black summer colony of Oak Bluffs. A number of upper-crust New York families maintain second summer homes in the old whaling village of Sag Harbor, on the eastern end of Long Island. The black joke is: "That's why they call it Sag Harbor. Everything is sagging."

But, in fact, though the black summer colony at Sag Harbor may have sagged a bit when it started two to three generations ago, it is very much propped up today. Homes in the enclave are large, attractive, and well maintained. A number have swimming pools, and several have tennis courts. Areas of Sag Harbor that were once known as Nineveh and Mount Misery have been stylishly renamed Azurest and Sag Harbor Heights. (Though the terrain of Suffolk County is notoriously flat, there are hilly spots in Sag Harbor that would qualify as "heights.") Sag Harbor's summer set is famously close-knit, clannish, and exclusive. Its leaders are members of New York's Pickens family (real estate), who have been summering here for many years, and New York State Supreme Court justice Edward R. Dudley and his wife, who own one of the houses with its own private pool. Newcomers with social ambitions find the going tough. "Money alone just won't do it here," says one summer resident. "There's one woman who's built a big new place, but no one's impressed with her sauna and her gymnasium and her bidets. To us, she's simply *nouveau*." In Sag Harbor Heights, the wooded lanes are unpaved to discourage rubberneckers or other unwanted visitors. There is a private beach, with a three-dollar parking fee for "outsiders." There is very little commingling with Sag Harbor's white summer colony, nor with any of the Hamptons beyond. Needless to say, there is no social intercourse at all with the large — and very poor — black population of nearby Bridgehampton.

At the oldest and most snobbish of the black summer resorts, Highland Beach — founded in the 1880's by Frederick Douglass's son — there was for years a rule, laid down by the light-skinned Establishment, that dark-skinned blacks could not join the club, or buy property there; this rule has since been eased, but only somewhat. At Oak Bluffs, where uppercrust blacks have also been going for years (Massachusetts Senator Edward Brooke has a large house there), life is also very staid and seemly. "Oak Bluffs is more formal," says Mrs. Paul Hough, whose family have had a summer home there for two generations. "We have bridge parties in the afternoon, small formal dinners in the evening. People bring their cars, and are driven to parties by their chauffeurs. We have a private beach, and a private tennis club. It amuses me to notice how, all at once, tennis has become such a big thing with white people. Why, my mother was having private tennis lessons at Oak Bluffs when she was a little girl!" No small amount of social rivalry exists, meanwhile, between Sag Harbor and Oak

Bluffs. A Sag Harbor resident says, "Oak Bluffs has become terribly *Middle West.* You know, those pushy Chicago people." A longtime Oak Bluffs resident sniffs and counters, "I hear that Sag Harbor these days has become completely *overrun."*

In 1946, two Philadelphia ladies, Sarah S. Scott and the late Margaret R. Hawkins, founded Links, Incorporated, which, though it is not as venerable as The Girl Friends, has become the most prestigious — and exclusive — black women's organization in America. Originally, the Links was simply a social group, centered about weekly bridge parties (members of Links were quite conscious of the black woman's traditional love of poker, but poker has long been relegated to the lower class; the upper-class black woman plays bridge). But as Links expanded, it took on philanthropic projects and it has become the black equivalent of the Junior League.

The name Links refers to links of friendship. Husbands of Links are called Connecting Links, and children are called Heir-o-Links. Membership in Links in any city is limited to thirty women (some cities have far fewer members) and most Links are so fair-skinned that some blacks wonder why Links call themselves a black group at all. The number thirty was selected as a ceiling for membership because "That was the maximum number that anyone could put up at one's house," according to Mrs. Hough, a former national president of Links. (In segregation days, when wealthy blacks traveled in the South, they could not stay in the best hotels; southern Links members were expected to hostess their visiting sisters.) Today, there are 130 Links chapters across the country, and their fund-raising projects involve education, medicine, and the arts. A popular Links fund-raising event is sponsorship of the *Ebony* Fashion Fair, a traveling fashion show that annually visits a number of cities across the country. Most Links husbands are members of *Boulé*. Nearly all Links members are AKA's, with a small sprinkling of Deltas.

For their choosiness and their grand ways, the Links are ridiculed and even despised by lower-class blacks. "They're nothing but snobs," says the outspoken Lina Fleming of Cincinnati. "Or let's just say they *try* to be snobs." Mrs. Fleming insists that she would not join Links if asked, and adds, "My sister was asked to be a Link. She turned them down. Being a Link means nothing." But it does mean something — if you are a Link.

At the same time, the Links and the other women's groups are — like the men's fraternal lodges — torn by inner strife, feuding, and clamboring for one-upmanship. Each Link, and each Link chapter, seems to spend much of its time trying to outdo the others, and to talk the others down. ("Those Washington Links think they're so *grand!*" sniffs one of the Detroit Links.) As for the Moles, they publish an annual magazine called *Molerama* and, in the 1974 edition, the publicity chairman for the Washington chapter was one Thersa Archer. In her annual report of her chapter's doings, which she wrote herself, Mrs. Archer described herself as "hard working, careful," and went on with a lengthy paragraph — one of the longest paragraphs in the article — describing her fourteen-day cruise to Nassau, Curaçao, Barbados, Martinique, and St. Thomas, a Fourth of July holiday spent in Norwalk, Connecticut, Thanksgiving with friends in Pittsburgh, and announced her and her husband's fortieth wedding anniversary. Thersa Archer, however, had obviously been having some sort of dispute with one of her publicity committee members, Beatrice Smith. She gave Beatrice Smith only a short, perfunctory paragraph, in which she described Mrs. Smith as "fickle, easily led." There must have been quite a row over this, because the words "fickle, easily led" were blacked out by the printer as the magazine went to press, though they are still legible through the ink.

Though many blacks tend to lay the blame for their woes at the feet of an amorphous white "Establishment," the infighting between and among their own many elite groups may have helped prevent them from having a true Establishment of their own. In any human society there has always been a pecking order, with an elite group gathered at the top. In New York, Mrs. Astor had her "Four Hundred." The uptown Jews had their "One Hundred." In Washington, the Links have their "Thirty," and Houston's Smart Set has its "Twelve." And of course the blacks have had a special need for their many tiny, closed social sets, clubs, secret fraternal and sororal orders, each with its secret rite and ritual, grip and password, each containing secrets within secrets. They have needed to bond together as a defensive shield against what they see as an inimical or, at best, indifferent white world. But in so doing the little clubs and orders have managed to erect tall barricades against each other as well. Perhaps this is at least one reason why promising black businessmen have had difficulty succeeding with what should have been promising black businesses. They don't quite like each other.

Though each of the little clubs and societies likes to think of itself as the Top, they are really a series of small tops cut off from any base. They are even ambivalent about the color of their skin. Most light-skinned blacks say that they are "not proud" of having white ancestors. Yet they are very proud of the light skin their white ancestors have given them, and often it is the main requirement to join the club. The view from the clubhouse is comfortable and cozy, but it does not take in what Barbara Proctor calls "those bottomless blacks" who, if they are aware of the elite groups, view them with scorn and consider their social pretensions ridiculous. A wry and bitter little ditty has emerged from

the bottom of the black world which reveals rather clearly
how this world regards the higher-ups. It goes:

> *Twinkle, twinkle, little nigger,*
> *All you do is sit and figger.*
> *Don't you know that if you get bigger*
> *All you'll be is a bigger nigger?*

Sometimes attempts are made to bridge the abysmal social
gap. One Links member tells of a young black man who
worked in her office. Though his origins were the ghetto, he
was college-educated, well-spoken, and "seemed nice." She
considered inviting him for dinner, but says, "I wasn't sure
how my friends would react, and how he'd react to them.
Still, I asked him. He came, and — I was really surprised —
he handled himself very well!" That, however, was as far as
it went. Another Link recalls shopping with her mother at
Rich's department store in Atlanta, and seeing, on an esca-
lator, an old black woman in split-out shoes, sagging stockings, a tattered shawl and a turban. She whispered to her
mother, "Look at that dirty old colored lady!" Her mother
reprimanded her. "You mustn't say things like that," she
said. "She may be just as nice as you and me." It was probably just what Charlotte Hawkins Brown would have said,
and that was as far as *that* went.

And so the fragmented elite of the black world, with their
clubs and societies each secretly at war with all the others,
has not yet achieved what might be termed true clout in
either the white world or the black. Among blacks, the elite
have achieved importance without real position. They have
become dignitaries, but without power, leading ladies and
gentlemen without much influence, figureheads, but not
leaders — shining examples, but not guides. As Lina Fleming puts it bluntly about the Links, "They're all chiefs but
no Indians."

9

"Let Us Pray...."

A CERTAIN AMOUNT OF DIVISIVENESS WAS, OF COURSE, ENCOUR-
aged by the white slave-owners of the antebellum South. It
was easier to control a divided people than a united one,
and plantation owners taught their house servants to believe that they were "better" than their fellow slaves in the
fields. To be sent to the fields was a form of punishment
and, if he did his job well, the house slave was rewarded
with better food, better clothing, and a generally easier life.
It amused slave owners to let their house slaves have periodic parties, dances, teas, and other "socials," for which
the slaves dressed up in their best clothes — invariably hand-
me-downs from the master and his wife — and which were
otherwise imitations of Southern white social activities.

An ex-slave named Austin Steward, who wrote and published his autobiography in 1857, gave a vivid description of
the status layers that existed on the plantation:

> It was about ten o'clock when the aristocratic slaves
> began to assemble, dressed in the cast-off finery of their
> master and mistress, swelling out and putting on airs in
> imitation of those they were forced to obey from day to
> day.

House servants were, of course, "the stars" of the party; all eyes were turned to them to see how they conducted, for they, among slaves, are what a military man would call "fugle-men." The field hands, and such of them as have generally been excluded from the dwelling of their owners, look to the house servants as a pattern of politeness and gentility. And, indeed, it is often the only method of obtaining any knowledge of the manners of what is called "genteel society;" hence, they are ever regarded as a privileged class; and are sometimes greatly envied, while others are bitterly hated.

But it would be an oversimplification to say that the house slaves and field slaves on all Southern plantations "hated" each other because of the caste system. In households where the slave-master or his wife was particularly despotic or demanding, there were often slaves who would have gladly changed places with the field workers and who misbehaved in an attempt to do so. And, in the end, it was always Slave Row — where every slave returned at day's end — and not "the big house" that was the heart and nerve center of the slave community.

Here the house slaves, quietly and steadily, brought whatever food and clothing could be pilfered from the house, and distributed it among the others. Since the slaves saw their own people as stolen property, they saw nothing wrong with stealing from their masters. Naturally, it is seldom pleasant to be on the receiving end of this sort of charity, and there was doubtless some resentment among the field hands against their benefactors. House servants were also able to provide a certain amount of after-hours entertainment to the other inhabitants of Slave Row — many of whom had never set foot inside the big house, or spoken to "Massah" or his "missus" — regaling them with tales and gossip of the doings of the household, mimicking and parodying their masters' speech, gestures, and mannerisms, often to the point of high hilarity. Most important, the house servants brought news of what Massah might be planning, picked up by eavesdropping at parlor doors and in back stairways. If, say, the serving maid at dinner learned that the master was planning to sell a block of slaves, that news was quickly reported to Slave Row. The house slaves earned respect as the plantation's spies.

It is quite clear that most slave-owners distrusted their house servants, as indicated by accounts of "spelling-out stories" — where the master and his family spelled out words and sentences that they did not want the slaves to understand. A woman who could covertly learn to spell was a valued agent to the community of Slave Row. Secrecy became a mode of life on the plantation, and most slaves made it a rule never to let the white man know what they were thinking. Slave-owners, meanwhile, tried to use their house servants as sources of information as to what the field hands were saying or contemplating. And naturally there were servants who, in return for bribes or special favors, became traitors to their fellow blacks, just as there were Jewish traitors in the concentration camps of World War II. When traitors were discovered, they were harshly dealt with, even killed. Once, at a kangaroo court that was set up on a Mississippi plantation, a black waitress was accused of telling her master about a planned slave revolt. In her testimony, she stood up dramatically among her fellow slaves and said, "I told the Massah, 'I'm going to tell you the truth, so help me God' — and then I told him *nothin'!*"

"Negro dialect," meanwhile, was another expression of the need for secrecy. Just as the Jews of Europe developed Yiddish, or Judeo-German, and the Jews of Spain developed Ladino, or Judeo-Spanish, as a way to keep their Christian enemies from knowing too much about their business, the slaves developed a language, full of allusions, innuendos and puns, that the white master could almost, but not quite, understand. Also, the slaves communicated with one another through music, and many harmless-sounding spirituals were actually skillfully coded messages being passed up and down Slave Row. "Steal away, steal away to Jesus, steal away, steal away home. . . . I ain't got long to stay here," meant that there would be an escape attempt that night. Other songs evoked battle and destruction: "Joshua fit the battle of Jericho, And the walls came tumblin' down." And others were direct challenges to the slavemaster: "Tell old Pharaoh, let my people go!"

The social hierarchy of Slave Row was much more complicated than simply a matter of house servants versus field hands. Age conferred status, among other things, and older people were addressed as "Uncle" and "Auntie" not because they were relatives but because these were terms of respect. Slave artisans were also a privileged class. Each plantation was in effect a feudal city-state and needed, in addition to laborers, skilled carpenters, cabinet and furniture makers, cobblers, tailors, stonemasons, blacksmiths, painters, plasterers, silversmiths, and ironmongers. Many of these slaves had brought the secrets of their crafts with them from Africa, and the beautiful grillwork of New Orleans is a particularly striking example of slave craftsmanship. These people composed an aristocracy of talent. Then, in each Slave Row community, there was another aristocracy based on the slave's relationship with his master. If a slave woman, for example, talked back to her mistress and got away with it, she was highly regarded. If a man stood up straight to his master, without bowing, and looked him straight in the eye (against the law in Louisiana), and was not punished for his uppityness, he became a plantation hero. An even greater hero was the slave who had made a brave attempt to escape, even though he might eventually have been caught and brought back to the plantation. The slaves who had made the most successful thefts from the masters, or who had carried off the most convincing deceptions, were also afforded special status, as were those who had become adept at seasoning their masters' food with urine, arsenic, ground glass, and "spiders beaten up in buttermilk."

The plantation also needed policemen, and often the most important man on the estate was the driver. The driver was the slave appointed by the slavemaster and charged with the responsibility of supervising the work of the slaves in the fields by day and patrolling the slave quarters by night. "The head driver," according to James H. Hammond, a South Carolina slavemaster, "is the most important Negro on the plantation, and is not required to work like the other hands. He is to be treated with more respect than any other Negro by master and overseer. . . . He is to be required to maintain proper discipline at all times; to see that no Negro idles or does bad work in the field, and to punish it [sic] with discretion. . . . He is a confidential servant, and may be a guard against any excesses or omissions of the overseer." He was, in other words, to be a combination majordomo and political liaison between the master and the other slaves, with a role rather similar to that of the straw boss of Jim Crow days.

The driver was also, quite often, the most feared and hated man in Slave Row — particularly if he abused his power and committed his own excesses or omissions. There was the case of a driver named Ely on a Mississippi plantation, who drove his slaves so hard and ruthlessly that they ambushed him and murdered him. But other drivers were genuinely admired, and even loved for doing what they could to soften the impact of slavery. Also in Mississippi, a driver named Solomon Northup conspired with his fellow slaves to outwit his master by faking whippings and other punishments, and successfully manipulated his master into giving his slaves shorter working hours and better quarters. Eventually, Northup managed to escape to the North.

In other words, an ability to deal with the white man — whether through deceit, clever bargaining, or other chicanery — was a thing much admired along Slave Row. The institution of slavery has been succinctly described as "a perpetual state of war," and, as in any war, anything was fair in this one. At the bottom of the slaves' pecking order were the humble and subservient who bent to their tasks unquestioningly. For these slaves, there was little but scorn.

The driver might be "the most important Negro on the plantation," but he was not necessarily the most important person in the slave community. Inevitably, that distinction fell to a more charismatic type, a spiritual leader with "powers" that verged upon the oracular. One slavemaster complained that it was a "notorious fact" that "on almost every large plantation of Negroes, there is one among them who holds a kind of magical sway over the minds and opinions of the rest. . . . The influence of such a Negro, often a preacher, on a quarter is incalculable." On one plantation, the leading high priest was called "Old Abram," and was said to be "deeply versed in such philosophy as is taught in the cabin of the slave." On another, in Mississippi, an ancient woman named Juba, who wore charms about her neck, was revered by her followers for the fact that she had had many visions and conversations with the devil. A Louisiana planter noted that Big Lucy had become the mystic leader of his slave community and "corrupts every young Negro in her power."

In New Orleans in the 1800's lived the legendary Marie Laveau, a tall, handsome "free woman of color" who was also a kind of voodoo priestess, credited with all sorts of extraordinary powers. At her command, blood would appear through a crack in an empty china teacup. She could, it was said, make men impotent at will, and her spells could make a woman barren. In the mulatto and black community, Marie Laveau was much feared and respected, and her influence in the white society of New Orleans was also awesome. By trade, Marie Laveau was a hairdresser, and she tended the ladies' coiffures in all the city's finest houses. Nineteenth-century women confided their secrets to their hairdressers as readily as women do today, and as a result Marie Laveau knew all the gossip, the scandal, the intimate details of marriages, liaisons, and love affairs. She used her knowledge well, trading tidbit for juicy tidbit among her clientele, and for years she ruled New Orleans, both black and white, and was considered one of the city's most powerful forces. Once, when General Lafayette came to New Orleans, a great ball was given in his honor. He failed to appear. It was because, so the rumor went, he was busy relishing the exotic pleasures of Marie Laveau. Marie Laveau had fifteen children, including one daughter to whom she imparted the secrets of her sorcery, and who took over for her in her image. The only portrait of Marie Laveau that is known to have existed was destroyed when the painting was stabbed through the eyes.

From the earliest days of slavery, the black priest was a pivotal plantation figure — the comforter of the sorrowing and bereaved, the interpreter of the supernatural, the guide to the here and the hereafter. From these men and women grew the Negro church, the fabled "invisible church of slavery," which rapidly became the first, and most powerful, black social institution in America. At first, it was by no means a Christian church, but an adaptation of African rites generally termed Obi Worship or Voodooism, over which had been spread a veneer of Christian ritual taught by the Baptist, Methodist, and Episcopal missionaries. Since slaves were not permitted to hold meetings on the plantation, and could not conduct religious services without a white witness present, the invisible church went underground. The worshippers slipped away, at night, to the fields or swamps to praise God in "hush-harbors." Their God, furthermore, was not the white man's God, nor was their devil the white man's devil. The devil, for example, was not the terror that he was in the European church, but a wily trickster, respected for his guile, who frequently competed with God and won. Intertwined with this was a belief in a world of spirits who could be manipulated, persuaded and inveigled to serve the living in various useful ways, and a belief in "hants," charms and taboos.

In a book called *From Slave Cabin to Pulpit,* Peter Randolph described a "hush-harbor":

> They have an understanding among themselves as to the time and place of getting together. This is often done by the first one arriving breaking boughs from the trees and bending them in the direction of the selected spot. Arrangements are then made for conducting the exercises. They first ask each other how they feel, the state of their minds, etc. The male members then select a certain space, in separate groups, for their division of the meeting. Preaching in order, by the brethren; then praying and singing all around until they generally feel quite happy. The speaker usually commences by calling himself unworthy, and talks very slowly, until, feeling the spirit, he grows excited, and in a short time, there fall to the ground twenty or thirty men and women under its influence.

The "invisible" church and its leaders and prophets became such a powerful force in the lives of American blacks that, when the slaves were freed in 1863, black Americans launched into frenzied church-organizing and church-building. The spiritual leaders of the plantations, almost none of whom had any formal religious training, had already been people of great influence. Now they found themselves in positions of considerable power. By 1876, the black South was linked by a network of churches of every denomination and persuasion. Because the churches were usually the largest buildings in the area, they were, at first, the only major buildings owned by blacks. They were social and spiritual centers. They were also centers of political, and substantial economic, activity. Money poured into the coffers of black churches as it did into the treasuries of the fraternal orders, and it has been estimated that, between 1870 and 1910, some $250,000,000 passed down the aisles of black churches in collection plates. Obviously some early black "preachers," who were merely self-taught orators and spell-binders who claimed a direct line to the Almighty, were less scrupulous than others, and used their positions for personal aggrandizement. Itinerant preachers, serving communities that had no regular church or pastor, also made money traveling about the country speaking for honorariums. And, in larger towns, as black religious institutions leapt from suppressed invisibility to jubilant visibility, it became an article of faith that the black preacher must have the handsomest horse and buggy (and, later, automobile) in town. He must have the finest house, the finest clothes, and the best-dressed wife. It was an honor for the women of the congregation to work for the preacher and his family as his cook, housekeeper, or laundress. Out of the black churches came the black colleges, and it was essential that the preacher's children be given a higher education. And so, in most Southern towns, it was possible for the black preacher and his family to become, if not the richest, at least the best fed and best cared-for people in the community. Many of today's black elite are descended from these early clergymen. And, as black preachers prospered, many of them bought or built their own churches, and rented them back to their congregations, thus providing themselves with a tidy source of income. This is currently the case with the Reverend Martin Luther King, Sr., of Atlanta, who owns his Ebenezer Baptist Church. The rent his congregation pays him has made Dr. King well-to-do.

The preacher, whatever his denomination, dealt with the fundamental problems of life — economic adversity, illness, death, and the question of the hereafter. And so, central to the theology of the post–Civil War black churches were their mutual aid and benevolent societies, which were life insurance and burial insurance companies in embryo. Practically every church of any size in the country had at least one benevolent society attached to it, and some had several. In general, these societies operated by assessing church members from 25 to 37 cents a month and, in turn, paying out sickness benefits of between $1.50 and $3.00 a week, and death benefits of between $10 and $20. The excess capital of these societies — which was often considerable — was banked or invested in real estate. These societies not only provided service, aid, and counseling; they also loaned money, at interest, in times of crisis and were therefore like miniature banks. At the same time, like the quasireligious fraternal orders, they offered business and money-management training to preachers and lay members of their congregations. They offered concrete proof of what individuals could do by pooling their resources. It was no coincidence that W. R. Pettiford, organizer and first president of the Alabama Penny Savings Bank, was pastor of Birmingham's Sixteenth Street Baptist Church. Nor was it a coincidence that, in more recent times, the late Elijah Muhammad, spiritual leader of the Nation of Islam, managed to create an economic empire of over $90,000,000 which includes 4,200 acres of farm land, a great deal of choice Chicago real estate, a weekly newspaper, and a nationwide chain of supermarkets, barbershops, restaurants and clothing stores.

Somehow, in the secret hush-harbors, the promise of freedom, including economic freedom to at least *some* blacks, had been held out:

Oh, freedom; oh freedom;
Oh, Lord, freedom over me,
And before I'd be a slave
I'd be buried in my grave
An' go home to my Lord and be free.

And yet, as black churches developed, they too, like the fraternal orders and secret societies, became divided into disagreeing factions. In the South, the black population became quickly bisected into two large religious communities — the Methodists and the Baptists. The Methodists, with their hierarchal organization, have tended to attract the wealthier and better-educated blacks — both as clergymen and parishioners — and Methodist bishops, in their various episcopal districts, exert great power over the lives of their ministers, who receive their church appointments from the bishops. The black Baptist congregations have attracted more than twice as many members as the Methodists, and the Baptist Church is considered the church of the black masses. On the other hand, without an organization with a centralized authority and hierarchy, the thousands of independent Baptist congregations, each of which selects its own minister, have provided a fertile arena for ambitious men and women who wished to become religious leaders and thereby move upward from the lower to the middle class. In some cities, in the process, Baptists have become split along color and class lines, as certain congregations decided to dissociate themselves from the emotional fervor of some Baptist rituals. Chanting, speaking in tongues, throwing oneself prostrate on the floor of the church in transports of religious ecstasy — such activities were considered "primitive" and "uncivilized."

Also, as blacks have moved up the social and economic ladder in their communities, they have tended to desert both the Methodist and Baptist churches, and to affiliate themselves with churches that middle-class America has long considered "nicer" — the Congregational, the Presbyterian, or the Anglican Episcopal. "My grandparents were Methodists, but we're Episcopalians" is a comment often heard among the elite, rather in the way that children and grandchildren of Orthodox Jews have tended to join the "more American" Reform congregations. At the same time, a number of upper-class black professional men — doctors, lawyers, dentists, and so on — have continued memberships in the Baptist or Methodist churches for business reasons. Their patients and clients are in these lower-class congregations. And it is common for upper-class black business and professional families to maintain two church memberships — one for social status and another for the financial advantage.

There are also a certain number of black Jews, many of them living in New York's Harlem to this day. Most of these are Orthodox, and observe the ancient Sephardic ritual that developed in medieval Spain and Portugal. This is because early Jewish plantation owners in the South were largely Sephardim who heeded the strictures of Deuteronomy 15. Deuteronomy implies that indentured servants or "bondsmen" in Jewish households should also be Jewish, and so Jewish slave-owners converted their slaves to Judaism. Deuteronomy also instructs that no slave should be kept for more than six years, and must be released in the seventh year — "And when thou sendest him out free from thee, thou shalt not let him go away empty." Many of these freed slaves kept their Jewish faith, and passed it along to their children and grandchildren. Black Sephardim are as fiercely proud of their ancient religion as white Sephardim, and consider themselves among the elite of Jewry. If their ancestors ever felt any spiritual kinship with the invisible church of slavery, the haughty Jewish blacks today have lost it altogether.

Whenever one moves upward, step by step along the American stairway of social class, it seems that something must be left behind. The Howard of Talladega graduate who sends his son to Princeton has deprived him of the special experience of the all-black college, and the perfumed meetings of the ladies of the Links, steeped in Good Works, lack the intimacy of the sewing circle that gathered around Grandmother's stove. When one climbs from Baptist prayer meetings to Episcopalian tea parties, the transforming magic of the hush-harbor in the midnight swamp has been lost forever.

Also lost, to many upper-crust blacks today, are the Negro spirituals. One woman says, "My grandfather was an itinerant preacher, who preached mostly in Baptist churches in the South. He did very well financially, and managed to buy a thousand acres of farmland in southeast Texas. I remember, when I was a little girl, that everywhere I looked and as far as I could see, it was Grandpa's land." (She has recently sold her share of the Texas land, wisely retaining the mineral rights beneath.) She adds, "They say that Grandpa was a wonderful preacher, and had a beautiful singing voice. I never heard him preach, and I used to wonder what he sang. I was raised an Episcopalian, and we never heard a Negro spiritual in our church. I never heard a Negro spiritual in our house. I never even heard *of* a Negro spiritual until I was practically a grown woman. The other day, I heard Roberta Flack and Donny Hathaway singing 'Come, Ye Disconsolate,' and I thought, 'What a beautiful song!' Someone told me it was a Negro spiritual, and I was *amazed*. I had absolutely no idea that black people ever sang songs like that!"

$\backsim$ *10* $\sim$

Business Ups and Downs

THOUGH IT IS COMMON FOR BLACKS TO ATTRIBUTE THEIR WOES
to slavery, it is important to remember that not all blacks
were slaves, and that there were free blacks in America from
pre-Revolutionary days.

And, though it is common for blacks to lay the blame for
their lack of great economic success at the feet of Jews and
other "foreigners," it is interesting to note that there were
free black entrepreneurs who were prospering in the New
World before any Jews had set foot on these shores. In 1634,
the year when the first tiny band of twenty-three Sephardic
Jews arrived in what is now New York, a black landowner
in New Amsterdam already had a large parcel of real estate.
In 1644, a group of eleven blacks was given acreage compris-
ing what is now New York's Greenwich Village, and this
area remained a black settlement for the next two hundred
years. Outside Boston, in Dorchester, Massachusetts, a black
man known simply as "Boston Ken" owned a house and lot
and several acres of wheat fields that same year. Several years
later, a man named Abijah Prince owned a hundred acres of
farmland in Guilford, Vermont, and received equal shares
of land in all six divisions of the township. These pioneer
landowners made their money raising and selling staple

crops — corn, wheat, rice, and tobacco. These black farmers bought and sold in the same markets as their white competitors, owned black and white indentured servants and, in at least one recorded instance, a black slave.

But, throughout the colonial period, days of relatively easy times for blacks were inevitably followed by periods of harsh reaction and repression. As more and more blacks were freed, or were able to purchase the freedom of others, and migrated into heavily settled areas, they began to be seen as an economic threat to the white majority. Beginning in the middle of the seventeenth century, nearly every colony started passing discriminatory laws and slave codes designed to limit the business opportunities of "free" blacks. In 1660, the Boston town meeting passed a law which forbade the use of black artisans. Ten years later, the Virginia legislature made it illegal for blacks to have white indentured servants. In 1712, the Connecticut Assembly decreed that no free black person could buy land or carry on a business in any town without the permission of the white residents.

Still, despite these pressures, some black businessmen persevered and prospered. In 1736, Emanuel Manna Bernoon and his wife, Mary, opened up the first oyster and ale house in Providence, Rhode Island (using, it was said, his wife's money; she had made a small fortune in the illegal whiskey trade). In pre-Revolutionary Newport, a black woman called "Duchess" Quamino became the seaport's leading caterer. During this period, blacks were also becoming the founding fathers of a number of American cities. Jean-Baptiste Pointe DuSable, a Haitian trapper and explorer, became the first non-Indian settler and landholder in what is now Chicago in the early 1770's. Of the forty-four founders of Los Angeles, twenty-six were black, and the heirs of these men inherited large tracts of land. Maria Rita Valdez, a granddaughter of one of these early California

blacks, owned Rancho Rodeo de las Aguas, which is better
known today as Beverly Hills. Another black, Francisco
Reyes, owned the entire San Fernando Valley. Unfortunately, he sold his property in 1790 and became the mayor
of Los Angeles. Had he held onto the valley, his heirs would
be among the richest people in the world today.

Free blacks virtually invented the catering business in
America. After the Revolution, a black Philadelphian
named Robert Bogle was said to be "the first man to advocate the organization of domestic service into a business."
Bogle, before 1810, opened a restaurant on Eighth Street
near Sansom and, from his establishment, ran all of Philadelphia's great weddings, banquets and balls, and became
not only an arbiter of food but an arbiter of taste in other
matters such as decor, flower arrangement and dress. Philadelphia matrons consulted Mr. Bogle, the Ward McAllister
of his day, not only before planning their menus but also
before composing their guest lists. "The Bogle touch" at
Philadelphia social events was adopted and enhanced by a
number of succeeding caterers, including Peter Augustin
and James Prosser — both black — and of the latter it was
said that "the name of James Prosser, among the merchants
of Philadelphia, is inseparable with their daily hours of recreation and pleasure." In 1845, Philadelphia society became
the virtual slave of three more black caterers, all operating
in the great tradition established by Bogle and Prosser. The
leader of this trio was Thomas J. Dorsey, of whom a Philadelphia reporter wrote, "Dorsey was one of the triumvirate
of colored caterers — the other two being Henry Jones and
Henry Minton — who some years ago might have been said
to rule the social world of Philadelphia through its stomach.
Time was when lobster salad, chicken croquettes, deviled
crabs, and terrapin composed the edible display at every
Philadelphia gathering, and none of these dishes were
thought to be perfectly prepared unless they came from the

hands of one of the three men named." Dorsey, like most of these black businessmen, was an ardent Abolitionist and, because he could afford to be choosy and "had the sway of an imperial dictator," he refused to offer his services in the homes of Democrats, saying, "I cannot wait on a party of persons who are disloyal to the government, and" — pointing to the portrait that dominated his reception room — "Lincoln is the government." Nor were these successful black men unphilanthropic. Henry Gordon, another Philadelphia caterer, contributed $66,000 to a home for "aged and infirm colored people." Stephen Smith, who at the time was probably the richest black in America — from his lumber and money-lending business he amassed an estate worth half a million nineteenth-century dollars — gave $150,000 to the same fund.

In New York, from the turn of the century well into the 1850's, the gustatory scene was dominated by a number of talented black caterers, including Thomas Downing, who ran a restaurant on Broad Street near Wall Street, and the partnership of George Bell and George Alexander, who operated a similar establishment in Church Street nearby. For many years, New York's most exclusive parties and weddings were put on by Thomas Jackson, who, according to James Weldon Johnson, was "in his day . . . the arbiter of New York."

For some reason, nineteenth-century blacks also excelled in matters pertaining to hair, and for many years the leading barbers and hairdressers in most eastern American cities were black. In New York, the most fashionable hairdresser was Pierre Toussaint, a former slave, who, according to his biographer, Hannah F. S. Lee, was held in such high regard for his tonsorial skills that "he had all of the custom and patronage of the French families . . . [and] many of the distinguished ladies of the city employed him." Still, however successful these tradespeople might be, they tended to keep a low profile, just as the nineteenth-century Jews did, and were aware that they were "outsiders." As a French traveler of the period, Jacques Brissot de Warville, noted, "Those Negroes who keep shops live moderately, and never augment their business beyond a certain point. The reason is obvious; the whites . . . like not to give them credit to undertake any extensive commerce nor even to give them the means of a common education by receiving them into their counting houses." Still, there were waves of reaction. In 1834, when the whites of both New York and Philadelphia rose up against black workers and black businessmen, there were major race riots. Philadelphia erupted again in 1838 and 1843, and there were black-white riots in Pittsburgh in 1839.

There were also wealthy free blacks in the South, including black planters like Cyprian Ricard, who owned a Louisiana plantation worth $225,000 and no less than ninety-one black slaves. In New Orleans in the 1840's there were at least eight black brokers who dealt in cotton futures and offered some of the services of commercial banks. There were prosperous cigar-makers in New Orleans too, such as George Alcés, who had a factory that employed two hundred workers, and a black inventor and engineer named Norbert Rillieux, who patented a vacuum cup that revolutionized the sugar industry. In Berne, North Carolina, a barber named John C. Stanley managed to accumulate properties worth $40,000, and a New Orleans merchant who loaned money at interest left an estate worth $500,000.

Though black wealth before the Civil War may not have been sufficient to constitute a great economic force, there were many blacks who were far from impoverished. In New York in 1853, it was estimated that blacks owned property worth $1,000,000 and had invested $839,000 in businesses in and around New York City. In Philadelphia, by 1856, blacks owned real estate worth $800,000. Just before the outbreak of the Civil War, blacks in Washington, D.C., owned property valued at $630,000. New Orleans, interestingly enough, was at that point the richest black city in America, with blacks in 1860 owning $15,000,000 worth of taxable property. The total personal and real wealth of free blacks in America that year has been placed at $50,000,000, and this is considered an estimate on the conservative side. Blacks owned nine thousand homes, fifteen thousand farms, and two thousand businesses.

But what happened? One might suppose, with their early lead in catering, that blacks by the 1970's would control the United States catering industry, and that they would dominate the barbering and hairdressing professions. Nineteenth-century blacks were also strong in New York's fashion industry, yet black designers and manufacturers are insignificant on Seventh Avenue today. They had also, at one point, prospered in the wholesale and retail grocery business, and yet they do not — as might have been expected — control major food or chainstore operations today. Racism is not the single, simple answer. To begin with, America's early black businessmen tended to concentrate in service businesses which depended on whites as customers. They had not yet discovered, as men like John Johnson did later on, that there was money to be made selling products to their "own kind." An element of snobbery had also entered the world of the free blacks in the 1850's. Perhaps because they had been spoiled by the attentions of white society ladies, black hairdressers would not dress the hair of other blacks. Black caterers did not care to cater parties at black homes, since their white trade carried more cachet. As for barbers, by the mid-1800's the "colored barber" had become a kind of ethnic joke, and he appeared in cartoons with a comb in one hand and a pair of scissors in the other. Many black barbers became self-conscious and embarrassed by their profession, and quietly withdrew from it. The barber's son did not want to be a barber like his father, and a promising family enterprise would be abandoned by the second generation in favor of something else. Something else, it often turned out, in which there was much stiffer competition. In the nineteenth century, competition was arriving in the form of some five million white immigrants from Europe who were hungry, ambitious, eager to hustle and to form trade unions that restricted blacks to menial occupations. All these forces combined to push black entrepreneurs backward from what had seemed a promising head start.

Ironically, the Civil War, which freed all blacks, was also a force that kept them economically imprisoned. Before the war, black businessmen in the North and South had had white competitors who were somewhat, but only somewhat, better off. The war, however, proved to be a field day for the profiteer and robber baron. All the great American fortunes — Rockefeller, Vanderbilt, Gould, Lehman, Schiff, Armour, Morgan — were amassed during the war years through government loans, war contracts, the expansion of the railroads, and the enormously inflated price of manufactured goods. It was open season for the speculator and the unscrupulous manipulator, and the Civil War made moguls out of men who had been small-time merchants and manufacturers. Yet, for some reason, no black moguls emerged from the war. Perhaps it was because, as has been argued, blacks found it distasteful to engage in profiteering from a war that was ostensibly being fought to free the slaves, though such scruples in such an amoral era are somewhat hard to credit. Perhaps it was because, at the war's outset, the economic position of the free blacks was still too weak. Perhaps it was because early black businessmen had received a poorer education than their white contemporaries and were, in some cases, illiterate — though men like Jay Gould, Cornelius Vanderbilt, and the original John D. Rockefeller were hardly intellectual giants and had had little formal schooling. ("If I had learned education I would not have had time to learn anything else," Vanderbilt once said.) Probably it was a combination of these factors, but the fact is that, at the war's end, black businessmen ended up with the same small businesses they had started out with, while their white competitors had improved their fortunes, and their arenas of power, enormously.

And of course white supremacist attitudes and racism cannot be ruled out as causes for the generally discouraging record of blacks in business. There were instances, like the case of the Freedmen's Bank, in which black enterprises were forced out of business through white chicanery, or even taken over by whites at gunpoint. In Cincinnati, a black furniture manufacturer named Robert Boyd did a thriving business throughout the South and West. One nineteenth-century night, a band of whites, angered at and jealous of Boyd's success, set fire to his factory and it burned to the ground. Boyd rebuilt his plant, and it was burned again. He rebuilt it a third time, and it was burned a third time. His fourth factory was his last. When that, too, was burned he could no longer get insurance and was forced to go out of business.

In Chicago, Mrs. Doris Lowe Zollar is very much a social leader in the black and white communities, and her name adorns the boards of some eighteen different civic, cultural, and social organizations. Her husband is a successful pediatrician with his own private clinic, and Mrs. Zollar is able to fly to Rome and Paris twice a year to shop for clothes. (*Ebony* voted Doris Zollar one of the ten best-dressed black women in America, an honor which she takes seriously, and for a while she served as Fashion Editor for Bettie Pullen-Walker's *MsTique*.) Dr. Zollar, the son of a laborer, is a self-made man, but Doris Zollar — fair-skinned, with ash blond hair and green eyes — is of the Old Guard South, and there has been money in the family for three generations. Her family, the Lowes, are prominent in Arkansas, where Grandpa Lowe owned a large tract of land outside Little Rock and ran an extensive farming and lumbering operation. As Little Rock grew, white developers began eyeing Grandpa Lowe's property, and presently a group of whites came to him with an offer to buy the land. But Grandpa Lowe refused to sell and, less than a month later, his house was set to the torch. He rebuilt the house, and it was burned again. Stubbornly, he rebuilt it a third time, and this time his white antagonists permitted it to stand. The Lowe family still has its Little Rock property, and Doris Zollar derives an income from the family lumbering operations.

But the family has suffered a misfortune common to many black families of property. Grandpa Lowe's will, when it was written, was vague and imprecise — the work, it seems, of a black attorney who lacked real expertise in such matters. There were at least two members of the family, for example, with the nickname "Buddy." It is impossible to tell, from Grandpa Lowe's will, which Buddy was intended to be his heir. There were also two Ernests in the family and, though an Ernest is mentioned in the will, the will does not specify which one. Grandpa Lowe's estate has now been in litigation for more than twenty years, and the family has begun to wonder if it will ever be settled and, if it is — after legal and court costs — whether there will be anything left.

Pride and Prejudice

~~~ *II* ~~~

Embattled Washington

PERHAPS NOWHERE IN AMERICA IS A BLACK OLD GUARD MORE
well grounded than in Washington, D.C. And almost nowhere else has the Old Guard come into such sharp conflict
with the more newly moneyed black middle class.

In Washington, which is now 75 percent black, one
speaks discreetly of "the black presence." It might be more
accurate to call it a black omnipresence. There are, however, within the omnipresence, at least three distinct and
separate presences. There is, to begin with, the mass of poor
blacks at the bottom. They are the most visible — idling on
street corners in the southeast quarter of the city, in vacant
lots, sitting on cracked stoops, and leaning against boarded-
up storefronts of the ghetto. A white feels uncomfortable in
these streets, where the blacks give him daunting looks, and
mutter unintelligible words to him as he passes by. It is said,
however, that a "foreign" black in these neighborhoods is in
even greater danger than a white outsider; he might be a
policeman in plain clothes, or a narcotics agent. He might
be armed.

Then there is a much smaller group, which might be
called the New Black Achievers — men and women who, in
recent years, have attained power, prestige, and no small

amount of money in politics (Mayor Walter E. Washington, for one), business, education and the professions. In large, expensive homes along such racially intergrated streets as Blagden Avenue — the main artery of Washington's so-called Gold Coast, which nestles between Rock Creek Park and Sixteenth Street — or on Kalmia Road, Argyle Terrace, and Colorado Avenue, these affluent blacks are less conspicuous behind their carefully pruned hedges and manicured lawns. They have, however, a significant voice in the community.

Then there is the Old Guard, Washington's black "cave-dwellers," people whose roots in Washington go back three, four, even five generations. These families, who have had money, social position, and — most important — education, since the turn of the century and earlier, live in three- or four-story town houses in quiet, tree-shaded streets in sections such as the Logan Circle area, a neighborhood that was once quite fashionable, went through a period of having seen better days, and is now on its way up again. Quiet, conservative, devoted to thrift, probity, and, for the most part, to the Episcopal Church, these families generally have not, though they could have, moved to glossier, newer neighborhoods. They have stayed where they are because their friends and relatives are there, just as their grandmothers' and great-grandmothers' friends were there. They might be said to form the backbone of the Washington chapter of Links. Some of the newer-rich blacks might like to join the Links but, since no Links chapter may contain more than thirty women, it is not easy, and the Links selects its membership strictly from the top. (The newer-rich blacks sniff, "A Link is a fur-bearing animal.")

The Old Guard is not unaware of the blacks in the ghetto. Much of the Links' fund-raising effort goes to support such organizations as the N.A.A.C.P., the Urban League, and the United Negro College Fund. But socially,

of course, they are beyond the pale, a painful embarrassment. Recently a woman from an Old Guard family demon-
strated the prevailing attitude toward ghetto blacks. Driving
with a friend through a run-down area of Washington, her
car was stopped by a traffic light at an intersection, and she
watched as a drunken young black man in a "Super Fly"
outfit reeled across the street, bottle in hand. "Disgusting,"
she whispered. "There is the cause of all our problems."
Her friend, more perceptive, said, "No, that is the *result* of
all our problems."

Of the newly rich blacks, the Old Guard is disdainful. It
considers these people gauche *arrivistes*. The Old Guard is
critical of their conspicuous spending — on big houses,
costly automobiles, and lavish entertaining. The new rich,
meanwhile, call the Old Guard Uncle and Aunt Toms, for
these are people who, after all, have lived quietly and peacefully, and have even prospered, for many years alongside
whites by adopting a don't-rock-the-boat philosophy. The
new rich would very much like to rock the boat—not only
the boat manned by whites, but also the one manned by the
Old Guard. The members of the Old Guard have no use for
black revolutionary movements, Africanism, Afro hair
styles, and even dislike the term "black." "Those people
who shout Black Power are not going to include people like
me when they get it," says one Old Guard member tartly.
Another says, "I do *not* think black is beautiful. Some black
people are beautiful. But a great many are not."

Mrs. Anne Weaver Teabeau is Washington Old Guard.
Though she has lived most of her seventy-odd years in other
cities, she returned several years ago as a widow to Washington, the city she has always considered home. After all, Mrs.
Teabeau is the great-granddaughter of Frederick Douglass,
the great Abolitionist who moved from Rochester to Washington in 1871. Mrs. Teabeau is a dainty, light-skinned
woman, and she sits in the equally dainty drawing room of

her Washington town house, surrounded by family memorabilia — portraits of the white-bearded patriarch, antique china and silver, photographs of the Douglass mansion on Capitol Hill and the twenty-room family country house, "L'Ouverture Villa," in Anacostia. Though Frederick Douglass died in 1895, before Mrs. Teabeau was born, she is full of tales of him that have been handed down — of his daring escape from a Maryland plantation, of how his name had been originally Frederick Augustus Washington Bailey, and how he changed it to Douglass after a favorite character in "The Lady of the Lake." She tells of the period when he joined John Brown, how he made his way to Canada and then to the British Isles, where he was taken up by London society, and why he first settled in Rochester — it was an Abolitionist center. Even in Rochester, however, there was discrimination. When Douglass's daughter, Mrs. Teabeau's grandmother, was first sent to school the principal made her sit in a cloakroom. When Douglass learned of this, he removed his daughter from the school and had her educated privately.

Frederick Douglass was, among other things, an avid croquet player, and the Anacostia croquet court was the scene of many family battles. Mrs. Teabeau produces an 1875 letter from Douglass to her grandmother, describing a contest between Douglass and his son: "Lewis is the son of his father and is mad as a March hare when he is being badly beaten. His voice grows hoarse and he fairly trembles with rage. The worst of it is, he always thinks that I presume upon my parental authority, and I in turn think that he presumes on his filial relation." Most of all, Mrs. Teabeau if filled with *hubris* and family pride. "A lot of people named Douglass claim to be related to us, but aren't," she says. "The other day a man telephoned me claiming to be a cousin. 'I'm descended from John,' he said. I told him, 'There was no John.' "

Of the younger, more vocal activist groups in Washington, Mrs. Teabeau says, "They stereotype us. They don't give us credit for all we've done for them. To hear them tell it, only the activists have done anything."

Mrs. Teabeau is a former president of the Washington chapter of Links, and once, when she suggested to her membership that it might be nice if the Links at least *visited* Washington's relatively new Museum of African Art, the Links, to a lady, politely refused. "We have nothing to do with Africa," one member told her. When the museum celebrated its tenth anniversary in the summer of 1975 with a large reception — honoring, among other notables, Hubert Humphrey, Chief Justice Warren Burger, and Henry Kissinger — over six hundred invitations went out, to all of the Old Guard. An attendance of at least a thousand had been hoped for. Fewer than three hundred people showed up, only one of them a Link — Mrs. Teabeau. Even she had originally not planned to attend the party, and knew that her appearance there would be unpopular with her friends. But the museum's director, Warren Robbins, finally persuaded her to put in a brief appearance. She was, he pointed out, on the museum's board of directors. Also, the museum is housed in her great-grandfather's A Street mansion.

The Museum of African Art is only one of the battlegrounds that have Washington's blacks divided against each other. "Nothing of interest or importance came out of Africa," says Mrs. Mary Gibson Hundley, another member of the Old Guard. "Our civilization gained from Greece, from Rome, from Europe and the Mediterranean, even from China. It gained from Egypt, but from nothing south of the Sudan." But this is only part of the problem. With no support from the Old Guard at the top, and no support from the ghetto blacks at the bottom, the museum is also getting only minimal support from the new-rich blacks in the middle. Partly this is because Mr. Robbins, the museum's founder, is white. In these black circles, it is also whispered that Mr. Robbins is Jewish. It is also suspected that Robbins is running the museum for his personal profit. (Actually, he has for some time been trying to turn the museum over to the Smithsonian because running it has become such a heavy financial drain.) Also, Mr. Robbins may have been unwise in choosing the Douglass mansion to house his collection. Frederick Douglass's place in black history has, over the years, grown somewhat shaky. Though an Abolitionist, he has become, in time, a symbol of Old Guardism. It was his son who established the exclusive summer resort at Highland Beach on Chesapeake Bay, which was and still is only for "certain" black people. And Frederick Douglass's second wife, who carried him into Washington society and dinners at the White House, was white. To some people, Frederick Douglass has become, of all things, an Uncle Tom.

Dividing Washington is more, however, than a simple conflict of the Old Guard versus the new, old money versus new, ancient family versus upstart, native Washingtonian versus out-of-towner — though that has a lot to do with the situation. Mayor Washington, for example, born in Georgia, is considered a parvenu. But his wife, the former Bennetta Bullock, is Old Guard and, according to a friend, "The Bullocks are an old and distinguished Washington family. When you say 'the *Bullocks,*' you lower your eyes to half-mast. Her father, Reverend Bullock, was *the* black minister." But another Old Guard Washingtonian sniffs and says it is more a difference in styles of living and styles of speech. "Her family came here from North Carolina in the twenties, only fifty years ago!" ("Mayor Washington talks like a Negro," one woman says, "but of course his wife doesn't.") But even more it is a difference in caste, and a caste based on texture of hair and color of skin and quality of facial features. Most of Washington's Old Guard blacks have straight hair, fair skin — some are even blond with blue eyes — and straight noses and thin lips. For these reasons, they set themselves apart. They are members of what is informally called "The Blue Blood Club" — that is, if one's skin is light enough so that the blue veins in the wrist show through, one is a member. The resort that Frederick Douglass's son established at Highland Beach was restricted to these people.

The Old Guard families include, in addition to the Douglasses and Bullocks, the Terrells, the Langstons, the Wormleys, the McGuires, the Bonds ("Max Bond's wife is a Clement from Atlanta"), the Bruces, the Gibbses, the Gibsons, the Syphaxes, the Cobbs, the Francises, the Brookes, and various combinations thereof as Terrells married Langstons, and so on. Though it is considered poor taste to mention it, most of these families have white ancestors of whom they are privately rather proud. Perhaps the most extraordinary black family in Washington — though they are not very black — are the Syphaxes. The first Syphax, William, was an itinerant preacher who arrived in Washington from Canada in the early part of the nineteenth century and settled in nearby Alexandria. As a minister, he was a spellbinder, and as a spellbinder he prospered. Whether he had ever been a slave, which is unknown, he had by 1820 purchased his freedom because his name appears in the census of that year as a free man. In ancient times, a Syphax was a Numidian king. A Syphax was also a general in Hannibal's army during the Punic Wars. William Syphax's name was originally Anderson, and so today's Syphaxes cannot claim these illustrious ancestors. But it is a point of family pride that their forebear was clearly a man of scholarship to have chosen such a distinguished, if unusual, name.

William Syphax prospered sufficiently to buy freedom for his wife and three daughters. His son, Charles, however, worked as a slave on the Virginia plantation of George

Washington Parke Custis, the grandson of Martha Washington, where, in his capacity as chief butler in the Custis dining room, he was quite happy. Charles was a great pet of the Custis family, and chose not to be manumitted. George Washington Parke Custis, meanwhile, had a daughter, Maria, by a woman named Arianna Carter, one of his house slaves. Charles Syphax and Maria fell in love and, saying that she would rather marry a black man than lead the life led by the other mulattos on the plantation, Maria asked for permission to marry Charles. Her father, Mr. Custis, was delighted, and gave the pair a formal wedding in the parlor of the great house, with an Episcopal minister presiding at the ceremony. Upon their marriage, furthermore, Custis freed both Charles and Maria and, as a dowry, gave Maria fifteen acres of his Arlington estate.

Custis had no white sons of his own, but he did have a legitimate white daughter, Mary, who became the heiress to the plantation. Mary Custis married Robert E. Lee, who was connected with all the great families of Virginia. The family-proud Lees of Virginia may be surprised to learn that they have black half-cousins named Syphax living nearby. And Barnaby Conrad, the author, lecturer, and San Francisco socialite, who also descends from Martha Custis Washington, and who takes his Eastern ancestors very seriously, was surprised not long ago to find a Sephardic Jew named Levy in his family tree. He may be amused to know that he also has black relatives.

Charles and Maria Syphax had ten children — William II, Elinor, Cornelius, Charles, Cobert, Shaulton, Austin, Ennis, Maria, and John — a sufficient preponderance of male heirs to assure a profusion of people named Syphax in the Washington telephone book today. Nearly all of Charles and Maria Syphax's children achieved an education and some degree of success. John Syphax, for example, was elected to the Virginia House of Delegates. William Syphax II was perhaps the most illustrious member of his generation. An outspoken civil rights activist, he was hired in 1850 by the Department of the Interior, where he worked for the next forty years as the chief receptionist in the offices of nine Secretaries. In his desk, William Syphax kept an autograph book which he asked each distinguished visitor to sign. The blue leather book, which has been preserved by the family, is dog-eared and worn, but the signatures are still vivid. The book contains the autographs of six United States Presidents, headed by a humble "A. Lincoln," as well as of Frederick Douglass, who wrote, next to his name, "Truth is of no color." After the Civil War, the Secretary of the Interior, who appointed the trustees of the newly established Colored Public Schools of Washington and Georgetown, selected William Syphax as the schools' first president and superintendent. A school is named after him today.

During the Civil War, the Custis-Lee estate was confiscated by the federal government for nonpayment of taxes, and with it went Maria Syphax's fifteen acres. But William Syphax, who had influential friends in Washington, succeeded in getting a Congressional investigation into the family's title to his mother's land. Congress passed a special bill, signed by President Andrew Johnson in 1866, returning the acreage to the Syphaxes. At the time, to avoid "sullying the name of the Father of Our Country," by affirming the fact of Maria's illegitimacy, Congress sidestepped the matter of her descent from Martha Washington, but did concede that George Washington Parke Custis obviously "had a paternal interest" in Maria.

For years, many Syphaxes had houses in the little compound in Arlington which, indeed, was a small village with a main street and a trolley stop called "Syphax." During those years, however, the Arlington Syphaxes became somewhat estranged from their cousins who lived in Washington because of Virginia's segregationist policies. The minute the trolley crossed the Potomac River, all blacks had to move to the last three rows of the car, a move the Washington Syphaxes were not willing to make, even if it meant not visiting their Virginia relatives.

Syphaxes have been prominent in Washington for four generations, particularly as educators, and they continue to be a force in the city today. Dr. Burke Syphax, for example, is chief of surgery at both Freemen's Hospital and the Howard University Medical School. John W. Syphax is a retired, Harvard-educated foreign affairs official with the State Department, and his father, another John, spent fifty-two of his seventy-odd years as a Washington school principal. William Custis Syphax, Jr., a grandson of Charles Syphax, Jr., attended Howard and American Universities, and for thirty-six years worked at the Department of Labor, specializing in veterans' affairs. His wife, Orieanna, has worked in Washington education and nursing programs for twenty-nine years. His aunt, Carrie Syphax Watson, was another influential school teacher. Syphaxes always marry well. Mrs. John W. Syphax, for example, was Melba Welles, whose father, James Lesesne Welles, was a prominent minister, and whose mother was a college dean of women. Though the Welleses are from Columbia, South Carolina, the family, on the Reverend Mr. Welles's mother's side, descends from ancient French Huguenot stock. With money on both sides, John and Melba Syphax live in a four-story town house in Q Street that was a family wedding present to them in 1920.

During World War II, when more land was needed for Arlington Cemetery, the Roosevelt administration persuaded the Syphaxes to part with their Arlington acreage, which adjoined the cemetery, in exchange for another piece of property. The Syphaxes feel that they got a much more desirable parcel in the trade, and the family cemetery in Syphax Village was moved to Lincoln Memorial Cemetery. It is on the new property that William T. Syphax now lives.

William T., whom the family calls Tommy to distinguish him from some half-dozen other Williams, is probably the richest Syphax, though he and his wife live in a modest, almost Spartan, brick house. In 1954, William T. Syphax and his wife, Marguerite, started Syphax Enterprises, Inc., a construction and management firm that today earns $8,000,000 a year, and is one of the twenty leading black firms in the United States. In Fairfax County, there is a Syphax Drive, where the company built a 324-unit apartment complex in 1965. In addition to managing apartment units that now number in the thousands, the Syphaxes are currently building the National Children's Center in Washington. It pleases the family, too, that Tommy's firm is handling the million-dollar reconstruction of the old Cairo Hotel, right around the corner from where the first William Syphax had his house at Seventeenth and P streets. Tommy Syphax, an urbane, pipe-smoking man in his middle fifties, says, "None of us has ever accepted being second-class. I set out to do something for the race. Even if it wasn't because of my family, as a black man I wanted to accomplish something in life." Both Syphaxes are members of more than twenty civic boards; for more than twenty years, Tommy Syphax has directed the choir at Mt. Olive Baptist Church (his father founded St. John's Baptist Church in Washington), and his chic, pretty wife is one of the two black women in the country who are certified property managers.

The only living descendent of the autograph-collecting William Syphax is his granddaughter, Mrs. Mary Gibson Hundley, a trim, light-coffee-colored widow with manners and bearing quite befitting the great-great-great-great granddaughter of the wife of the first President of the United States. Mrs. Hundley lives in a small, elegant town house in a residential block on Thirteenth Street, where she is surrounded by antiques and other family heirlooms, including her maternal grandfather's autograph collection.

Mrs. Hundley, an honors graduate of Radcliffe who for years taught languages at Washington's prestigious Dunbar High School, had no children because she was a victim of another kind of prejudice; women teachers used to lose their jobs if they became pregnant. Still, she is enormously family-proud and, speaking in a broad-A Boston accent, is a woman of strong opinions. "I am *not* black," she says, "and I do not like to be called black. I don't have black features, hair, color, or speech. I don't like to be called Negro, either, because 'Negro' is simply the Spanish word for black. I like the expression the French use. I am an *Américaine de couleur.*" Mrs. Hundley produces a portrait of her grandfather, an arrestingly handsome man with piercing eyes and high cheekbones. "Do you notice the thin lips? That's his Custis inheritance, and he was very slim and tall — like the Custises. His wife was a Miss Mary Browne, another very old and distinguished family here — there's also a school named after her — and the Brownes were part Cherokee Indian. The finest Indians, of course, were the Cherokees. In fact, when Grandmother Syphax died, she was listed as an American Indian on her death certificate. So I am part white, part black, and part red, and it is simply *incorrect* to call people of mixed ancestry black, and I *deplore* the term. I deplore people who go around looking like savages with their bushy hair. It is *not* an African style, and anybody who knows anything about African history knows that the African tribespeople kept their hair cropped short, for cleanliness. At Radcliffe, I was just another one of the girls. Why, I was invited to parties in Boston houses where they wouldn't even receive the Irish!"

Mrs. Hundley recalls that Grandpa Syphax was "always impeccably tailored, and terribly pious. He had a quotation from the Bible for every occasion. The children had to be at the table every morning at eight A.M. for an hour of prayer. He was even opposed to going to the theatre, and they say that the only time he ever went inside a theatre was to pull one of his brothers out. My mother was more liberal. She tried to convince him that some theatre was like a sermon. Once, as a girl, when a young man had taken Mother to the theatre, and she told Grandpa about it, all he said was 'My, you're getting worldly.' "

When she was a child, Mrs. Hundley's model for decorum and behavior was her mother's close friend, Mrs. Mary Church Terrell. "Notice how Mrs. Terrell speaks," her mother would advise young Mary. "Notice how Mrs. Terrell does things. She does everything with perfect ease." One thing that Mrs. Terrell did with perfect ease, it may be remembered, was to walk into a segregated Washington restaurant several years ago, sit down, and demand to be served. Her lawyer, Charles Huston, had discovered an obscure District of Columbia statute which stated that no public restaurant could refuse service to any "respectable" customer. It had been decided that of all the women in Washington, black or white, Mary Church Terrell was one who *no one* could say was not respectable. She won her case. "She was magnificent," says Mrs. Hundley. Mrs. Terrell, an educator, lecturer, and the president of the National Association of Colored Women, had a celebrated feud with Mrs. Mary Bethune. Said Mrs. Bethune to Mrs. Terrell, "I'm glad I'm black because I know I'm legitimate." Said the light-skinned Mrs. Terrell to Mrs. Bethune, "I wouldn't be too sure about that." They never spoke again. "Mary Bethune was highly overrated," says Mary Hundley. "She latched onto Mrs. Roosevelt and hung to her coattails. Now, Charlotte Hawkins Brown was something else again — she was of Mrs. Terrell's breed. But Mary Bethune did more to spread prejudice among black-skinned people against light-skinned Negroes than anybody I can think of. She used to talk about 'my black girls,' and she started that whole 'black is beautiful' nonsense. She said that she used to look into her mirror and say, 'Mary, you're black and you're beautiful.' Beautiful! She was ugly as sin. But Mrs. Terrell was a *lady*."

Like Mrs. Hundley, Mary Church Terrell came by her ladylike ways through both training and inheritance, and it is worth spending a moment to consider Mrs. Terrell's extraordinary background. Though she made her home in Washington, she was "a Church of Memphis," and the Churches of Memphis are often considered — and certainly consider themselves — the grandest black family in America. For nearly three quarters of a century the earthly remains of various illustrious Churches have reposed in the vast marble Church mausoleum in Memphis's Elmwood cemetery, which is now regarded as something of a family shrine. Mary Terrell's father, Robert R. Church, was born in slavery and, as a youth, worked as a cabin boy on the Mississippi River steamboats. After the Civil War, he settled in Memphis where, working quietly and with the required amount of obsequiousness within the framework of the black power structure, Mr. Church started his business rise. He began as a saloon-keeper, and soon he acquired a hotel. In the riots of 1866 he nearly lost his life when he was shot in the back of the head and left for dead on the floor of his saloon. But he recovered and went on gathering up more parcels of Memphis real estate. He built a large auditorium, which became the city's leading meeting-place for black organizations and was, at the time, the largest black theatre in the United States. He also developed an amusement park on Beale Street, which became the black recreation center, and opened the city's first — and for many years only — black bank. By the turn of the century, Robert R. Church was unquestionably the richest black man in Memphis and was touted as "the first black millionaire in the South." The huge gingerbread Church mansion at 384 South Lauderdale Street was a Memphis landmark. After the city of Memphis was devastated by a yellow fever epidemic, Church was the first person to purchase a City of Memphis municipal bond, as a token of his faith in the town's economic recovery. He was the first black in Memphis to be selected for grand jury duty and, as a power in the Republican Party, he served as a delegate to the Republican national convention in 1900.

After divorcing his first wife, who was Mary Terrell's mother, Robert R. Church made an imposing second marriage to the former Anna Wright, who became Mary Terrell's stepmother. The new Mrs. Church had a dizzying ancestry, and was descended from a Kentucky colonel who was related to the Kentucky Breckenridges; from an English-born Philadelphia Quaker named Benjamin Wright; from a wealthy Memphis plantation owner; as well as from a Chickasaw Indian family who were distinguished not only by the fact that they owned a prosperous brickyard but also by the fact that they had a relative who lived to be a hundred and ten years old. Anna Wright's Grandfather Wright, in fact, was a man of such consequence that he imported white private tutors from the North to educate his children. Though Anna Wright Church was so fair as to be hardly recognizable as a Negro, she became the unquestioned leading *grande dame* in Memphis's black society.

Robert R. Church himself could boast of a heritage that was every bit as colorful and illustrious as his wife's, and which included nothing less than royalty. On the distaff side, Mr. Church's first American ancestor was his grandmother, a slave who was simply called Lucy. But Lucy's upbringing had been far from simple. When Lucy was first brought to the slave block in Norfolk between 1805 and 1810, she attracted great attention. She was described, somewhat wonderingly, as "a beautiful bright red young girl with very long straight hair." For reasons no one could understand, Lucy spoke perfect French. Also, when she went on the block, she was wearing a pair of heavy gold earrings in her pierced ears, and an exquisite necklace of coral tipped with gold was at her throat. Because of her beauty and regal bearing and her jewels, Lucy was the object of heavy bidding and was sold at a "fancy price" — to a rich Norfolk tobacco merchant.

The exotic Lucy, it turned out, was not African at all but Malaysian, and in her native islands she had been a royal princess. As a result of civil strife, she had been taken prisoner and sold. In the tobacco merchant's home, her Church descendents like to point out, Lucy worked as a seamstress and "was never treated as a slave" or required to do menial chores. She was regarded almost as a member of the family, and was treasured for the stories she used to tell of the court life she had known in her faraway Oriental palace. The earrings and necklace are still in the family.

By his second wife, Robert R. Church had a son, Robert R. Church, Jr., who inherited his father's money and expanded the family real estate interests. He became even more active in Republican politics than his father. In 1916, he founded an organization known as the Lincoln League, the purpose of which was to encourage blacks to take part in the electoral process. He had been educated at private schools in the North, and was a dapper, fastidiously tailored man whose trademark was the spotless white handkerchief that always blossomed from his breast pocket. He was also a gifted orator. In 1912, at the age of twenty-six, Church attended his first Republican national convention, an event which he never missed for the next forty years, until his death in 1952. During the 1920's, Church was at the height of his political powers and was considered one of the most influential black Republicans in the country. Through his Lincoln League, Church and his Black and Tan wing of the party succeeded in wresting control of the Shelby County Republican organization from the whites and, during the Coolidge and Hoover administrations, whenever it was necessary to make a political appointment in Tennessee, Washington's advice was, inevitably, "Ask Bob Church."

Bob Church's power declined considerably during the New Deal era, however, and when many blacks began switching their traditional allegiance from the Republican to the Democratic party, Church and his family remained staunchly Republican. In fact, it is said that pressure from the Memphis Democrats caused Bob Church to leave the city in 1940 and move with his family to Washington, where his half-sister Mary made her famously dignified restaurant entrance.

Bob Church's daughter, Roberta Church, is also well known in Republican circles. She has served as Special Consultant for Minority Groups to the United States Department of Labor, and was appointed by Richard M. Nixon to the National Advisory Council on Adult Education. She continues to be prominent in Washington public affairs though, as she says, "I will always consider Memphis my home." In Memphis, they say, "The Churches *are* Memphis." And, in the hierarchy of the American black Old Guard, the Churches stand very near the top, if not at the top, of the list of the black Four Hundred — or, as the blacks themselves often put it, "The black Three Hundred and Ninety-Nine." This is not to say, of course, that the Churches are all that tight-knit a family. The two sets of children by Robert Church Sr.'s two wives did not always get on with one another. (For one thing, the children by the first Mrs. Church had much darker skins.) Mary Church Terrell and her half-brother Bob seldom saw eye-to-eye. And in Roberta Church's privately printed history of the family, *The Robert R. Churches of Memphis,* which deals primarily with the achievements of her father and grandfather (and does not overlook Miss Church's own accomplishments) , she gives short shrift to her half-aunt, Mrs. Terrell. She merely notes that, "Since two books have been published about Mary Church Terrell, daughter of the first marriage, and her family, this book will limit itself to the second marriage of Robert Church, Sr. to Anna Wright Church."

If Mary Church Terrell was the early model of decorum for Mary Gibson Hundley, Mrs. Hundley learned her lessons well. Like her mentor, she is aristocratic in bearing, a spirited conversationalist, a woman of strong opinions, and a trifle aloof in the presence of those she feels to be of inferior intelligence or breeding. Like Mrs. Terrell, Mrs. Hundley is also a doughty fighter over matters of civil rights — though, like Mrs. Terrell, she goes about doing what must be done in a ladylike way. A number of years ago, using the same lawyer who had represented Mrs. Terrell in her restaurant case — and won it — Mrs. Hundley and her husband went to battle against their all-white neighbors in order to buy their Thirteenth Street house, which had been under a "restrictive covenant" forbidding sale to blacks or even *Américaines de couleur*. The Hundleys lost in the lower court but, on appeal, won, and the case, *Gorewitz* v. *Hundley,* was cited in the 1948 Supreme Court desegregation decision. "I believe Grandpa Syphax would have been proud of our victory," Mrs. Hundley says, even though the long legal fight cost many thousands of Syphax dollars. As a result, she remains somewhat bitter about the N.A.A.C.P. "We had been members of the N.A.A.C.P. for years," she says, "and they didn't help us with a plugged nickel."

Currently, Mary Hundley is involved in another battle — another of those that, like the one to save the Museum of African Art, have divided Washington's Old Guard light-skinned families against the newer-rich, darker-skinned majority. It is over the fate of the old Dunbar High School, where Mrs. Hundley taught for so many years. Dunbar High School is an altogether unique institution. Established in 1870 by federal charter, it was originally called

PRIDE AND PREJUDICE   143

The Preparatory High School for Colored Youth, and its original trustees, who had influential friends in Congress, were members of Washington's old-line black families, including a number of Mary Hundley's ancestors. Dunbar was, for many years, the only free public high school for blacks who wanted a college education, and blacks who could afford to — and wanted higher education for their children — moved their families to Washington so that their sons and daughters could go to Dunbar. There were no special entrance examinations for Dunbar, but youngsters were thoroughly interviewed to see whether they could do the work. Most important, Dunbar's charter stipulated that the federal salaries paid the black teachers at Dunbar must equal those paid to white teachers in the District of Columbia. At the time, there were a number of black graduates from Northern colleges like Oberlin, Amherst, Dartmouth, and Harvard. But academic posts were closed even to those blacks who had completed graduate work, and black teachers had been forced to accept low-paying jobs at all-black schools.

The creation of Dunbar appeared to black educators as a kind of salvation, and the best black teachers from all over the country competed for posts at Dunbar. With the best faculty available, and the best students that could be found, Dunbar was indeed a school for the upwardly mobile elite. Generations of black achievers attended Dunbar, and went on to shine in the best colleges of the Ivy League. Massachusetts Senator Edward Brooke went to Dunbar ("I taught him Latin," says Mrs. Hundley), as did Ralph Bunche, the late Dr. Charles Drew, who organized the first Red Cross blood banks, along with numberless judges, doctors, lawyers, and professors, in addition to Washington Terrells, Syphaxes, Wormleys, and Cobbs. It carried great cachet to go to Dunbar, and its alumni today — like the more expensively educated alumni of Palmer — consider themselves a special breed, and hold regular reunions once a year and sing the old school song. Needless to say, many Dunbar alumni are light-skinned — like Senator Brooke, who claims descent from Thomas Jefferson.

Later, led by women like Mrs. Hundley and her friends, the school's faculty resisted efforts to turn Dunbar into a manual training school of the kind advocated by Booker T. Washington, and insisted that Dunbar remain a college-preparatory high school, of the kind Booker T. Washington's archrival, W. E. B. Dubois, endorsed. Washington and Dubois squabbled over educational matters almost as much as Mary Terrell, Mary Bethune, and Charlotte Brown did, but most of Washington's Old Guard are Dubois admirers, since he stressed "excellence." Booker T. Washington they regard as a spokesman for the lower classes.

Today, with Washington's schools integrated, and blacks able to attend — and teach at — any American private school or college, there is no real need for a school like Dunbar. Dunbar is now in a slum, and there is another, newer, college-preparatory high school, Woodrow Wilson, in another part of town. Dunbar High School will retain its name, but will move into a new modern building close by, and Washington's Board of Education wants to tear the old building down and turn it into a football field. Dunbar alumni and former teachers like Mrs. Hundley are outraged and up in arms. To them, Dunbar is a symbol — *the* shining symbol — of black higher education, prestige, and success in the capital. They have tried to have the old building declared an architectural treasure or monument, though the building is no more than routine Tudor. What the building is, of course, is a nostalgic treasure and yet, the Old Guard feels, if all else goes, this building, where so much was done for so many people, must remain.

The board of education, meanwhile, an eleven-man board consisting of seven blacks and four whites, is heavily

𝔓𝔲𝔟𝔩𝔦𝔠 𝔖𝔞𝔩𝔢 𝔬𝔣 𝔑𝔢𝔤𝔯𝔬𝔢𝔰,

By RICHARD CLAGETT.

On Tuesday, March 5th, 1833 at 1:00 P. M. the following Slaves will be sold at Potters Mart, in Charleston, S. C.

Miscellaneous Lots of Negroes, mostly house servants, some for field work.

Conditions: ½ **cash, balance by bond, bearing interest from date of sale. Payable in one to two years to be secured by a mortgage of the Negroes, and appraised personal security.** *Auctioneer will pay for the papers.*

A valuable Negro woman, accustomed to all kinds of house work. Is a good plain cook, and excellent dairy maid, washes and irons. She has four children, one a girl about 13 years of age, another 7, a boy about 5, and an infant 11 months old. 2 of the children will be sold with mother, the others separately, if it best suits the purchaser.

A very valuable Blacksmith, wife and daughters; the Smith is in the prime of life, and a perfect master at his trade. His wife about 27 years old, and his daughters 12 and 10 years old have been brought up as house servants, and as such are very valuable. Also for sale 2 likely young negro wenches, one of whom is 16 the other 15, both of whom have been taught and accustomed to the duties of house servants. The 16 year old wench has one eye.

A likely yellow girl about 17 or 18 years old, has been accustomed to all kinds of house and garden work. She is sold for no fault. Sound as a dollar.

House servants: The owner of a family described herein, would sell them for a good price only, they are offered for no fault whatever, but because they can be done without, and money is needed. He has been offered $1250. They consist of a man 30 to 33 years old, who has been raised in a genteel Virginia family as house servant, Carriage driver etc., in all which he excels. His wife a likely wench of 25 to 30 raised in like manner, as chamber maid, seamstress, nurse etc., their two children, girls of 12 and 4 or 5. They are bright mulattoes, of mild tractable dispositions, unassuming manners, and of genteel appearance and well worthy the notice of a gentleman of fortune needing such.

Also 14 Negro Wenches ranging from 16 to 25 years of age, all sound and capable of doing a good days work in the house or field.

Charlotte Hawkins Brown with Palmer pupils

Publisher John H. Johnson and his mother, Gertrude Williams
(left)

Mrs. John H. Johnson with Marc Chagall in
front of her Chagall painting

Mrs. Lowell Zollar outside her Chicago home

Best-dressed Mrs. Lowell Zollar at the new Chicago Ritz-Carlton

Bettie Pullen-Walker chats with friends at a kickoff party for MsTique *magazine given at New York's St. Regis Hotel in November 1973. Left to right: Jack Scott, president of Ideal Publishing Company; Carole Bartel, writer; and Ms. Pullen-Walker, Chicago publisher of* MsTique

A Links dinner in Chicago

At a Links Cotillion

*Advertising executive
Barbara Proctor with her
son*

George E. Johnson (left) and Illinois Senator Charles Percy

Mr. and Mrs. George E. Johnson of Chicago, and friends

Ebony *Fashion Fair model*

The audience at Ebony's Fashion Fair

The late big-game hunter, Dr. T. R. M. Howard of Chicago

Grande dame Mrs. Mary Gibson Hundley, a descendant of Martha Washington, in her Washington, D.C., sitting-room

Washington's Mr. and Mrs. William T. Syphax in front of the Lee mansion, which belonged to one of their ancestors

District of Columbia Congressman Walter E. Fauntroy in his Washington office

Strivers' Row, an architectural gem in Harlem

*Socialites Dr. and Mrs. Winston Churchill Willoughby in their
Washington, D.C., home*

Planning New York's Beaux Arts Ball are (left to right) Mrs. Robert F. Wagner, Baron Theo Von Roth, Robert David Lion Gardiner, Mollie Moon, Mrs. Ralph Bunche, and Marietta Tree (ca. 1970).

New York: Mrs. Mollie Moon being escorted from a mock champagne bottle at her annual Beaux Arts Ball for the Urban League

The John Wesley Dobbs family of Atlanta,
with Mattiwilda Dobbs at center

Mr. and Mrs. Henry Cooke Hamilton in their garden overlook-
ing the Atlanta skyline

Jewel Lafontant in the "white tie and tails" costume she designed when she became the first woman of any color to present a case before the United States Supreme Court

The late Mary Church Terrell and Haley Douglass, a descendant of Frederick Douglass

Jewel Lafontant in her Chicago home

Three generations of Atlanta Yanceys: (from left) Arthur H. ("Aytch") Yancey, Arthur H. Yancey II, and Asa G. Yancey, M.D.

A Vaughan family reunion in Africa. Jewel Lafontant is back row center

Some of the guests at a luncheon given by the Coalition for a United Community Action in Chicago. From left to right: Bill Berry, Al Johnson, Jesse Jackson, Carl Lattimore, and Muhammad Ali

Mary McLeod Bethune

representative of the newer-rich, black-skinned group. They are equally determined that, at all costs, Dunbar must go, must vanish from the face of the earth. To them, Dunbar is a symbol, too, but of something they have hated and resented for years — Uncle Tomism, black elitism, the Old Guard "Dunbar snobs," the light-skinned blacks. And so the battle lines are drawn over an empty and unused building. "It's the same as in the days of slavery," says Mrs. Hundley. "The slaves who worked in the fields hated the slaves that worked in the house. If the housemaid consorted with the master or the master's son — which she was often willing to do because it was one way for her to get her freedom — she had light-skinned children. My great-great-grandmother was a house slave, which is why I'm the color I am. The board of education represents the old field hand mentality, and they hate me for what I am."

The fact is that the black Establishment in Washington has changed. Families like the Syphaxes, Terrells, Cobbs, and Wormleys, who used to stand at the top of the city's Negro pecking order and rule the roost, no longer do, and their power has been usurped by a younger, hungrier, and larger group who have come to Washington from other cities and struggled upward from the bottom. They are supported by a working middle class — government workers, bank and department store clerks, nurses, pharmacists, and the like — who have tended to move out of the central city into the surrounding suburbs. The Old Guard, needless to say, dislikes seeing the old order change.

It used to be said in Washington that "Syphaxes speak only to Wormleys, and Wormleys speak only to Cobbs." The Wormleys have certainly had a rich history in the city. The founding father of the family, James T. Wormley, a former steward on a Mississippi River boat, was induced by white friends in the 1850's to start a catering business, and by the eve of the Civil War he was a rich man, with his services as much in demand as those of Messrs. Augustin, Prosser, Dorsey in Philadelphia, and Downing in New York. In addition to catering for some of Washington's grandest parties, he owned a restaurant and several large houses downtown, one of which was occupied during the first year of the war by "Old Fuss and Feathers," General Winfield Scott, making Wormley one of the earliest black landlords with a white tenant. Later, Wormley owned and operated the Wormley Hotel, which was the Washington home for Vice President Schuyler Colfax, and was a popular meeting place for foreign diplomats and dignitaries, as well as for makers and shakers of American politics. Ironically, this black-owned hotel was the scene of a historic political deal in 1877 that brought the Reconstruction Era to an end, and ushered in the Era of Segregation. At the conference, Democratic leaders agreed to end the dispute over the election of Rutherford B. Hayes, the Republican candidate, if the Republican leaders would agree to withdraw federal troops from the South. Wormley's descendents have been prominent businessmen, educators, and clergymen, and consider themselves very much out of the top drawer among the Old Guard.

The Montague Cobbs trace their family history back to William H. Montague, who was born in Georgetown in 1820. He later migrated to Springfield, Massachusetts, where he made a tidy fortune as a manufacturer of black hair preparations and cosmetics. In the Panic of 1873, however, he lost his business and returned to Washington where, in spite of his early success, he could find jobs only as a laborer and watchman. But his son, who had started work as a messenger in 1884, had, by 1900, risen to the position of assistant tax assessor for the District of Columbia, an unusually high post for a black man in those days. He married the wealthy daughter of a man named Cobb, who owned a job-printing shop, and their son, in European fashion, was named W. Montague Cobb. Dr. W. Montague Cobb today is a distinguished anatomist, professor of anatomy at Howard University, and editor of the *Journal of the American Medical Association*. It was Dr. Cobb who, several years ago, conducted a study which revealed that the graduates of Dunbar High School, his alma mater, more than held their own in Ivy League colleges against graduates of the finest New England private schools.

Then there are the R. Grayson McGuires, owners of one of the most successful black funeral homes in Washington. Founded by Mr. McGuire's father, McGuire's has been offering, as its slogan states, "Distinction at Its Finest" since 1912. The McGuire family's roots in Washington go back four generations, and a McGuire was in the first graduating class at Howard, while another owned the first black pharmacy in the capital.

But the old families, and their institutions, are being eclipsed by the newer group. The annual December Debutante Cotillion, for example, which the old Guard Bachelor-Benedicts Club and the Girl Friends co-sponsored, was more or less abandoned in the 1960's when it was accused of Uncle Tomism. One of the most prominent of the newer-rich families are the Winston Churchill Willoughbys and, typically, they are not native Washingtonians. Dr. Willoughby is a dentist who was born in Trinidad and who came to Washington, after a sojourn in Zanesville, Ohio, in 1935. In 1975, the District of Columbia Dental Society named Winston Willoughby "Dentist of the Year." Anselee Willoughby is from South Carolina and was brought to Washington by an ambitious mother who sent her to Howard University, in hopes that she would meet a Howard medical student, which she did, and marry him, which she also did. Winston Willoughby is tall, dark, slender, and handsome, with a small black moustache and, though he is dark-skinned, his racially mixed Trinidadian ancestry (one of his great-grandfathers was a Lord Willoughby) is responsible for the fact that seven of his brothers and sisters live in New York as white people. His wife is dark, slender, pretty, and vivacious. The Willoughbys live in a large house on Colorado Avenue, where they have become very social. It all started several years ago when Winston Willoughby began to get patients from the Australian Embassy. Soon he was the pet dentist of the "Embassy Row set," and his patients now include diplomats from most of the African nations, and some of the non-African ones as well. The next step was when the attractive Willoughbys began to get invitations to embassy social events.

Anselee Willoughby sits in her spacious drawing room today, spreading out scrapbooks of clippings of her current social doings like any professional society woman anywhere. She has been pictured in *Vogue* and in the New York *Times,* and her name and photograph appear regularly in the Washington papers. She is up to her ears in charity work, toiling for the District of Columbia Mental Health Association, for the Meridian House Foundation, and for crippled children. She organized the Women's Year for foreign students and diplomats. She is on the Women's Committee of the Washington Performing Arts Center. In 1974 she chaired the S.O.S. Ball for the benefit of drought-stricken African nations, where she succeeded in getting Mrs. Nixon to give a tea at the White House (and in getting herself photographed being hugged by Mrs. Nixon). The President himself came to the ball, which netted close to $70,000, which was distributed to the thirsty African countries for food and clothing.

"We were the only private people invited to the last official Agnew party," says Anselee Willoughby. "The Elliot Richardsons have had us to dinner. We've been invited to Nancy Kissinger's party in honor of the Kaundas from

Zambia. Every year, we give a party for the Australian Embassy — Sir James Plimsoll is a patient of my husband's — and this year's theme was 'An Australian Night in Trinidad.' I've entertained for the Argentine Embassy. I entertain all the time. I usually do a buffet dinner for fifty with a tent in the garden, or seated dinners for fourteen in the house. Once a year, I have a big surprise birthday party for my husband in the summer. It's a surprise because he never knows where it will be held or what the theme will be. I invite all the Senators, diplomats, cabinet officers, and visiting dignitaries. We mingle with all societies here. They've started calling me the black Perle Mesta!" In 1972, for all their social activities, the Willoughbys became one of the first two nonpolitical black families to be listed in the Washington *Green Book,* considered to be a much more important guide to who is who in the capital than the *Social Register.* The other family, the William Beasely Harrises, are also non–Old Guard. Both Harrises are lawyers, and Mrs. Harris, who was United States Ambassador to Luxembourg between 1965 and 1967, is dean of the Howard University Law School. (The *Green Book* points out that it has always listed all ranking government officials and diplomats stationed in the capital, regardless of color; the Willoughbys and Harrises are, however, the first civilian black families to make the little book.)

And, of course, at an economic level much lower than the Willoughbys' are the black activists, militants, and revolutionaries, crying "Black Power Now!" and chanting about Africanism. "It's sad," says Mary Gibson Hundley, sitting in her tiny parlor surrounded by her Syphax heirlooms. "It's the ignorant people who yell about Africa. What happened was that the cotton-pickers were replaced by machines, and so they flocked up to big cities like Washington. They were illiterate and poor. They have no idea, no comprehension or understanding, of what we've been doing here, quietly, peacefully, but steadily, for years. They have no idea of what people like Mary Church Terrell did in breaking segregation in restaurants, or what my husband and I did when we succeeded in breaking the restrictive covenant in housing. They have no idea of how to let white people be their friends. When Fred and I were fighting our court case, our strongest support came from a white Radcliffe graduate on the school board. They've no idea what Dunbar High School has been doing for more than a hundred years. Or what Grandpa Syphax did. We're proud of what we've done — but they simply have no idea."

As though to prove her point, when Mrs. Hundley's kinswoman, Orieanna Syphax, ran not long ago for election to the powerful District of Columbia Board of Education, she lost. The Syphax voice is no longer wanted.

And, though Anselee Willoughby graduated from Dunbar, she doesn't bother attending the sentimental reunions of Dunbar alumni, nor does she particularly care what happens to the old school building, which will, in all likelihood, be razed. Nor is she a Link. "My mother was," she says offhandedly. "It's an old ladies' club." Nor has she heard of Mrs. Hundley. "Who is she?" she asks. "Is she someone I should know?"

12

South of the Sudan

BLACKS WHO ARE DESCENDED FROM SLAVES WHO WORKED ON
the plantations of Virginia and the Carolinas tend to think
of themselves as several cuts above those who toiled for
planters farther south, in Georgia, Mississippi, and Louisiana. This somewhat tenuous assumption is based on the
theory that when blacks arrived from Africa or the West
Indies at such slave ports as Charleston and Newport News,
the planters of those states had first choice of the lot, and
naturally picked men and women who seemed strongest,
healthiest, brightest, and best-looking. Other Southern cities were then offered the remainder. For this same reason,
descendents of slaves in Cincinnati consider themselves superior to those from Louisville, while Louisville looks down
on those from Memphis, and Memphis looks down on
Natchez. Again, it is assumed that as the slave boats made
their way southward down the Ohio and Mississippi Rivers,
stopping at river ports along the way to display their wares,
the upriver slave-buyers were offered the best selection.
When the boats reached the Mississippi delta, only the dregs
of each shipment were left. Since it was not economical to
ship these people north again, these leftovers were often
sold at bargain prices.

In the slave trade, of course, family ties were ripped apart, and it is commonly assumed that no black Americans today know anything of their African antecedents. But this is not entirely true, and a number of American families have elaborately traced their ancestry back to tribal Africa, where they have found interesting and in some cases distinguished relatives. There is the extraordinary Vaughan family of Camden, South Carolina, for example. A man who took the unusual name of Scipio Vaughan was born around 1784 in the Owu district of Abeokuta, which is now a city about forty miles north of Lagos, the capital of Nigeria. He was a member of the Egba family of the Yoruba tribe, who were noted warriors, and it is claimed that he was related to the tribal chieftain, or king. This is possible, because many tribal leaders sold into slavery various of their relatives who displeased or threatened them. Scipio was captured and sold around 1805, and became the property of Wilie Vaughan, a Camden planter whose surname he assumed.

Scipio was an artisan of unusual talent, a skilled ironmonger who became famous throughout the Carolinas for his beautifully crafted wrought-iron gates and fences. He married a Cherokee Indian woman, who bore him thirteen children, and, over the years he endeared himself to the Vaughan family. When Wilie Vaughan died in 1820, his will stipulated that an equivalent to wages of "my negro man Scipio" be set aside for the education of Scipio's children, and added, "Should Scipio survive the first day of January 1825, my will and desire is that he shall be freed and have the use of his time thereafter: That he shall also have his carpenter tools and one hundred dollars at that time." It is not clear whether or not the terms of Mr. Vaughan's will were carried out to the letter. Scipio's name did not appear on the census of Kershaw County as a free man until 1850, and he may have voluntarily remained in slave capacity for Vaughan's widow, Sarah. His name had disappeared from the census by 1860, indicating that he had died in the years between. Two of his sons, however, used to tell of a deathbed scene at which Scipio made the young men promise to leave the South and "its oppressive laws against colored men," and return to their ancestral home in Yorubaland. The two men, first Burrell Churchill Vaughan and then James Churchill Vaughan, with money saved from doing odd jobs, purchased their freedom and sailed for Liberia.

Burrell remained in Liberia, where he married and established a branch of the Vaughan family. James, however, joined a band of Baptist missionaries and traveled southward to Yorubaland and joined the family he had never known. It was not easy for the young alien, who spoke a foreign tongue, bore strange American Indian features, and practiced a religion called Christianity, and it is likely that James Vaughan felt himself a part of the African culture and yet remote from it and, perhaps, a bit superior to it. Though he was a carpenter by trade, he was also a self-styled man of God, and preached his Baptist faith in various outposts in Ijaiye and Ogbomosho. He fought on the side of the Egbas in the Yoruba civil war that was then raging, but married a princess from the Benin tribe, whom he renamed Sarah. The slave trade was still flourishing on Africa's West Coast, and kidnaping was a constant threat. Still, James Churchill Vaughan was able to establish the first Baptist church in Nigeria. His property was plundered twice — first by the "Ibadan dogs of war," and again by members of his own Egba tribal family, when an attempt was made to drive all Christians out of Abeokuta, where his father had been born. He and his wife walked for three days to Lagos with James carrying their tiny son on his back. In Lagos, his first home was destroyed by fire. Though he was now penniless, he started over again as an ironmonger, and gradually branched out into the hardware business. He eventually owned two stores, which sold palm oil, coconuts, ivory, and other products to the growing European market. By the 1880's, James Vaughan was a rich man.

Vaughan made two visits to his American relatives in South Carolina, and a ninety-two-year-old cousin, Mrs. Bessie Boykin Rayford, who was then a little girl, remembers the excitement when "the African" returned, the second time, in 1889. "He wore a jacket of several different colors with a top hat to match," Mrs. Rayford recalls. "The whole town, both black and white, turned out to see him, and there was a parade for him down the main street of Camden." Back in Africa, Vaughan continued to correspond with his American cousins. He also sent gifts, including small canvas bags of gold coins to his niece, Harriet Josephine Carter.

When Vaughan died in 1893, he was buried under a tall, imposing monument of imported Italian marble in Lagos's Ikoyi cemetery, and his two sons, who had been educated in Europe, took over the business. His daughter, lyrically named Aida Arabella, also educated in Europe, married a Lagos lawyer named Eric Moore. In 1922, Mrs. Moore decided that it would be nice to invite her American cousin and namesake, Aida Arabella Stradford, to visit Africa, and offered to send for her at the Moores' expense. Mrs. Stradford was unable to make the trip, but she sent her sister Sara in her place, and thus a granddaughter and a great-granddaughter of Scipio Vaughan met on the African side of the Atlantic. Soon afterward, Mrs. Moore brought her daughter Omotunde to the United States to be entered in a private school, and there was another family reunion. The African and American branches of the Vaughan family have remained in close touch over the years, and, since Scipio's descendents have been prosperous on both continents, there has been a good deal of jetting back and forth between the United States and Lagos.

Aida Arabella Stradford never got to Africa, but she became the family's chief historian and genealogist of both the American and African branches, working with the Kershaw County Historical Society, from family Bible records, inscriptions on old tombstones, and questionnaires to fourth-, fifth-, and sixth-generation Vaughans all over the world. Before she died in 1972, she completed a biography of her great-grandfather Scipio, in which she wrote: "I have related some of the facts concerning my family tree, not only because I regard it as interesting, but also for the purpose of proving that while genealogical trees do not flourish among us, nonetheless, there are some of which we may be justly proud." Mrs. Stradford's daughter is the Chicago lawyer Jewel Stradford Lafontant, who became the first woman United States Deputy Solicitor General.

Mrs. Lafontant was also the first woman attorney of any color to present a case before the United States Supreme Court, and that occasion presented her with an unusual problem. Lawyers presenting cases before that august body have always, by tradition, worn white tie, striped trousers, and tailcoats. Mrs. Lafontant consulted with various males in her profession, but none of them had the slightest idea of what a woman in that position might wear. One actually suggested that she appear before the Supreme Court in a long white evening gown. In the end, Mrs. Lafontant solved the problem herself by designing an outfit of her own. It consisted of a slim-cut skirt of gray-and-white striped material, with a hemline just below the knee; a modified tailcoat; and a white blouse with a white jabot at the throat. The justices complimented her on her appearance.

"Mother was always talking about our African relatives," Mrs. Lafontant recalls, "and as a small child I knew that Africa was not all a jungle, and I was very proud of my African cousins. But when I mentioned them to my friends, nobody believed me." In 1956, Mrs. Lafontant met one of her several-times-removed cousins from Lagos, when Mrs.

Ayo Vaughan-Richards visited the United States. Mrs. Vaughan-Richards, another of Scipio's great-great-grand-daughters, is Nigeria's principal nursing officer and the hostess of her own Nigerian television show. Married to a white architect whom she met while studying in Scotland, Ayo Vaughan persuaded her husband to add her name to his with a hyphen.

Ayo Vaughan-Richards and Jewel Lafontant became friends, and Mrs. Lafontant repaid the visit in 1964 when she went to Africa for the first time. "I was so excited about going to see my people," she says, "that I cut my hair and wore it natural. When Ayo met me at the airport, she cried, 'Cousin Jewel! What happened to all of your lovely hair?' I told her about 'black is beautiful,' and about hair. 'Of course black is beautiful,' she said impatiently, 'but why do they have to do that to their hair?' " Mrs. Lafontant has revisited Lagos several times and, in Lagos, Mrs. Vaughan-Richards says, "We've kept in touch through the years. But I have a commitment to persuade *all* of our relations in the states to come home. Those who have visited us had tears in their eyes when I showed them the graves of their ancestors."

If all the Vaughans and Vaughan-connected families in the United States did return to Africa, it is estimated that a migration of some 115,000 people would be involved, as the descendents of Scipio's remaining eleven children have proliferated across the American countryside. Today, there are Vaughns as well as Vaughans, and they are all considered to be in some way, however dizzyingly, "connected." When the question was asked if jazz singer Sarah Vaughan was part of the family, "Probably" was the reply. In Lagos, the descendents of James Churchill Vaughan have been equally prolific and have become bewilderingly interconnected with the great tribal families of Nigeria. Ayo Vaughan-Richards's maternal grandfather, for example, was Chief Taiwo

Obowu, who is buried in a huge mausoleum in the heart of Lagos. There is a street in Lagos called Vaughan Lane. Lagos Vaughans have exotic names like Kehinde, Adeyinka, Lawunmi, and Apinke, and there are also titled Vaughans. Lady Kofo Ademola, wife of Sir Adetokunbo Ademola, the former chief justice of Nigeria, is a Vaughan cousin. She was the first Nigerian woman to graduate from Oxford. The "oldest living Vaughan" in Lagos is said to be Michael Ayo Vaughan, seventy-seven, a retired banker, and, in the present generation, James Olabode Vaughan, supply and distribution manager for the Mobil Oil Corporation, who is forty-seven, is another of Scipio's great-great-grandsons. James Olabode Vaughan has black skin, but his half-brother, James Wilson Vaughan, a London-based film-maker, has the features of those on the head of an old American Indian nickel — a "throwback," it is assumed, to his Cherokee great-great-grandmother. All Vaughans can recite the inscription that is carved on all four sides of James Churchill Vaughan's marble tomb in Lagos:

> *Sacred to the memory of James Churchill Vaughan, Native of Camden, South Carolina, born April 1, 1828. He migrated to Africa in the year 1853, leaving behind a large family, owing to the oppressive laws then in force against colored men in the Southern States.*
>
> *His life in Africa was characterized by many vicissitudes in all of which he proved himself equal to the attendant difficulties. He died on the 13th of September, 1893.*
>
> *And though after my skin worms destroy this body, yet in my flesh shall I see God. Job XIX. 26*

In America, Vaughans have not only married Carters and Stradfords, but also MacLaughlins, McDonalds, Robinsons, Rayfords, Moseleys, Jacksons, Mouzons, Gants, and Lees. Through the Lees, the Vaughans are also connected to the Dibbles, another old-line Camden family. Sallie Rebecca

Lee, a Scipio granddaughter, married Eugene H. Dibble, and the Dibbles claim to be descended from an African prince. The Dibbles, the family is careful to point out, did not come to the United States as slaves. They came as merchants from Africa, settled in South Carolina, and went into the wholesale grocery business. The first Eugene Dibble's grocery business became one of the largest in the South, and with his profits he bought acreage in what is today much of downtown Camden. The family still owns this property, and has been renting it for years, peacefully, to white tenants.

Today's most prominent Dibble is probably Eugene Dibble III of Chicago, who, though he is not a Black Muslim, has the lucrative position of chief financial consultant to the Nation of Islam, for whom, among other things, he is putting together the financing of a new 500-bed hospital, a $50,000,000 undertaking. Mr. Dibble is also Muhammad Ali's advisor on money matters. Mr. Dibble's father was a doctor at Tuskegee Institute and was a friend of George Washington Carver, and his Grandfather Dibble was a friend and neighbor of Bernard Baruch; they had adjoining farms in South Carolina. Eugene Dibble, a tall, powerfully built man who admits that, if he wished to, he could easily "pass" for white (and, when it's convenient to do so, he does), is as family-proud as his multitudinous relations. "My mother was a Taylor," he says. "My Grandfather Taylor was a builder, and built all of the buildings at Tuskegee. He was the first black man to graduate from M.I.T. My uncle, Robert R. Taylor, was a prominent Chicago businessman. The Taylors, like the Dibbles, were never slaves. My brother, Robert T. Dibble, is a doctor in Washington, and one of my sisters is on the faculty of Howard, and another is with the University of Chicago." He can also rattle off genealogical facts about the family of a sort that would be beyond most white families, such as: "Jewel Lafontant's mother was my grandfather's first cousin."

Equally well versed in genealogy, surprisingly, are the Dibbles' five children, who range in age from twelve to twenty and whose skin colors range from the light side to the dark. Not long ago, the children drew up an enormous family tree in an attempt to gather all the members of the family on one sheet of paper, those in Africa as well as those in the United States. It took many sheets of paper, Scotch-taped together, and, when spread open, it nearly covers the entire living room floor of the Dibbles' large Chicago apartment. Proudly looking over the monumental work of Rochon Dibble, twenty; Clyla Dibble, eighteen; Eugene Dibble IV, seventeen; Andrew Dibble, fourteen; and Hilary Dibble, twelve, Eugene Dibble III says, "We have figured out that over the years there have been twenty-three Dibbles at the Mount Hermon and Northfield Schools in Massachusetts. It would be safe to say that there has *always* been a Dibble at Mount Hermon or Northfield. Eugene the Fourth is headed for Yale. I have a little motto that I've passed on to my children: 'Genealogy determines the eye, and environment creates what the eye can see.' "

Not to be outdone is Mrs. Eugene Dibble III. She was a Campbell, and Campbells are related to Lees and Reeds (making the Dibbles in some way related to each other), and she points out, "My great uncle, Lee Reed, was a Supreme Court Justice in South Carolina." She adds, "My family has been traced back to the Tudor Kings of England." With equal pride, Mrs. Dibble, a Wellesley graduate, also adds, "My maternal grandfather was a servant. But he saved enough money to buy a home in a good neighborhood. I think that's pretty good for a man who never went beyond the third grade!"

13

Passing

WHETHER OR NOT IT IS AN ATTITUDE IMPLANTED WITHIN them by generations of a dominant white society, most upper-class blacks have deep feelings of inferiority because of the color of their skin and their general "visibility" as black people. Though most would not admit it, they would really rather be white. To the brave cry of "Black is beautiful" could be added, in an almost inaudible whisper, "but white is still better." Even in the proudest black families, the little whisper is there, expressing itself in the search for white ancestors or, if none can be found, at least American Indians. Furthermore, black secret self-loathing is no new phenomenon, and was apparent among the black elite over a hundred years ago, as a mulatto black writer named John E. Bruce observed satirically shortly after the Civil War:

> There is another element in this strange heterogeneous conglomeration, which for want of a better name has been styled society and it is this species of African humanity which is forever and ever informing the uninitiated what a narrow escape they had from being born white. They have small hands, aristocratic insteps and wear blue veins, they have auburn hair and finely chiselled features. They are uneducated as a rule (i.e.) the largest number of them,

though it would hardly be discovered unless they opened their *mouths* in the presence of their superiors in intellect, which they are very careful not to do. In personal appearance, they fill the bill precisely so far as *importance* and pomposity goes — but no farther. They are opposed to manual labor, their physical organization couldn't stand it, they prefer shuffling cards or dice or "removing the spirits of Frumenta from the gaze of rude men" if somebody else becomes responsible for the damage. Around the festive board, they are unequalled for their verbosity and especially for their aptness in tracing their ancestry. One will carry you away back to the times of William the Silent and bring you up to 18 so and so, to show how illustrious is his lineage and pedigree. His great, great grandfather's mother-in-law was the Marchioness So and So and his father was ex-Chief Justice Chastity of S.C. or some other southern state with a polygamous record.

Upper-class black families tend to have fewer children than blacks in the ghetto, partly because, according to middle-class American standards, it is not "nice" to have large families, but also because children are just another daily reminder of the fact of blackness. One woman, light-skinned, tells of her distress and disbelief when she was first shown her baby in the hospital. It was so black. "That's not my baby!" she cried. (Another woman, also light-skinned, was equally dismayed to see that her baby was, to all appearances, white.) The children of parents of mixed ancestry can, of course, turn out to be of any shade, like the Dibble children, who range from quite light to quite dark, and this in itself can create problems: one little boy may be accepted by his white contemporaries, while his brother may not be. A number of wealthy black families, including the John Johnsons of Chicago, have adopted children just to avoid this situation. At least there will be no question of what color a child's skin will be.

Black families often go to elaborate lengths to "protect" their children from finding out that they are black, or "different." Often, in the home, the terms "black" or "colored" or "Negro" will never be used in front of children, and children's friends are carefully screened to be sure that they meet only their "own kind," and do not learn that there are people of any other color in the world outside. One woman recalls, "When I was a little girl and overheard an adult say someone was black, I assumed it meant that that person was dirty." The word "white" is also often taboo in front of children, and Victoria Sanders, a Chicago stockbroker whose mother and aunts were cleaning women, says, "I knew that my mother cleaned for white people, and so I assumed that this meant white people must be dirty."

In much the same way, upper-class Jews who have moved away from the Orthodoxy often keep the fact of their Jewishness a secret from their children — sometimes until they are almost grown. Geoffrey Hellman, the New York writer, tells that he was not told that he was Jewish until it was time for him to go to prep school, when he was taken aside by his father and told the sober facts of life. With blacks, of course, the terrible news comes earlier — usually when they start the first grade at school — and it comes with shattering, almost traumatic effect. In countless households there has been repeated the scene where the child, in tears, comes home from school and says, "Mommy, what's a nigger, and am I one?" Sometimes, despite the most careful secrecy, the news that a child is different comes earlier. A Cincinnati woman remembers that, as a little girl, she was traveling by bus with her mother to the South. The fact that they were sitting in the back of the bus made no impression on her. She was too young to read the sign printed above the driver's head, and all the people seated around her were her own color. But when the bus made a refreshment stop along the highway, and she and her mother were refused service at the lunch counter, "I'll never forget the look on my mother's face when the waitress said, 'We don't serve colored,' " she says. "She looked so desperately sad that I thought she was going to die, and I was so frightened that I began to cry."

Such early bruises do not heal easily, if they heal at all. When asked if he felt inferior to white people, one seventeen-year-old boy from a well-to-do black family said, "Offhand, I'd say no, but actually knowing all these things that are thrown up to you about white people being superior — that they look more or less down on all Negroes — that we have to look to them for everything we get — that they'd rather think of us as mice than men — I don't believe I or any other Negro can help but feel inferior. My father says that it isn't so — that we feel inferior only to those whom we feel are superior. But I don't believe we can feel otherwise. Around white people until I know them a while I feel definitely out of place. Once I played a Ping-Pong match with a white boy whose play I know wasn't as good as mine, and boys he managed to beat I beat with ease, but I just couldn't get it out of my mind that I was playing a white boy. Sort of an Indian sign on me, you know."

Though young black people insist that they are proud of being of the upper, or at least more privileged, class, they have definite mixed feelings about being black at all, as another young man says: "Knowing that there are difficulties that confront us all as Negroes, if I could be born again and had my choice I'd really want to be a white boy — I mean white or my same color, providing I could occupy the same racial and economic level I now enjoy. I am glad I am this color — I'm frequently taken for a foreigner. I wouldn't care to be lighter or darker and taken for a Negro. I am the darkest one in the family due to my constant outdoor activities. I realize of course that there are places where I can't go despite my family or money just because I happen to be a Negro. With my present education, family background, and so forth, if I were only white I could go places in life. A white face holds supreme over a black one despite its economic and social status. Frankly, it leaves me bewildered."

Bewildered — it is as good a word as any to describe the way well-educated, well-off black families view themselves in relation to white society. It is with the same ambivalence and uncertainty that blacks view interracial marriages. Black women, for example, are nearly always opposed to black men marrying white women. It is not so much that they hate and resent the whites, nor is it because of the reasons usually given — that when a black man takes a white wife, he becomes subservient to her and, at the same time, usually marries someone beneath his social class. It is more likely to be because black women feel that, since there are so few eligible black males, they should save themselves for black women. At the same time, in a number of upper-class black families, a wife will accept the fact that her husband has a white mistress and even, at heart, be a little proud of it; it does not threaten her position socially, a position she tends to regard as somewhat shaky. Black women see nothing wrong with white men who take black wives, particularly if they are *rich* white men. This is taken as a tribute to the "secret charms" of black women. But when Adam Clayton Powell, Jr., married New York socialite Beryl Slocum, even though she was rich and social, the black communities of New York and Washington were up in arms.

Because of their mixed feelings about being black at all, most blacks are not quite sure how they feel about the many light-skinned people who manage to move out of the black world and "pass" as whites. No statistics are available, but it has been estimated that thousands of black people cross over the color line each year, and it is assumed that because men are more mobile, more black men than women are passing as whites, and that they do so for economic reasons. Some black men have left their black wives and children to move upward and outward into the white business world. There is the case, for example, of Harry Murphy of Atlanta. The son of a printer, Harry Murphy, and not James Meredith, was actually the first black person to graduate from "Ole Miss." Murphy attended the University of Mississippi as a white man, and no one ever knew the difference. He is now living and working in New York. And Robert Johnson, an editor at *Ebony* (and no kin to John Johnson), remembers that at Great Lakes Naval Training station, a schoolmate, who Johnson knew was black but who had fair skin, approached him and said, "Listen. This is the last time we'll ever talk about this, but I'm passing. Just don't blow my cover. Don't blow my gig." Johnson insists that he was delighted to hear of his friend's good fortune. "My theory is," he says, "that if you can fool the white folks, more power to you!"

But one wonders whether such sentiments are, in the last analysis, sincere. The word "pass" has two meanings in the black world. When someone says, "He passed," it does not usually mean that the person referred to has become assimilated with whites. To pass is also to die. Even the best-educated blacks refer to death as "passing," the way lower-class whites will use the euphemism "passed away." In other words, it is possible that light-skinned blacks who have disappeared to join the whites are considered as good as dead.

A number of upper-class blacks have, of course, made noble efforts to come to grips with their black identities, and to rid themselves of their insecurities and feelings of inferiority. One of the most articulate of these is Dr. Margaret Burroughs, an assistant professor at Kennedy King City College in Chicago and the director of Chicago's DuSable Museum, which is devoted to black art and culture. Dr. Burroughs, a doughty, wirily built lady who looks as though nothing would faze her, has long been concerned about her fellow blacks' poor self-image, and long ago decided to do something about it. Early in her teaching career, for example, a group of black students came to her office and complained about a white teacher who had asked her pupils to sing "Old Black Joe." Dr. Burroughs, a woman not without a sense of humor, thought about the problem for a moment, then turned and faced a window and said, "Now listen. I'm not talking to you, I'm talking to this window. I'm not telling you what to do, I'm telling you what *I'd* do. I'd do as the teacher told me, but whenever I got to the chorus of that song, I'd sing it, 'Old *white* Joe.'" The students followed her suggestion and, though the other teacher was not amused, she got the point.

In 1952, long before the natural or "Afro" style in hair became fashionable among blacks, Dr. Burroughs decided, for no particular reason, to stop "pressing" her hair. "It was expensive, and it was time-consuming," she says, "and I thought, why should I go to so much fuss just to make my hair look like white people's hair?" So she let the natural kinks emerge. The reaction among her friends, associates, and students was strong, even hostile. She was criticized and ridiculed and got anonymous letters. In her classroom, a student placed a note on her desk that read, "Maizie's Beauty Parlor: You go!" She took the note up with the class, and asked them if they could think of any reasons why she might be wearing her hair as she was. One student suggested, "You've got a scalp disease." Dr. Burroughs explained, "I think I look more beautiful this way. I think all people look more beautiful when they look like themselves."

Still, wherever she went she was jeered and mocked. Ironically, for letting one of the traits of her race show, she was called "a disgrace to the race." The most violent criticism came from her fellow blacks. On her way to a lecture she was giving at a black college in the South, she passed a dormitory window and heard a student say, in a loud voice, "What's *she* trying to prove?" And at the lecture she was booed, not for what she had to say but for her choice of coiffure. As a result of this experience, Margaret Burroughs wrote a poem that has become something of a black classic, called "What Shall I Tell My Children Who Are Black":

Let it be known to all, the story
Of the glorious struggle of my people.
Let it be known that black men and women
Helped to build this, our country.
Let it be known that black men and women of the past
In an effort to make this country
What it ought to be, gave up their very last
To make America a real democracy,
A true homeland of the free.
Let our leaders of today go back into the past
And come fighting forth envigored with the spirit
Of Turner, and Vesey, Douglass, Tubman and Truth.
Let our stalwart black youth lift their heads in pride
As they tell of their fathers' fight for freedom
To the white youth by their side.
Yes, let it be known, let all the old folks tell it.
Sing it to the babes yet in arms.
Let us read the glorious story
Right along with our Bible. Let it be known to all,
The story of the glorious struggles of my people.
Too long . . . Too long has it been kept from us.

Margaret Burroughs's hairdo became not only her personal trademark but her personal symbol of protest. "To me it began to have a deep meaning," she says. "It meant that black people *must* be proud of what they are and who they are, and not try to hide their lights under wigs, and hair straighteners and bleaching creams. I hope it also meant that what goes on inside a person's head is more important than what sits on top of it."

Building her DuSable Museum of African American History has been another "glorious struggle" for Margaret Burroughs, and she has faced problems similar to those of the Museum of African Art in Washington. Though Chicago had an American Indian Museum, a Jewish Museum, an Oriental Institute, and a Polish Museum, there was vociferous opposition to the idea that a museum of black culture should be established. Much of the criticism came, again, from leaders of the black community, one of whom wrote to say, "We have nothing to be proud of." The white community was also opposed, claiming that a black museum would constitute an instrument of segregation. Still, the DuSable Museum was formally inaugurated in October 1961, in Dr. Burroughs's living room.

It was not until thirteen years later that the museum was able to move out of her living room and into a building in Washington Park with 25,000 square feet of exhibition space, donated by the city of Chicago. The museum's collection is still almost pathetically small, and the building, with cracked plaster and peeling paint, is sadly in need of repair. Its cleaning and maintenance staff is meager, and the museum presents an appearance of honest, if untidy, poverty. Dr. Burroughs and her husband do most of the work themselves, and they put in long hours without any compensation. The museum offers a number of unique services. It will supply suggestions to parents who want to give their babies African names. It will demonstrate techniques for wrapping skirts and turbans in various African styles, and it will advise couples who want to get married with an African theme. In 1974, the DuSable museum put on a wedding where the minister wore a dashiki, and the bride and groom stood at an altar decorated with African sculpture. If a group of children cannot come to visit the museum, the museum will come to visit them — in the form of a lecturer, usually in the person of Margaret Burroughs, with a suitcase full of artifacts. Though most museums shut off their telephones after 5:00 or 5:30 P.M., the DuSable Museum keeps its switchboard open until late at night to answer questions on African history. Usually, these come in forms of calls from barbershops and corner taverns from men and women who need a fact to settle a bet. But the museum is desperately in need of funds, and Dr. Burroughs is currently trying to raise $2,000,000 for operating costs, renovations, and new acquisitions — a modest enough sum, compared with budgets of other museums. "If every black person in Chicago would contribute just one dollar, we would reach our goal," Dr. Burroughs says. So far, however, these dollars have not been forthcoming.

In Washington, one of the problems facing the Museum of African Art is that its director, Warren Robbins, is white. In Chicago, the situation facing the DuSable Museum is, if anything, even more acute because Margaret Burroughs is black. So deeply rooted is black self-doubt that the majority of blacks simply cannot accept the possibility that a fellow black, such as Margaret Burroughs, might be doing something worthwhile. Such is the competitiveness of black versus black that blacks actually resent and seek to belittle other blacks, such as Margaret Burroughs, who have achieved some degree of recognition and status above them. The result is a large segment of the black population that would rather submit to the authority of whites than to accept the leadership of other blacks.

In fact, middle-class blacks often seem to have difficulty cooperating in any endeavor. It has been noted that black scholars and educators often tend to turn to a white "authority" in their field for advice, that black doctors turn to white doctors when they need a confirming opinion, and that black lawyers would rather confer with white members of their profession than with blacks. A black client often feels more secure with a white lawyer, and a black patient feels he is in better hands if his doctor is white.

In a study by sociologists Abram Kardiner and Lionel Ovesey, it has been pointed out that blacks' frequent failures in professional, social, and business relations with other blacks is because "in every Negro, he encounters his own self-contempt." It is as though the black were saying, "You're only another black man like me. So why should you be in a position above me? Why should I listen to you?"

Or perhaps, in even more human terms, it is because in small, daily ways, even the most successful blacks are reminded that, though *some* black people have made great and important strides, *most* have not. It is what the Washington lady, from her car, saw in the drunken young man dressed like "Super Fly." It is what Doris Zollar sees when she looks at her wedding book. When she married Lowell Zollar, a young doctor, it was a great social event in Little Rock, and was given large coverage in the society pages of the black press. There was a huge reception, with many gifts, each one carefully listed in the wedding book. Among the gifts of Lenox china dinner plates, vermeil table settings and silver tea services, are listed such gifts as this one:

"Mr. and Mrs. B——: $5.00"

~ 14 ~

The Power of the Press

IN 1957, A BLACK SOCIOLOGIST NAMED E. FRANKLIN FRAZIER published a book called *Black Bourgeoisie,* the contents of which still raise hackles among upwardly mobile blacks. Frazier, who died in 1962, was chairman of the Department of Sociology at Howard University, and among his assertions, repeated throughout the book, was the statement that Negro society lived "in a world of make-believe." Primarily, Frazier was critical of the new middle-class blacks who had achieved some degree of affluence during their lifetimes — in the professions or white-collar occupations — and whose lives had become an abject, and usually second-rate, imitation of the doings and attitudes of the white upper-class social structure they saw around them. This imitation, as Frazier saw it, was more like a dreadful parody. Frazier pointed mockingly at the then-current phenomenon of black debutantes, in long white dresses and opera-length gloves, being presented at cotillions in rented hotel ballrooms by tail-coated fathers who were druggists, bank clerks, or electricians. These new-rich (or comparatively rich) blacks, Frazier claimed, tried to compensate for their innate feelings of inferiority by buying expensive automobiles — even then, the Cadillac had become the black status car — which were nearly always financed; on houses that they could not afford; on clothes, furs, and jewelry that they did not need; on costly and tasteless furnishings that they never used; and on luxury cruises and other travel undertaken not so much for pleasure as for a way to flaunt their new wealth. Needless to say, Professor Frazier's book made a number of black people, who could see themselves reflected in his pages, very angry.

This new class, Frazier said, had no economic or cultural base. They had "sloughed off the genteel tradition of the small upper class," and had similarly rejected "the folk culture of the Negro masses." Lacking "cultural roots in either the Negro world with which it refuses to identify, or the white world," which refused to let the black bourgeoisie share its life, "most black bourgeoisie live in a cultural vacuum and their lives are devoted largely to fatuities." Frazier concluded, "The black bourgeoisie suffers from 'nothingness' because when Negroes attain middle-class status, their lives generally lose both content and significance." It was a stinging indictment and, it must be admitted, important parts of Frazier's 1957 thesis still stand, particularly as they pertain to certain segments of the new middle class. Professor Frazier, however, failed to mention that new-rich whites are often just as guilty of imitative vulgarity and conspicuous spending. And his is a rather limited definition of what social "class" consists of in America. Class is not simply defined by money, material possessions, or even manners. It is more a matter of self-assurance, dignity, and a commonality of interests within a common organization. In any social class — high, low, or middle — there must be give-and-take. But, in the end, an upper class emerges from people who have the deepest and most solid feelings of their own self-worth, and of the worth of their similarly situated and similarly thinking peers.

Professor Frazier claimed that black attitudes were sustained by two "myths" — the myth of black business, and the myth of black society. These myths, he asserted, were both created and promulgated by the black press. It is an interesting notion, and bears some looking into. The first black newspaper, *Freedom's Journal,* was founded in 1827 by two free blacks, one of whom, John Russworm, was the first black to be graduated from an American college. Twenty years later, Frederick Douglass's *North Star* — later renamed *Frederick Douglass's Paper* — appeared. Both these newspapers were essentially Abolitionist tracts, aimed at white as well as black readers, and concentrated on reports of mistreatment and injustice to blacks in the South. After the Civil War, a number of black newspapers came into existence, particularly after 1880, when blacks began migrating from the South to Northern cities. By 1900, the two most influential black newspapers were the *Guardian,* published by William Monroe Trotter, a Harvard graduate, and the *New York Age.* The *Guardian* was a mouthpiece for Negro intellectuals, while the *New York Age* plumped for the theories of Booker T. Washington, who wanted to build a strong black labor force.

In 1905, the Chicago *Defender* appeared — first as a simple handbill. By 1910, however, the *Defender* was appearing regularly and, at first, the paper concentrated on sensationalism to attract readers. But by the end of the first World War, the *Defender* had become the leading black voice in the country. Due, in large part, to the huge migration of blacks to Chicago, the *Defender*'s circulation reached 100,000 by 1922. The *Defender* was also one of the primary causes for this migration, because the *Defender* was the first of what would be many black publications that romanticized the scale of the opportunities — business and educational — that blacks could find in the big Northern cities. To the poor black in the South reading the *Defender,* Chicago sounded like a second Eden. In Chicago, he was told, life was fast, rich and stimulating. Good-paying jobs were to be had. There were superb schools and colleges for his children. In Chicago, blacks owned their own homes and automobiles — some employed white chauffeurs — and there was a gay social life in opulent restaurants and at lavish private parties. In the *Defender*'s pages, Chicago was advertised as the Land of Milk and Honey, and the *Defender* received thousands of letters a week from rural blacks asking nothing more than how to get to Chicago. When they got there, of course, they often found something quite different as they crowded the city's relief roles.

Between World War I and World War II, dozens of new black newspapers came into existence, most of them published in big cities, and most of them dealing with city life. By 1943, there were 164 active black newspapers, most of them published in large cities with black populations of 50,000 or more. Nearly all were weeklies, and they had a combined circulation-per-issue of close to 2,000,000. During World War II, three new important black news organs appeared — the Pittsburgh *Courier,* with a weekly circulation of about 270,000; the Baltimore *Afro-American,* with 230,000; and the Norfolk, Virginia, *Journal and Guide,* with 78,000. The Chicago *Defender,* meanwhile, held strong with a circulation of 160,000. In 1956, the *Defender* became a daily and instituted a national edition that circulates throughout the country. As black newspapers proliferated, black newsgathering agencies came into existence, the most important of which is the Associated Negro Press, which was established in 1919. All these newspapers, to entice their readers, covered international and national affairs only in a way that had a black "slant." During the Korean War, for example, less attention was paid to the defeats and victories — or even to the cause — of the war itself than to the heroic deeds of certain black soldiers. From the slant, it was possible to get a slanted view — that all black soldiers

were shining heroes, for example. What readers were reading was often less news than it was romantic fiction and
escape literature.

In 1945, John Johnson's *Ebony* appeared, and it gradually became the most influential black news magazine in the
country. Though John Johnson originally intended his
publication to be one that chronicled the lives of "ordinary" black men and women, it has become something a
little different, which undoubtedly accounts for *Ebony*'s
success and for the fact that the Johnsons who own it have
become very rich. It is easy to fault *Ebony*. It is often slop-
pily edited, and few issues are without a number of typo-
graphical errors. There are errors of syntax too, as well as
errors of plain fact. Also, *Ebony* can be accused of being a
bit parochial. Published in Chicago, it pays a great deal of
attention to Chicago people, their lives and doings. But it is
the quality of life reflected in *Ebony* that is most interesting.

Ebony also publishes "The Ebony Success Library,"
which includes such volumes as *1,000 Successful Blacks,* and
Famous Blacks Give Secrets of Success. Success is *Ebony*'s
theme, and it is nothing if not inspirational. It has become,
in other words, a magazine devoted to the back achiever, the
extraordinary black. In the pages of *Ebony,* success is romanticized and glamorized, given an extra coat of luster and
excitement. Everything in *Ebony* is heightened, and the
magazine abounds in adjectives and superlatives. A Chicago
doctor is described as a "brilliant" surgeon. A young econo-
mist with a university post is described as "world-re-
nowned," and a lawyer is "internationally famous." Nikki
Giovanni, generally recognized as one of the best black
poets, is called "extraordinarily famous." A California
couple — she a schoolteacher and he the director of a boys'
camp — are written up in *Ebony* in terms of their "beautiful" home with its "spacious bar." Actually, in the accom-

panying photographs, the house looks like an attractive but modest California bungalow and the den looks hardly spacious but rather cluttered and crowded. A Harlem couple have fled the city to enjoy "the affluent good life" of a Westchester suburb, and their Irvington home is also "spacious" — though, in the photographs, the house looks on the small side. The Irvington couple, *Ebony* points out, have white neighbors who treat them nicely.

People whom *Ebony* writes up are nearly all, it would seem, "executives" or "highly paid executives." *Ebony* — as well as its readers, one assumes — has an obsessive interest in salaries. This or that prominent "executive" in an accounting firm earns $35,000 a year. Another earns $80,000 a year. In higher brackets, men are simply "millionaires" or "multimillionaires." *Ebony* is equally interested in what people pay for things, particularly houses, and every piece of black real estate is provided with its price tag. (The Irvington couple, for example, live "in a neighborhood of $100,000 homes.") Other possessions are listed. If a man "drives a Cadillac," that fact is noted. Another couple has two Cadillacs and a custom-built Mercedes. Still another man drives a $27,000 Rolls-Royce. If a man has bought his wife a $25,000 diamond necklace, *Ebony* reports that fact, along with what she pays for her clothes and he pays for custom-made shoes at "world-famous Peel's of London." In the pages of *Ebony,* all men are "dapperly dressed," all women are "chic," and all living rooms are "elegant." (*Ebony* also always counts the rooms of houses.) Perhaps *Ebony*'s emphasis is an extension of John Johnson's personal philosophy, but the message emerges that "success" is measured in money and possessions.

Ebony devotes a good deal of space to black Society, to its parties and charitable doings. *Ebony* also chronicles the successes of black entertainers. To upper-crust and even middle-class blacks, the entertainers exist on an interesting social stratum all their own. Blacks are proud of their entertainers; most, after all, are attractive-looking people and make decorative additions at parties. Also, most are people with proven talent. And yet a distinction is drawn between people like Marian Anderson and Mattiwilda Dobbs, who are opera singers, and such people as Diana Ross, a pop singer. An upper-crust black mother would much prefer her daughter to study opera, ballet, or concert piano to having her sing with a rock group or dance in a Broadway musical. This was exactly Charlotte Hawkins Brown's attitude when her niece married Nat "King" Cole — he was a "popular" performer, who sang in nightclubs. He was not even Paul Robeson, who performed in Shakespeare. It is an attitude currently expressed by Mrs. Winston Willoughby of Washington, who, talking of a recent Washington party, commented, "Pearl Bailey was there — big deal!" She would be a very big deal, of course, at a white party.

Charlotte Hawkins Brown would have been even more aghast had her niece wanted to marry Roy Campanella or Joe Louis. The black upper crust is much less proud of its professional athletes. Partly, it is because the athletes are assumed to be people who have made a great deal of money through the sheer good luck of having been born with long legs or strong arms, who have needed no education and possess no artistic talent. Many black athletes, furthermore, have "made their way up from the street," and have few of what are considered the social graces. Also, the number of blacks who have become successful athletes are a somewhat painful reminder of one of the cliché beliefs which whites have expressed about blacks — that they have "a natural ability" at sports, just as they are supposed to have "natural rhythm."

In *Ebony*'s *1,000 Successful Blacks* (actually a biographical listing of a little over 1,100 names), which is sort of a black *Who's Who,* there are sketches of a number of entertainers. Only a smattering of black athletes is listed, including Althea Gibson, Hank Aaron, Vida Blue, Arthur Ashe, and Willie Mays. But where are O. J. Simpson, Lew Alcindor, Roy Campanella, Oscar Robertson, John Brockington, Joe Frazier, Frank Robinson, and Sugar Ray? Apparently, *Ebony's* editors considered none of these athletes sufficiently "successful" for inclusion in the book. Every year, *Ebony* publishes another, smaller list, *The 100 Most Influential Black Americans.* The criteria for inclusion in this list are, according to *Ebony,* "Does the individual affect, in a decisive way, the lives, thinking and actions of large segments of the nation's black population? Does the individual command widespread national influence among blacks, and/or is the nominee usually influential with those whites whose policies and practices significantly affect a large number of blacks?" There are no entertainers, and no athletes, it seems, who meet these criteria, for there are none among the "100 Most Influential."

Perhaps the most exclusive and prestigious list is contained in *Ebony's Famous Blacks Give Secrets of Success.* There are only seventy-two names on the "Famous" list, and each listee is given a fairly extensive biography. (Interestingly enough, *Ebony's* publisher, John Johnson, is given a six-page profile, while only four pages are devoted to Thurgood Marshall.) The sketches are arranged in alphabetical order, from Milton B. Allen, state's attorney for the city of Baltimore, to Andrew Young, Jr., Congressman from Georgia. Of the seventy-two, a healthy majority of forty-one are either businessmen, politicians, judges, doctors, educators, clergymen, lawyers, or civil servants. Fifteen are entertainers. Two are members of the military —Major General Daniel James, Jr., Deputy Assistant Secretary of

Defense, and Rear Admiral Samuel L. Gravely, Jr., the first black admiral in the United States Navy. There are only two black athletes — Wilt Chamberlain, perhaps because he is a college graduate, and George Foreman, perhaps because he was an Olympic Gold Medalist or because, as *Ebony* points out, he is now a "businessman" as well as a prize-fighter.

Incredibly, the man who is probably the most famous black in the world today, Muhammad Ali, is not included among the "Famous" (surely he is more famous than John H. Johnson). In George Foreman's sketch, furthermore, Foreman is permitted to make a slurring reference to Ali and his penchant for making speeches. "Ali is qualified to explain physical fitness," says Foreman, "but not philosophy. To make statements, I think, is the job of intellectuals, not athletes." Muhammad Ali is probably also more successful and has made more money, than John Johnson. But he is not even included in *1,000 Successful Blacks*. He is probably more philanthropic. "One of the problems with Ali," says his business manager, Eugene Dibble, "is keeping him from giving all his money away, and trying to get him to build up an estate for his children." The former Cassius Clay is also probably more devoutly religious. He wanted to give the entire purse from his fight with Foreman to the Nation of Islam, to which he is a celebrated convert (instead, under Mr. Dibble's guidance, the $5,000,000 — considerably reduced by taxes — went into a couple of high-rise apartment houses in Chicago). True, he once went to jail — but for a cause many people found admirable.

Of course Muhammad Ali would never have been accepted by Mrs. Astor's Four Hundred. But because he is an athlete, and therefore not quite "respectable," he has not made it into the black Seventy-Two, the black One Hundred, or even the black One Thousand. Some blacks say,

"It's not so much because of his profession or his color. It's his religion."

At the same time, *Ebony* publishes a regular feature called "Strictly for Laughs," a page of black-oriented cartoons. As in any publication, the cartoons get the highest readership, and yet these "Laughs" project a somewhat different image and style of life. In a recent issue, for example, a cartoon showed a young black doctor telephoning his mother to say, "Hello, Mom! I've got this pain in my stomach. What do you think I can take for it?" — a fun-poking attempt to deal with black matriarchal society but one which, in the process, makes the doctor seem ignorant. Another cartoon depicts a black couple visiting a home-improvement loan agency; the wife has a large nose and protruding teeth, and her husband explains to the loan officer, "It's for my wife. I want to send her to a plastic surgeon." Another cartoon shows a black woman wielding a feather duster in front of the face of a white man. The man says, "You must be the new cleaning woman." Still another depicts a black controller in the tower of an airport, speaking on the radio to the pilot of a plane that seems headed directly for the tower. The controller says, "You're not upset about my winning that card game last night, are you, Fred? . . . Fred!!!" — a reference, of course, to blacks' proclivity for poker-playing.

The vicissitudes of black businesses, as well as blacks' fondness for tavern life, are mocked in a cartoon showing a child manning a lemonade stand. His sign, "Lemonade 10¢" has been crossed out and replaced with a sign that reads "Beer 25¢." He explains to a police officer, "Well . . . I couldn't make any money with lemonade." Still another shows a housewife, her hair in rollers, surrounded by small children in what is clearly a slum tenement. Rats crawl across the floor and across the newspaper she is reading, and the only visible luxury is an ancient refrigerator. Pointing to the paper, the wife calls out, "Hey, honey, look! It says here we're part of the middle class." And so it goes in "Laughs."

Editorially, *Ebony* seems to have become a "shelter" magazine, and this impression is supported by its advertising as one turns the glossy color pages showing glamorous black women dancing in moonlit Acapulco, and black couples, looking young and wealthy, building sand castles on Aegean beaches with bloody Marys at their sides. (White advertisers and their agencies have discovered the power of the black consumer market, providing many jobs for black men and women as models and mannequins. But, according to Beverly Johnson, a leading black fashion model, "The minute the economy takes a down turn, jobs for black models get scarce.") White shelter magazines like *Vogue, Town & Country,* and *House & Garden* also deal with the perfumed never-never world of the very rich, but somehow, in these magazines, it is all taken less seriously; we know that most people do not have drawing rooms decorated with $100,000 *trompe l'oeil* walls and so we smile at *House & Garden*'s fantasy-land. But *Ebony* takes success with deadly seriousness. *Ebony* says, *"This is what black life is like, and here is how much it costs,"* which makes it all seem somewhat joyless and rather crass.

As for humor, white magazines like the *New Yorker, Playboy,* and so on that publish cartoons also poke fun at human foibles and problems, but they do so in a gentle way. Ebony's humor — whether one considers "Laughs" funny or not — is bitter and harsh. Certainly, in contrast to *Ebony*'s editorial text, it does not seem designed to improve the blacks' self-image. Instead, "Laughs" portrays blacks as ineffectual, irresponsible, and vindictively ashamed of the way they look. *Ebony*'s "Laughs" seem more like cartoon *Angst.*

In New York, the *Amsterdam News,* published in Harlem — "America's Largest Weekly," as its slogan proclaims — is also intended to reflect the quality of Negro life and thought in America's largest city. With its newspaper format, the *Amsterdam News* makes for somewhat livelier reading than *Ebony* — one learns, in screaming red headlines, that one of Elijah Muhammad's sons has been arrested for selling heroin. But, like *Ebony*, the insides of the *News* are filled with the gossipy doings of Society — who has been seen where with whom, and what the Alpha Kappa Alphas and Elks are up to. Marriages are given a great deal of space in the *News*, and from reading the *News* it is possible to believe that everyone in Harlem is sipping wine, dressing up, and stepping out. Backgammon, we learn, has taken the upper West Side by storm, just as it has the fashionable white world in Gstaad and Palm Beach. "All the 'in' singles are playing backgammon every Monday evening at Rust Brown (96th & Amsterdam)," declares the *News*.

Like *Ebony*, the *Amsterdam News* is given to heady adjectives, and to counting, pricing, and measuring costly luxuries. The Guardsmen's weekend at the Cavalier Hotel on Chesapeake Bay will be "fabulous," and guests will arrive not just on a boat but on a "72-foot ChrisCraft." Every bank teller is an "executive," and everyone is "prominent" or "famous" and "brilliant." In Betty Granger's column, "Conversation Piece," we read that at "the 50th anniversary of Martha Graham featuring Dame Margot Fonteyn and the fabulous Nureyev, your friends were right there sipping champagne, rubbing shoulders with the veddy, veddy rich. . . . Among them was the brilliant and handsome doctor Maurice V. Russell (he's PROFESSOR OF PREVENTIVE MEDICINE — Community and Social Medicine — at New York State University Medical Center) and also veddy, veddy rich who after party and reception that followed wonderful Roselyn McDonald and Dr. Lonny MacDonald (he's the famous psychoanalyst whose patients include the

top of the crop of show business and musical personalities)
and also well-known Godfrey Cambridge. . . ."

In another column, "Swinging Around Town with
Audrey Bernard," we learn that "among the beautiful
people who joined in a champagne toast . . . were Adam
Wade (host of Musical Chairs), models Evonne Swann and
Barbra Prysock, Cordell Thompson (Jet Magazine), Katy
Jones, G. Kieth Alexander (WBLS), Jean Habersham
. . ." and that Jean Habersham's morning radio talk program will be "focusing on 'our' in people." Later, "The
beautiful people gathered once again at the St. Regis penthouse at a press reception hosted by tennis ace, Arthur
Ashe, Whitman 'Grady' Mayo of Sanford and Son fame, and
officials of the Jamaican government and Reynolds Alumi-
num." "Swinging Around" also includes blind "teaser"
bits: "What prominent female banker has a foot fetish?
Think about it! What prominent young man on the West
Side's '10 Best Dressed List' is 'bout to ease down the aisle
again?"

Perhaps this land of champagne and feathers and Suzy
Knickerbocker chitchat of the "in" places where the "in"
people are going to play the new "in" games with famous
psychoanalysts and rich and handsome medical professors is
what Harlem's readers most want to hear about. Perhaps
success in America, for blacks, is what *Ebony* and the
Amsterdam News seem to think it is: money and goods and
nothing more. Perhaps, as *Ebony* and the *Amsterdam News*
seem to suggest — and as Professor Frazier insisted — under-
neath whatever black success may be can be found that deep
underlying layer of racial shame.

It would be too bad if this were always to remain true.
But, at the moment, with their emphasis on sheer acquisi-
tiveness, both these popular publications seem a long way
from encouraging, or even defining, true "class," or dignity,
or intrinsic human worth.

In the world of white journalism, meanwhile, a number of American newspapers and magazines have begun integrating news of black affairs into their pages. A number of years ago, the New York *Times* quietly started reporting black engagements and weddings in its Sunday Society sections. And even in the South, white newspapers are making a noticeable effort to report news from the black community. The Memphis *Press-Scimitar,* for example, now gives black and white social news virtually equal space. Some thoughtful blacks wonder whether the black press might follow this lead, and gradually move away from its present parochialism, and stop limiting itself exclusively to stories concerning blacks. If this were eventually to happen, then one fine morning we might wake up to a world where there was no "black press," and no "white press" — but merely an American press devoted to the daily doings of all of us.

Strivers' Row

DESPITE *Ebony*'S EMPHASIS ON MONEY AND STATUS, BLACK self-pride and dignity do exist. They can be found, furthermore, in some unusual places, such as right in the middle of Harlem in the pocket of citified self-assurance known as Strivers' Row, an area of Manhattan that most New Yorkers do not know exists, and that few have ever seen.

Strivers' Row — or, more properly, the St. Nicholas Historic District, which is also called the David King Model Houses — comprises two parallel blocks, West 138th and 139th Streets between Seventh and Eighth Avenues. It is an anomaly and a bit of an anachronism, a neighborhood within a neighborhood, a reminder of what Harlem once was and, perhaps, might have remained. Today, most New Yorkers tend to think of everything north of Ninety-Sixth Street — where the Penn Central Railroad's New Haven line emerges from its tunnel under Park Avenue into the open air — as "Harlem." This is not accurate. Strictly speaking, Harlem was the area between 130th Street and 143rd Street, and between Madison and Seventh Avenues, an area, in other words, of fifty-two square blocks. One Hundred and Forty-third Street was the northern boundary, and beyond that the neighborhood was Irish. As older black Harlemites recall, "If the Micks caught you north of a Hundred Forty-third, they beat you up." The Jews who lived on the eastern side of the border were less bellicose, but still unfriendly.

In the early days of New York, of course, Harlem was a rural area of fields and farms, where old New York white families had properties. What is now Strivers' Row once belonged to such families as the Cadwalladers, Lynches, Pinckneys, and Delanceys. As the city grew, Harlem became a kind of middle-class suburb, where real estate values were somewhat depressed since Harlem was considered a difficult place to get to. In 1891, a builder named David H. King, Jr., commissioned a number of leading New York architects — including McKim, Mead & White and its famous partner Stanford White — to design a series of elegant four-story row houses on West 138th and 139th Streets, to be called the King Model Houses. The houses had handsome entrances and facades, casement windows and balconies, balustraded roofs. Behind the houses were courtyards, gardens and fountains, connected by an interior alleyway that ran the length of both blocks. The houses were built of brick, terra-cotta and Belleville brownstone, a special stone gathered from the banks of the Passaic River north of Newark. The King Houses were to be, according to Mr. King's sales brochure, for "millionaires." At first, they were — white Christian millionaires, such as the first Randolph Hearst.

But in the late nineteenth century, as huge migrations of Russian and Polish Jews flooded into the city fleeing the pogroms of Eastern Europe, Harlem became predominantly Jewish. By 1910, an overwhelming majority of the people who lived between 110th Street and 155th Street and between the East and Hudson rivers were either foreign-born or had foreign-born parents. Russian Jews dominated the 1910 census figures. Next came the Italians, then the Irish, then the Germans, then the English, Hungarians, Czechs, and others coming from the Austro-Hungarian Empire. In addition, there were 75,000 native whites, and only 50,000 blacks.

Blacks did not arrive in New York in any large numbers until after World War I, and they followed the lead of foreign immigrants, and moved to Harlem. Most were from the South, and most were poor. As blacks moved in, the Jews moved out — north into the Bronx or, if they could afford it, to the South Shore of Long Island. They remained, however, in many cases as landlords. Landlords charged, many people still feel, exorbitant rents, and it is said that if a landlord wanted to raise his rent fivefold, he rented to a black family. For this, many blacks still hate the Jews. "I was brought up believing that all white people were Jews," one woman recalls. Not only was the landlord Jewish, but his agent who came to collect the rent was Jewish. To meet their rents, black families doubled up. Large houses and apartments were divided into tiny rooms. As many as fifty people could be found living in a two-room apartment. Building and plumbing facilities were strained. Buildings began to deteriorate. Harlem was on its way to becoming a slum.

At the same time, throughout the 1920's and early thirties, Harlem was also becoming a popular tourist spot, as well as a place New Yorkers from downtown flocked up to visit. There was "stompin'" at the old Savoy Hotel, there was the famous Cotton Club. Speakeasies abounded that offered lively black entertainment. Harlem in those days was also, ironically enough, a place where discrimination against blacks was rampant. Blumstein's store was the only store where blacks could shop. If a black wanted to go to the Apollo Theatre, he had to sit in the balcony, in "nigger heaven," and Harlem's Victoria Theatre didn't admit blacks at all. Childs Restaurant in Harlem, rather than serve blacks, closed its doors. Frank's Restaurant, once a fine eating place on 125th Street, did not welcome blacks and if a black insisted on going in, he was seated in the back of the room. When black Catholics tried to enroll their children in Harlem parochial schools, they were refused. Even the great Universal and Apostolic Church, it seemed, did not want Negroes. Harlem's public schools became the dumping ground for the misfits, the incorrigibles, the hard-to-educate — both black and white. Only a teacher who could not get work anywhere else in the city would accept a job in Harlem. Police officers were punished for misconduct or incompetence by being assigned a Harlem beat. Black-owned nightclubs, set up to entertain a white trade, would not admit blacks. To get into the Cotton Club, a black had to be known, and eventually the Cotton Club abandoned Harlem and moved downtown. The Jews and other white immigrants in Harlem had had the advantage of the settlement houses, designed to speed their Americanization. There were no such facilities to ease the Negroes' transition to city life.

In the early 1920's, one by one, the King Model Houses began to be sold to blacks who were, for the most part, professional people and therefore relatively affluent — doctors, lawyers, and educators. And the new black residents of these houses decided, at the outset, that their two streets would not be sucked into the burgeoning slum beyond. The trees were tended, the hedges clipped, the stone vases and window boxes were kept filled with flowering plants. Entrance railings and balustrades were painted, brass doorknobs and knockers were polished. Gardens and courtyards were maintained. Each neighbor tried so hard to compete with the others for the best-clipped shrubbery, the best-polished brasswork, the best-washed steps, and the prettiest garden that the two parallel blocks were humorously given the name "Strivers' Row."

"It could have been done in other parts of Harlem, too,"

says one long-time resident of the Row. "There used to be many lovely old streets up here. Even when a house is broken up into tiny apartments, the facade and the appearance of the neighborhood can be kept up. It doesn't take that much money or that much time just to give doorways and window frames a regular coat of paint. Garbage doesn't have to be thrown in the streets or down airshafts. It's people who don't care who create slums, and then the slums create more people who don't care. It becomes a vicious circle. Attractive surroundings help make attractive people."

Of course, what was intended as a shining example to other blacks of what could be done to create a pleasant neighborhood very quickly had the opposite effect. The more attractive and manicured Strivers' Row became, the more it found itself the object of mockery, jealousy, and bitter hostility among the other blacks of Harlem. A black playwright named Abram Hill, who died in 1939, and who wrote a play about the Row, used to recall how he had to pass through the neighborhood on his way to school and developed, with no real knowledge of the people who lived there, a terrible resentment of these blacks who clearly lived better than he — just from passing the grilled entrances and looking up at the carefully curtained windows of the Row. Meanwhile, as though afflicted with a kind of mass paranoia, the rest of Harlem all around the Row disintegrated into a horror of filth and poverty. "It's as though the rest of Harlem wanted to *force* us into becoming a ghetto," says one Row resident. "They developed this blind hatred of us as society snobs. We weren't snobs. We just wanted to live in a nice neighborhood. There was no way to reach those people, but we resisted them. We've held on." In resisting, Strivers' Row became more insular, withdrawn into itself, more inbred, proud, and prejudiced against ghetto blacks.

When the first black families began moving to the Row, there was the usual flurry of panic selling, and three- and four-story town houses could be picked up for bargain prices. James W. Banks, who is president of the 138th Street Block Association and an associate administrator of the Board of Elections — his father was one of New York's first black dentists — has lived on the Row for nearly all of his fifty-four years and recalls, "We were the sixth black family to move in. My father bought our twelve-room house for nine thousand dollars." Today, Row houses sell in the $50,000 range, compared with town houses of similar size and construction at more fashionable East Side Manhattan addresses which go for $100,000 and up. Another early Row resident was Dr. Louis T. Wright, the first black doctor at Harlem Hospital and later its Chief of Surgery, whose family lived on the Row for thirty-two years. Then there was Dr. Charles H. Roberts, another early New York black dentist, and Vertner W. Tandy, the first black architect to be licensed in New York State, and Lt. Samuel J. Battle, Manhattan's first black police lieutenant. Gerri Major, the former society editor of *Ebony,* grew up on the Row in the 1930's and remembers that "the social life was gay and wonderful, with luncheons, bridge parties, and formal, white-tie dances. Everyone seemed to have everything — cars, boats, summer homes. You have to remember the times. The 'Black Movement' as such didn't exist."

The oldest resident of Strivers' Row is probably eighty-six-year-old Mrs. Robert Braddicks, the widow of a banker and real estate broker, who has lived in the same fourteen-room house on West 138th Street for fifty-three years. Mrs. Braddicks insists that she has no intention of ever leaving the street. "Where would I go?" she asks. "I haven't lived in an apartment house for over fifty years, and I'm not about to start now. No, I don't feel as though I live in a ghetto. I live in my *home.*" Mrs. Braddicks, who also maintains a summer and weekend home in New Jersey, has become a symbol of the enclave's stability.

At one point, Strivers' Row was a popular address for successful show business personalities, and Fletcher Henderson, W. C. Handy, Stepin Fetchit, Eubie Blake, Noble Sissle, Flannery Miller, and Sidney Bechet all had homes on the Row at one time or another. More recently, Strivers' Row has become popular with young executives, businessmen, and professional people who work in Harlem, such as Jean Wade, the advertising director of the *Amsterdam News,* Walter Legall, who is an officer with a computer firm, and educator Charles L. Sanders. Booker T. Washington III, an architect, has become a Row resident, as has New York Supreme Court Justice Oliver Sutton. Today, there is a long waiting list for houses on the Row.

If anything, Strivers' Row today is more attractive and house-proud than ever. In 1967, New York's Landmark Preservation Commission declared the Strivers' Row houses a landmark, meaning that no exterior changes can be made to any of the houses without the permission of the commission. This distinction has added to Row residents' feelings of security and self-satisfaction. Still, Strivers' Row remains a tiny island of comfort and affluence in the middle of a seething sea of desperation, danger, and urban indifference. Step around the corner, and you are in Harlem's lowest depths. In this situation, the Row has become a prime target for Harlem's criminal element. Mrs. Braddicks's house has been burglarized twice. Still, with the help of two powerful neighborhood associations, Row residents have been able to secure extra police protection for their little Andorra (it hasn't hurt to have judges and retired police officers living on the Row). Elaborate burglar alarm systems have been installed, along with powerful lights to illuminate the once-shadowy backyards at night. And a group of Row residents, consisting mostly of retirees, has been organized as a volunteer watch force "to keep an eye on things." Thus Strivers' Row hangs on. "This has been a nice place to live for over fifty years," says one resident. "It's going to remain that way for another fifty."

Strivers' Row, then, has been more than a social whirl of elegant black-tie dinners, ladies' bridge parties, and balls. It has been the American Dream formed into a kind of reality to the families who live there. It was proof that the Dream, which had always been the property of white people, could be achieved by blacks as well, if they seized it — and held on. It was proof of the theories that W. E. B. DuBois advanced, that a "talented tenth" of the black population, by committing themselves to America and American ways and rejecting the "Back-to Africa" ideas of men like Marcus Garvey, would rise, like cream, to the top. "We were brought up to believe that one could make it if one was determined enough," one Row resident says. "We had our own world here." In this world, the Row turned its back on the nightmare of the rest of Harlem. It didn't matter that murder, prostitution, and drug-dealing were going on within shouting distance of Strivers' Row. All this was placed out of sight and out of mind.

Strivers' Row's two block associations have rigid rules which are rigidly enforced: no trash or litter thrown in streets; keep hedges uniformly clipped; keep brasswork polished; no children playing in the streets; no peddlers or solicitors admitted through front entrances; all pickups and deliveries to be made through back entrances, courts, and alleyways; beautify gardens and window boxes; replace dead or ailing trees, and so on. In its pride, Strivers' Row has become extraordinarily exclusive. In a survey conducted by the Landmarks Preservation Commission, it was noted that forty-one percent of the people living on Strivers' Row socialize only with their immediate neighbors on the Row. A mere twelve percent venture outside the area for any social activity. Nearly half do not socialize at all.

Recently there have been a few voices raised along the

Row that have questioned the Row's encapsulated, ostrich-like existence, and that have suggested that Strivers' Row is painfully out of touch with the reality of modern times. Instead of an island, Strivers' Row might step out of its cocoon and become a responsible, involved leader of the total Harlem community. One such man is James Banks, Jr., who has tried to move the little community outward into the affairs, and terrible problems, of the much larger one. But so far he is in the minority. Others, happy as they are, see Strivers' Row as a symbol of what black people *could* have done with Harlem if they had cared enough, been bright enough, worked hard enough. Why didn't blacks do it in other neighborhoods? "Shiftless. Lazy," sniffs one Row woman. "They're no good, those people. No good at all." She turns immediately to the special amenities and luxuries that Strivers' Row provides. "Do you know that ours is the only neighborhood in *all of Manhattan* where you don't have to put your garbage out in the street in cans for collection?" she asks. "It's picked up, as it should be, from back alleys, the way it's done in Beverly Hills."

Another Row resident, a young doctor named Raymond Ransom, says that he likes living on the Row and considers it an excellent place to raise his children. But he is also concerned about the "other" Harlem. "It's a little ludicrous," he says, "to spend so much time and energy on the beautification of two blocks, and to turn the corners of Seventh and Eighth Avenues to be visually assaulted by some of the worst conditions in urban living, and not to have even a nodding acquaintance with any of those people, or any idea of what it is they're thinking about, or what they want or need."

But, for the most part, the older residents of Strivers' Row do not even go so far as to say they see no hope for the "other" Harlem. To them, it might as well not exist.

⌒⌒ 16 ⌒⌒

... And Other Good Addresses

STRIVERS' ROW USED TO TAKE PRIDE IN THE FACT THAT THE two-block area was treated with "respect" by the rest of Harlem. Occasionally, a Harlemite might take a visiting friend from out of town for a stroll along the Row — to show it off, and to demonstrate that Harlem was not *all* a ghetto. But, for the most part, pedestrian traffic was low — much lower than in the rest of Harlem — and was limited to the comings and goings of the residents themselves, and their friends and to patients visiting the various doctors' and dentists' offices along the Row. Vehicular traffic was also light, which contributed to the quiet, parklike, turn-of-the-century atmosphere of the place. There was even a proposal to ban vehicular traffic from the two streets — residents with automobiles could always enter their houses and garages through the alleyways — but this plan was vetoed by the city on the grounds that the two streets provided necessary emergency access to nearby hospitals.

By the mid-1970's, however, there were some disturbing signs of change. At night, the little streets were increasingly being used as dragstrips, as owners of "hot" cars raced down Strivers' Row testing the power of their engines, their brakes screeching at the corners. Despite the addition of high-intensity streetlamps along the streets themselves and in the alleyways, incidences of mugging, burglary, and other crimes have increased alarmingly. The many doctors in the area are a particularly prime target for burglars, since they are assumed to keep large amounts of cash in their offices and also, rightly or wrongly, are supposed to keep stores of amphetemines and narcotics in their refrigerators. Knocking on wood, Dr. George D. Cannon — of an old-line New York family, who owns a town house on West 139th Street and keeps his offices on the two lower floors of the house — says that he is the only physician in the neighborhood who has not been burglarized at least once. To maintain the security of his office, Dr. Cannon employs a full-time guard for six dollars an hour who does nothing but sit in his waiting room. Dr. Cannon also carries a loaded pistol in his hip pocket.

The Landmarks Preservation Commission, meanwhile, can do nothing to control the use to which the interiors of Strivers' Row houses are put, and, by the early 1970's, some forty-one percent of the buildings on the Row, though privately owned, had become rooming houses. Strivers' Row people who take in roomers tend to make genteel excuses for doing so. The older people, whose children have grown, married, and moved away, say they take in roomers for security, for companionship, to ward off loneliness. Others claim that a fifteen-room Manhattan town house is just "too much house" for one family. Few will admit that, as taxes and the cost of New York living have gone up, coupled with the effects of an economic recession, taking in roomers has become, for many, an important source of added income. Owners of rooming houses insist that Strivers' Row roomers are meticulously screened, must be people with legitimate occupations, with clean habits and of high moral character. Residents proudly point back to the year 1925, when they succeeded in having closed a 100-gallon still that was operating in the basement of 235 West 139th Street, and when, a year earlier, a building around the corner on Seventh Avenue was padlocked because it had been leased to a bootlegger. Still, the block associations have recently had to add another rule to their little list: "Roomers in houses should not be permitted to lean out of windows or to dress without pulling down shades." Rooms to Let signs placed in windows must be of a uniform size and lettering. But as more and more of these signs appear in Strivers' Row windows, more and more of the older residents like Dr. Cannon have begun to feel that preserving Strivers' Row may be a losing battle.

Though Strivers' Row is still considered "the best two blocks in Harlem," there are other choice addresses, constituting small pockets of black wealth and prestige, in northern Manhattan. For years, fashionable blacks have also favored the area nicknamed "Sugar Hill," which is more properly known as Harlem Heights, an amorphous neighborhood between Edgecombe and St. Nicholas Avenues and West 143rd and 155th streets. There were the Dunbar Apartments, for example, at Seventh Avenue and 150th Street. Originally built as cooperative apartments for middle-income families, the Dunbar quickly became a stronghold of the emerging black bourgeoisie. W. E. B. DuBois and Walter White, among others, lived in the Dunbar for a while, and the buildings, which had large interior gardens, were exceptionally staffed and protected. A drawback of the Dunbar was that the apartments, though many of them had fine views of the city from the bluffs, had rather small rooms and were walk-ups. An even more prestigious Sugar Hill address was 409 Edgecombe Avenue, a tall elevator building, which, from the 1930's on, was something of a Harlem showcase in that it boasted not only an elegantly canopied entrance but also a full-time uniformed doorman. Bus tours of Manhattan used to point out 409 Edgecombe, where a number of black entertainers and athletes — including several New York Giants players — made their homes. It was said that if a black person got into a taxi in Manhattan, all he had to say was, "Take me to Four-Oh-Nine"; the driver would know he meant 409 Edgecombe. To live there was a symbol that a black had "arrived" in New York. W. E. B. DuBois also lived for a while at 409, as did Thurgood Marshall, Roy Wilkins, and W. H. Braithwaite.

There are newer semiluxury apartment houses in other parts of Harlem that have tended to replace 409 Edgecombe in terms of desirability and fashionability. There are the Esplanade Gardens, between 137th and 138th Street on Seventh Avenue. There is also the Lenox Terrace, on 135th Street just west of Fifth Avenue, where Manhattan Borough President Percy Sutton lives, and the Riverton, at 2235 Fifth Avenue. Other well-to-do black families have moved into large apartments in fine old buildings on upper Fifth Avenue, north of Ninety-sixth Street, which have become peacefully integrated. Dr. Cannon, for example, lives at 1200 Fifth Avenue, at 101st Street, with a view of Central Park. His was the first black family in the building. Now there are two others.

New York, unlike Washington and other cities of the South, does not have a pronounced black Old Guard. Like most white New Yorkers, most black New Yorkers were born elsewhere, and many migrated to Harlem from Southern cities. But New York's leading black families would include the Austins (Augustin A. Austin, a real estate man, was called the richest black man in New York). Today, that distinction probably belongs to Mr. J. Bruce Llewellyn, who operates a chain of supermarkets called Fedco Foods Corporation, which is ranked as the fourth largest black-owned business in America (behind Motown and Chicago's two Johnsons). Mr. Llewellyn is president of a New York organization called One Hundred Black Men, Inc., which was formed to impress the white business community with the vitality of black enterprise in the city. Membership in One Hundred Black Men is limited to the city's top black businessmen, including John Procope, publisher of the *Amsterdam News,* Earl Graves, publisher of *Black Enterprise,* F. W. Eversley, Jr., a leading building contractor, and Eugene H. Webb, a real estate broker.

One of the crusades of One Hundred Black Men is to try to refute the claim, which is often made, that black people, when they become successful, "do not take care of their own kind." They point to such philanthropists as the late Dr. Arthur C. Logan, who was extremely community-minded. (The old Knickerbocker Hospital in Harlem has been renamed the Arthur C. Logan Memorial Hospital.) Members of New York's Bishop family have also been generous, along with the Bradfords, Billupses, Sanderses, Riverses, Wrights, and Weavers — all prestigious New York names. The late Dr. Godfrey Nurse was a noted philanthropist who gave $100,000 to Columbia University; Dr. Lloyd Freeman was a benefactor of both Columbia and Fisk Universities, and Dr. C. B. Powell, emeritus publisher of the *Amsterdam News,* contributes heavily to the Y.M.C.A. and the N.A.A.C.P. New York's black leaders also point out that less well-to-do blacks contribute to philanthropy as well, albeit indirectly, when they pay dues to unions, which, in turn, give from their treasuries. Business leaders stress that blacks have always been generous to their churches, and that the thousands of black churches in the United States could not exist, and provide the services they do, without black philanthropy. In Harlem, the richest church is probably Abyssinian Baptist on West 138th Street, a block from Strivers' Row. "Abyssinian thinks of itself as very fancy," says one woman, "simply because it's got air conditioning." The elite black church, however, is St. Philip's Episcopal, on West 134th Street.

A great deal of black philanthropy is carried on by organizations. The black Elks in New York, for example, give $15,000 a year to charity and support between forty and fifty scholarship students annually at Eastern colleges. The Masons contribute $25,000 a year to black causes, and the two leading women's organizations, the Links and the Girl Friends, have each given $100,000 to both the N.A.A.C.P. and the National Urban League.

In New York, blacks have prospered in supermarkets, publishing, insurance brokerage, and real estate, but they have not, for some reason, been particularly successful in banking. There are six black-owned banks in Chicago, two in Washington, but only one in New York City, the Freedom National Bank in Harlem, which was incorporated as recently as 1964. Harlem's black elite, furthermore — though a number are stockholders — won't bank at the Freedom Bank. It is considered "the poor man's bank." In 1928, an experimental bank was opened in Harlem which was the brainchild of John D. Rockefeller, Jr. It was Mr. Rockefeller's philanthropic notion that a bank should be established which would provide banking services for the black community, which, at the time, could not get loans at white banks. The bank was also designed to provide banking training to young blacks, and to strengthen New York's banking ties with black-owned banks in the South. It was called the Dunbar Bank — like Washington's Dunbar High School, after the black poet Paul Laurence Dunbar — and it failed after barely five years.

One reason for the bank's failure was the Great Depression that hit the American economy within a year after its founding — but that was only a contributing cause. The real reason for the Dunbar Bank's failure was that it got no support from the black community of Harlem. Partly, this was because Harlem was suspicious of Mr. Rockefeller's motives; it was assumed that here, again, was a case of a rich white man trying to exploit poorer blacks in order to get richer. Mr. Rockefeller might claim to have high-minded aims, but this was doubted. Also, of the bank's nine employees, three were white — the three at the top: the president, the vice president, and the cashier, which again created an impression of white exploitation. Mr. Rockefeller also employed a black man at the Dunbar Bank named Roscoe Conklin Bruce. Mr. Bruce was supposed to "keep a finger on the pulse of Harlem"; he was distrusted by Harlem.

Other things were wrong with the bank. It was probably placed in the wrong location, in the "snob area" hard by the Dunbar Apartments, at 148th Street and Eighth Avenue. Had it been placed on Harlem's main artery, 125th Street, where most of Harlem shopped and did business, and where the new Freedom Bank is located, it might have done better. But, as it was, it drew its employees from the neighborhood and the "Dunbar Apartments crowd." And, as Mr. Guichard Parris, an early employee of the bank, recalls, "People here didn't like the idea of going to a party and running into the teller they just made a deposit with the day before. People don't want their business to be told to other people. When it comes to banking, Negroes want secrecy. They don't want the rest of Harlem to know what they're doing, what money they're making, how big their deposits are. You have to remember, too, that this was during Prohibition, and a lot of Harlem money was being made illegally. At a white bank like the Chemical, you could at least be sure of privacy and anonymity." Rockefeller, after four unsuccessful years, tried to reorganize the bank. Augustin A. Austin, Harlem's richest man, was persuaded to place his funds in the Dunbar Bank, and was advertised as the bank's largest single depositor. Nothing worked. The bank folded and, ever since, the Rockefellers and their various foundations and philanthropies have been noticeably wary about going into anything in the areas of housing or banking.

Much of black fund-raising and philanthropy in New York is in the hands of several capable women. There is Mrs. Louise K. Morris, for instance, who works furiously for a variety of black causes and heads the Utility Club, Inc., which raises and disperses between $15,000 and $20,000 a year for charity. But probably the leading black society woman in New York — though some criticize her for her love of publicity and her fondness for hobnobbing with white society folk — is Mrs. Henry Lee Moon. Plump, fair-skinned, animated, with a flair for startling and exotic clothes and jewelry, Mollie Moon is certainly one of New York's more colorful ladies. In her pretty apartment in Queens — the Moons moved out of Sugar Hill several years ago in quest of more space and cleaner air — Mollie Moon arranges herself against a large bouquet of gladioli and sips champagne. A program from the Bolshoi Ballet sits on her coffee table, and it is not one of the free handout variety but the kind you pay for. It is clear that Mollie Moon is a woman of taste and consequence, and that her status symbols are the same as any white woman's in her station.

Mollie Moon has been much photographed by the press, and has a huge stack of eight-by-ten glossy prints to prove it. She has been photographed being bussed by former Mayor John V. Lindsay, chatting with the late Mrs. Robert Wagner, with Marietta Tree, Marian Anderson, Ralph Bunche, Lena Horne, Sammy Davis, Jr., Jeanne Murray Vanderbilt, the late Winthrop Rockefeller, Robert David Lion Gardiner (sixteenth Lord of the Manor of Gardiner's Island), and Pope Pius XII (with whom Mollie Moon, a Catholic, had a private audience — all of whom she counts among her many friends. Mollie Moon adores champagne, and it matches her effervescent personality. She never used to drink wine and once, on an ocean voyage to Europe, she said to a steward in the dining room, "No wine for me, thank you." A friend turned to her in amazement, and said, "Mollie, are you turning down champagne?" She cried, "Was that *champagne?*" She tried some, liked it, and has been sipping it ever since from a stylish tulip glass.

Mollie Moon was born in Hattiesburg, Mississippi, but "escaped at the age of nine months — obviously not under my own steam." The person who engineered her escape was her mother, an energetic lady who brought her to Cleveland and who for years was active in Republican politics there — remaining a Republican long after most blacks transferred their allegiance to the Democrats under Roosevelt. Mollie Moon was educated at Rusk University and at McHarry Medical School, where she earned a degree as a registered pharmacist, a profession she has never practiced. She also studied at Columbia, and took courses in German and biology at the University of Berlin. Mollie Moon, clearly a woman of the world, says, "If you ask me, the main difference between upper-class Negroes and upper-class whites is that the Negroes are better educated." On travels that took her into the segregated South, she was undaunted by discriminatory regulations. "I just put on a sari, painted a red dot on my forehead, and said I was an Indian."

Back in Cleveland, she met her husband, an erudite man who is a graduate of Ohio State School of Journalism and who wrote, briefly, for the New York *Times* — where old Mr. Sulzberger refused to give him a press card, saying that the *Times* was "not ready for that" — and later for the *Amsterdam News*. Henry Moon is now retired and is now known, according to his wife, as "the best martini-maker on the East Coast." In New York, where the Moons have lived for the last thirty-five years, Mollie Moon threw herself into good works, and her name has decorated any number of boards and committees. At the moment, she is on the board of the Advisory Drug Committee, which reports to the Commissioner of Food and Drugs in Washington. But her main philanthropic endeavor has been in behalf of the National Urban League, and for a number of years she has been chairman of the Urban League Guild.

In New York, though she is unaware that she has a rival in Washington with the same title, Mollie Moon is known as "the black Perle Mesta." She is also known as the "Queen of the Cocktails-five-to-nine Set." She loves parties, and there has been quite literally no one of importance in New York in the last three and a half decades who has not been to one of her entertainments. In her apartment, the telephone never stops ringing with party invitations. Her favorite party guest was Dr. Bunche, who also loved parties. "Oh, how that man loved parties!" she says. "Even when he was old and ill and losing his eyesight, he'd drop everything to go to a party. He'd come to my house for cocktails at five and stay until two in the morning."

Mollie Moon's most celebrated party is New York's annual Beaux Arts Ball, which she inaugurated in 1942 in behalf of the Urban League and which has been a New York society feature ever since. Mollie Moon is considered a genius at getting leading white socialites to dress up and sit down at dinner with celebrities from the black world of society, sports, and entertainment. One might not think that Josephine Baker and Marian Anderson would both turn up as honored guests at the same party, but Mollie Moon did it. And when Josephine Baker met Marian Anderson, Mme. Baker performed a deep curtsy. The Beaux Arts Ball used to be held in the old Savoy Hotel in Harlem — "in the days when Harlem was safe, and gay, and fun to go to" — but in recent years it has been held in the Waldorf-Astoria, always in February "to relieve the midwinter doldrums." Though 1975, because of the recession, was not a banner year for the Beaux Arts Ball, its profits usually yield the Urban League about $20,000 annually and, over the years, has netted the League over half a million dollars.

The Beaux Arts Ball is famous for the dazzling spectacle of the costumes people turn up in and, at every ball, the most spectacularly dressed person of all is its chairman. She appears in glittering headpieces of towering tinsel, fur, feathers, jewels, and gowns bedizened with sequins and gold paillettes. At a recent ball, the glamorous chairman was presented to the audience stepping out of a huge mock-up of a champagne bottle, wearing a gown of silver lamé with a jeweled breastplate and a crown of white ostrich plumes.

Some black New Yorkers criticize Mollie Moon and call her a social butterfly. But she has her serious side. Not long ago, for example, she attended an Urban League conference in Atlanta, and a diversion offered to the conferees was a tour of the homes of the many wealthy blacks in the city. Mollie Moon demurred. "Why should I be interested in going to see the homes of wealthy blacks?" she says. "I said no. I told them I'd rather go to the museums, or visit some of the local historical sights." She is aware that she has critics, but pays them little heed. Poring through her huge collection of glossy photographs of herself and her famous friends, of her many public appearances in her extraordinary costumes over the years, she says, "My only regret is that I'm not a size twelve anymore."

Taste

WHITE VISITORS TO HOMES OF AFFLUENT BLACKS ARE OFTEN struck by a puzzling, and yet pervasive, "difference" in the appearance of things. Louis Auchincloss, the novelist and Manhattan Brahmin, whose favorite philanthropy is the Museum of the City of New York, has been called on to visit the homes of wealthy blacks in Harlem in the course of fund-raising, and says, "It's very hard to describe. These were gracious, cultivated people, but there were things in their houses and apartments that — while obviously expensive — I just wouldn't want in mine." Another New York white, a woman, says, "I noticed little things, small details, that just struck me as somehow — well, not wrong, but still not quite right. I remember, for example, noticing a huge Steuben glass bowl in the center of a coffee table. I know the cost of Steuben, and I'm sure that bowl must have cost at least twelve hundred dollars. It was filled with gold-painted walnuts." Others have noticed other subtle differences, which raise bemused questions among white people. Why, for example, should Bennetta Bullock Washington, the wife of Washington's mayor and a woman of aristocratic background, satisfy herself with plastic plants in her house and settle for brightly colored glass ceiling fixtures that would strike some as garish? And why, though she is a woman with a Ph.D. degree, does she live in a house that seems to contain not a single book? Why (as *Ebony*'s success stories never fail to note) has the ownership of a Cadillac automobile become the ultimate black success symbol — to the point where less rich blacks often go heavily into debt simply in order to drive a Cadillac? The Cadillac has become such an important ornament to black life that blacks themselves make jokes about it. There is the story of the black man who bought a new Cadillac but was careful always to park it across the street — so his house wouldn't topple over on it. Then there is the tale of the wealthy black who directed in his will that he be buried in his Cadillac. As the great car and its departed passenger were being lowered into the grave, a spectator at the funeral murmured, "What a way to go!" Wealthy whites tend not to favor Cadillacs and, instead, would tend to buy an equally expensive, but smaller and less ostentatious, Mercedes. At issue here is the complicated question of black *taste* or, perhaps, lack of it. Or the subtle difference between using wealth and simply spending money.

Should, for instance, a white visitor to the home of a well-to-do black be surprised — or slightly put off — when his hostess asks him politely, "Will you have apple juice, milk, or ginger ale?" At least one New York man found this selection of drinks a trifle odd. Why do so many black cooks add two cups of sugar to the cake recipe when one would do? Do blacks really "like different foods," and is that why many Southerners still insist that "blacks smell different"? (The theory of black body odor is as difficult to assess as the theory that black males have larger sexual organs than do whites. Body odor is a black obsession, as attested to by the number of deodorant ads carried in *Ebony,* but the answer is probably that some black people have an unpleasant body odor at some times, just as some white people do.) Why is Kool-

Aid such a popular drink among blacks? And, for that matter, why do so many black people smoke Kool cigarettes? At least one psychologist, Dr. Edward Lahniers of the University of Cincinnati, feels that the associations of the words *Kool* and *cool,* as in "keeping one's cool" and "playing it cool," have much to do with this. As for alcoholic beverages, the more expensive brands of Scotches, such as Chivas Regal, are often served in the households of well-to-do blacks. At the same time, liquor distributors have long been aware that whiskies with the word "white" in their brand names are extremely popular in black bars — White Horse Scotch, and Dewar's White Label, for example. A Scotch with an integrationist label — Black & White — is not a popular drink with blacks, nor is expensive Johnnie Walker Black Label. That, of course, is one kind of taste. It has nothing to do with why the Harry Belafontes, in their large New York apartment on West End Avenue, have a living room dominated by a huge, curving, mirrored bar (whereas, in a white home, one would tend to find a small rolling table for drinks), or why Berry Gordy, Jr., the mogul of Motown Records, has — or had an interior decorator who let him have — a California house draped with gold lamé curtains, or why Mrs. Martin Luther King, Jr., who is certainly a woman of a high degree of sophistication, contributed exactly one dollar to a recent Cancer Crusade in Atlanta, and then demanded to know how much other people were giving. Each to his taste, of course. But the divergence between black tastes and white has certainly been a factor that has contributed to the apartness of the races, and that has made the white, when encountering the black in his home or his world, feel that he is entering alien, puzzling, and not particularly compatible territory.

Many whites feel, along with Professor Frazier, the black sociologist, that blacks, when they become successful, immediately want to flaunt their success — not merely to whites, but also to less fortunate blacks. One white New York woman, who has been involved with various committees involving the black community, made this observation: "The first time I was invited to dinner in a black home, I was a little bit overwhelmed. I knew the family had money, but I was completely unprepared for what I found at the dinner table. The food was delicious, but there was so much of it! Course after course after course. I got the definite feeling that this wasn't the way they usually ate, but was a spread that was put on just for me, because I was white. And the table setting. I've never seen so much silver and china in use at one dinner table. Even though there were all those courses, there was more silver laid out beside my plate than I could possibly use. I had the feeling she was using every piece of silver and every piece of china she owned. A few weeks later, I had this same woman to my house for dinner. I had what I thought was a nice menu, but I could tell that she was somewhat surprised that I wasn't serving as much food as she had. After all, she had served a turkey, a ham, *and* a roast of beef, and all I was offering her was a roast. At one point, she pointed to some dishes that I keep displayed in a dining room china cabinet, and said. 'That's lovely china. Why don't you use that?' She seemed actually a bit put out that I wasn't using *all* my best things. Oh, and another thing I remember about the dinner at her house. The dining room was quite attractively furnished, but there was a television set in the room. At seven o'clock, even though we were eating dinner, she turned on the news."

Partly, the difference in taste that white people find odd and foreign may stem, as Professor Frazier suggested, from the fact that middle-class blacks try desperately hard to "do things" the way white people do, and to conform with what they see as white upper-crust standards (including, perhaps unconsciously, drawing an association with whites from such products as White Horse and White Label whisky) . At the same time, even the wealthiest blacks have had only a limited opportunity to observe, at first hand, white upper-class life on a daily basis, and to absorb the small nuances of white social behavior that whites take for granted and therefore practice with ease.

For their ideas of what upper-class white tastes and manners are like, most blacks have had either to rely, as house servants, on occasional backstairs, behind-the-scenes glimpses, or on the heightened version of white life that is presented in films or on television. Understandably, with Hollywood as a model, the black imitation of white high life often seems — to white eyes — garish or even grotesque. A curious loss of communication between blacks and whites is the result. In Cincinnati, for example, a white hostess telephoned a prominent black couple and invited them to her house for cocktails, and was disappointed when the couple did not appear. Later, she learned the reason: the black couple had been offended because the hostess had not mailed out a printed invitation. In the eyes of the black couple, the white hostess had been guilty of a social *gaffe*. The proper black hostess — as the white hostess would have known had she read Charlotte Hawkins Brown's little etiquette book — mails out her invitations. In her section on "Invitations," Dr. Brown wrote: "A formal invitation is printed or engraved to be elegant, while an informal invitation may be given on the telephone. The receiver of such an invitation is sometimes at a disadvantage because he is not given time to consult his or her calendar. . . . The telephone is a most convenient substitute for informal invitations [but is] recommended for school boy and girl affairs."

With the wide gap that exists between black and white society, certain details of behavior, certain "social graces," that come naturally to upper-class whites either elude the blacks or, when they try to employ them, seem stilted, forced, and — to a white's way of thinking at least — in poor taste. In very much the same manner, Old Guard Christian families regard the habits — in terms of dress, home decorating, and speech — of newly rich Jews as gauche and tasteless. Similarly, old-line German and Sephardic Jewish families who have learned to dress conservatively and live quietly look askance at their newly rich coreligionists from Eastern Europe who wear clear plastic sling-back shoes, mink stoles, and diamonds on the beach at Miami. As one German Jewish woman put it, "I have diamonds, too, but I've never taken them out of the bank." Of course Charlotte Hawkins Brown had a word on this too: "Don't make the mistake of trying to be too elegant. It is exceedingly bad taste to overdo at any time. Neatness and simplicity are often preferred to showy elegance."

But, even more important, black taste may be related to the rather special way blacks regard and interpret social "class." In a series of interviews with successful black businessmen, each was asked the question, "How do you define class and what, to you, constitutes class?" An overwhelming majority immediately answered that class was a matter of clothes, and how a man dressed. Clothes, the feeling was, definitely made the man. One young man, the first black to be made an executive with a leading white accounting firm in Chicago, went on at length as to how important his clothes were to him. He not only bought his suits at the finest stores — Brooks Brothers, Saks Fifth Avenue, and Marshall Field — and his shoes at Bally and Gucci, but he was also deeply concerned with the care of his clothes. "Dry cleaning ruins a good suit," he said earnestly, "and so does repeated pressing. I try to take care of my suits in such a way that they never need to be dry cleaned more than once every six months. As for pressing, if a man hangs up his clothes properly every night when he takes them off, making sure that the trousers hang straight from the cuffs in a clamp-type hanger, with the seams matched, and his jacket on a padded hanger, a suit will stay in press. If I have a spot on a necktie, I never have it cleaned. I simply throw it out. The same thing with socks. I've never worn darned socks. When I have a hole in a sock, I throw out the pair. Underwear too, and shirts, and shoes. I spend a dollar a day on shoeshines."

Blacks have always been extremely fashion-conscious. In fact, blacks have become genuine fashion leaders and any number of styles, later adopted by white people, were first popularized and worn by black men and women, including men's flared trousers and wide-lapeled suits, body shirts, sandwich-soled shoes, women's high boots, mini skirts, dyed furs and pants suits. Both Paris and Seventh Avenue are well aware of blacks' trend-setting role. In terms of decorating and home furnishings, however, they have been much less influential. Perhaps this is because blacks have had less opportunity to display their homes to white people. A mirrored ceiling or a huge lamp with a pink-ruffled shade would impress another black, but it would not be admired by a white person with "good taste" — nor would it have much chance to. Clothes are another matter. A well turned-out black man or woman on the street is noticed by everyone, and some status, after all, is determined by how others regard you, which may be related to how you regard yourself — and how well you can keep up your front. How you protect yourself, in any case, will determine how others will regard you and, to a black, fine, stylish clothes are the easiest, most obvious form of protection.

On the white side of the racial divide, there is a tendency to think of "middle-class blacks" as middle-class people with dark skins. This is far from the fact, and class in the black world is determined by other, somewhat different, distinctions. To a white of the middle or upper class, his class is determined by his occupation, income, the quality of his residence, his prestige, life-style, and personal identity. In addition to the way he dresses and the way he presents himself — including the important matter of the way he speaks — black status is conveyed by home ownership and education. Blacks tend to attribute far greater importance to education as a means of maintaining and keeping status than white people do. Most educated whites tend to assume that their friends on their own social level were similarly educated, and give no more thought to it. "Oh, did you go to Yale? So did I" is the common white reaction whenever the subject comes up, which is seldom. Educated blacks, on the other hand, discuss and compare their educations — and their parents' educations, and their children's educations — endlessly. To have a son or daughter who is a college dropout is a sorry disgrace to a black family, while a white family shrugs it off as no more than a minor mishap. A college degree is the goal of every black achiever, and to have a graduate degree beyond that is regarded as a passport to the loftiest social strata in the black community. Black doctors, dentists, lawyers, druggists, teachers, ministers, psychologists, nurses, social workers, and even undertakers stand at the pinnacle of black society because they are, by virtue of their professions, recipients of higher education and special training. These professionals are much more highly regarded in the black community than mere money-makers. A black college professor earning $12,000 a year would be held in higher esteem by other blacks than the unschooled merchant earning $100,000 a year. A woman such as Mrs. Mary Gibson Hundley of Washington, a retired high school teacher who looks forward to her monthly Social Security check, considers herself of a much more refined cut of cloth than Chicago's John H. Johnson with his $40,000,000-a-year publishing business — partly because she graduated from Radcliffe and Johnson never got to college. Berry Gordy, Jr., might head a record company with $50,000,000 in annual sales, but he, again, never went to college and is an ex-prizefighter to boot. It is doubtful that Mrs. Hundley or others in her class would even care to meet him.

Education, of course — with its Latin derivation meaning "a leading out" — has been the traditional avenue out of the ghetto for all minority groups. And it is certainly true that, when little-educated blacks have been able to educate their children, the children have usually done better, financially, than their parents. But some critics have felt that blacks have stressed education, culture, and intellectual refinement too much and that education snobbery, in a capitalist society, helps account for the fact that there are so few successful black business enterprises, and even fewer people who could be called black capitalists. There is a limit, after all, to how much a Ph.D. social worker, teacher, or even physician can earn. By placing so much emphasis on education and the collection of multiple college degrees, blacks have failed to develop any strong tradition of setting up their own businesses, accumulating property and business assets, or inheriting wealth — all of which are preoccupations of white capitalist society. In fact, it has even been suggested by at least one black sociologist that blacks' education fever, promoted by black colleges in the South — most of which were established by white missionaries — was part of a sinister white conspiracy to keep black people in the professional class and to prevent them from ever joining the ranks of the capitalists.

Dressing well, being well groomed, owning your own home and car, having an education — these are the main criteria for status in black America. There are, of course, some regional differences in the way the struggle for status is waged. Northern Negroes tend to be more concerned about the goals of integration. In the South, old-line black families who resisted the rush to Northern cities in the 1920's and thirties tend to have a longer history of institution building, to have more status consistency, to place more stress on lineage and family background, and to have more feeling of having been "born into the class." It is a sad fact, though, that many blacks all over the United States seem not to have realized that having a sense of personal identity is also a hallmark of class. Perhaps it is because, as many blacks claim, white Americans place more emphasis on race than on class, that white Americans look upon the black college professor with the same disdain, and even alarm, as the black hoodlum, that whites cannot yet perceive blacks as individuals but only as *blacks*. But if this were true, the result of this kind of treatment might have been to teach blacks that they have a community of interest with one another. Thus far, however — as blacks continue to try to outdo and out-dress each other, and out-educate each others' children in the scramble for class and status, a true community of interest and taste does not seem to have developed.

Any scramble can become unmannerly, and good manners, too, are a part of having class. White upper-crust society places great emphasis — perhaps too much — on good manners and is frequently put off by black abruptness. As one white man puts it, rather despairingly, "Why do they seem to have a perpetual chip on their shoulders?" Not long ago, a white hostess in New York was entertaining a black woman — the owner and publisher of a successful black newspaper, a woman with a postgraduate degree. The black woman opened the conversation with "Mrs. S——, I'll bet you don't remember where we met."

"I certainly do," said her hostess, "It was four years ago at a League of Women Voters' meeting."

"That's not true!" replied her guest. "I met you twenty years ago, when I was working my way through college cooking for white people. I was cooking a dinner for Mrs. B—— on Sixtieth Street, and you came back into the kitchen to tell me that you enjoyed my meal. You see? You're just like all white folks. To you, all black people look alike." Very much put off, the hostess fell silent, and the brief drawbridge that had been lowered between the races clanged shut. Charlotte Hawkins Brown would not have approved. As she used to tell her privileged pupils, hoping that they would one day become the peers of privileged whites, "Manners must adorn knowledge and smooth its way in the world. Without them, it is like a great rough diamond, very well in a closet by way of curiosity, and also for its intrinsic value. But most prized when polished."

⌐~ 18 ~⌐

"Sweet Auburn Avenue"

IF THE MOOD IN NEW YORK AND WASHINGTON IS EDGY, UN-certain and uncomfortable, the mood in Atlanta is, by comparison, serene. Georgia's bustling, booming capital — "the fastest-growing city in the United States," Atlantans say — has long taken pride in its "un-Southernness," and in a more moderate, liberal, and enlightened attitude toward blacks than can be found in other cities of the South. Atlanta likes to compare itself with such cities as Houston and Los Angeles, rather than with Savannah, New Orleans, Memphis, or Mobile. Though a street in Atlanta is named Margaret Mitchell Avenue, gone are the days of *Gone with the Wind* and Scarlett O'Hara in her crinolines with her eye-rolling colored Mammy. Even during the hard, cruel days of segregation, Atlantans say, there was a "deep undercurrent of understanding and respect" between the whites of Atlanta and their black neighbors. The under-current may not have been as deep or as solid as white Atlantans like to suppose, but it is true that, for the most part, race relations in Atlanta have been peaceful. The last major race riots occurred here in 1910. Atlantans claim that this is because Atlanta is a city of colleges and educators. There are more than a score of institutions of higher learning in the city, including six major black colleges, such as Spelman, Morehouse, and Atlanta University. This has created an atmosphere of mutuality and morality, high-mindedness and tolerance. Atlanta University, for example, for years had a racially mixed faculty. White and black teachers dined with each other, entertained each other, and when the Ku Klux Klan attempted to invade the Atlanta University campus, the white teachers joined with the blacks to stop the Klan at the college gates.

Some black Atlantans, on the other hand, claim that the generally good relationship that exists between blacks and whites can be attributed to other factors. Mrs. Grace Hamilton, who, among other things, was the first black woman to be elected to the Georgia State Legislature, believes that it is because so many prominent white Atlanta families have blood relatives who are black living in the same town. Mr. David T. Howard, for example, who for years ran a leading black funeral home, is said to have been some sort of cousin of Mr. Pierre Howard, a prominent white attorney and member of the State Senate. Another white Atlantan is said for years to have kept two families — one black and one white — on opposite sides of town. In the manner of a true Southern gentleman, he is equally generous to both families. His white wife is aware of, and accepts, the situation, as does his black mistress; the two women even smile and speak to each other when they encounter each other on the street. "Everyone in town," as they say, understands the arrangement, as they understand other similar arrangements. Of course it is not considered quite "fitting" to talk about it much.

Such situations have become quite common in the South, where there has been more *sub rosa* interracial mixing than one might suppose would have been the case. (Just as prominent Southern white men have discreetly kept black mistresses, so have prominent Southern blacks kept white mistresses; it is considered a bit of a status symbol.) In Charleston, South Carolina, there is the case of the Grimke family. Charleston's Grimkes, who are white, consider theirs to be "one of the noblest names of Carolina." Therefore, Mrs. Angelina Grimke Weld of Charleston was somewhat surprised, in 1868, to read in her newspaper of a young black student at Lincoln University in Oxford, Pennsylvania — the first college for Negroes — named Archibald Henry Grimke, who had been cited for his extraordinary "erudition." Mrs. Weld wrote to young Grimke and, saying that since Grimke was such an uncommon name, she was curious as to how he had come by it. Archibald Grimke wrote back to say that he was one of three children of Henry Grimke, Mrs. Weld's brother. After Henry Grimke's wife had died, he had taken his white children's black nurse, one Nancy Weston, as his common-law wife, and had three mulatto children by her.

At Henry Grimke's death, he had said to his black wife, "I leave you better than free because I leave you taken care of." His will had stipulated that Nancy should be provided for and her children educated. But his white son, E. M. Grimke, had disobeyed his father's orders. He had thrown Nancy and two of her children out. He had kept young Archibald, his own half-brother, as his slave and then, heaping insult upon injury, sold him to another planter. After the Emancipation, the little family was reunited, and Nancy had been able to earn and save enough money to send two of her boys, Archibald and his brother Francis, to Lincoln University.

Mrs. Weld was astonished with the revelation that she had Negro nephews. She had been a staunch Abolitionist, had moved from South Carolina to Massachusetts in order to carry on her crusade, and she was shocked to think that her white nephew — or any of the noble Grimkes, for that matter — could have treated his own flesh and blood so shamefully. She immediately went to Lincoln University to visit her newfound black kinfolk. In order to atone for what her relative had done, she offered to pay for Archibald and Francis Grimke's education.

The white Grimkes and the black Grimkes became friends. Angelina Grimke Weld and her husband invited the boys to visit them in Massachusetts and, when they arrived, though they had little money, their mother had seen to it that "each carried a cane, wore a high silk hat which had been made to order, and coats that were custom made." Both boys graduated from Lincoln in 1870, and Francis Grimke was valedictorian of his class. With their Aunt Angelina's support, Archibald went on to Harvard Law School, and Francis went to Howard Law. When Archibald Grimke finished Harvard, Angelina and her husband helped him get placed with a Boston law firm. From 1894 to 1898, Archibald Grimke was United States consul to Santo Domingo. He later joined W. E. B. DuBois in the Niagara Movement, and the N.A.A.C.P., which grew out of it. Francis Grimke switched to theology, and graduated from the Princeton Theological Seminary. For the ardor of his sermons, he became known as "The Black Puritan." Thus, to some extent, the stain that had been placed on the noble name of Grimke was erased on both sides of the racial fence, and Aunt Angelina had atoned for the misdeeds of her relatives.

In Atlanta, Grace Hamilton is an excellent example of a Southern black lady of cultivation and refinement. Atlanta-born — as every true "Atlantan" must be in order to consider himself such — as was her mother, Mrs. Hamilton's maiden name was Towns. Her paternal grandfather's great-uncle was George Towns, and he was governor of Georgia in the late 1850's — and he was white. When Mrs. Hamilton was first elected to the Legislature in 1966 amid a certain amount of fanfare and publicity, she rather startled people by offering to pose for a photograph under a portrait of her distinguished white ancestor. Mrs. Hamilton's husband, Henry Cooke Hamilton, is a tall, courtly gentleman, the retired admissions director at Morehouse and former professor at Atlanta University, and is so fair that, during segregation days, he had no difficulty passing as white and was therefore spared many indignities and inconveniences as he traveled about the South recruiting Morehouse students. (An uncle, Cameron Hamilton, actually moved to California and became a white; one of Mrs. Hamilton's uncles also "passed.") Once, when Mr. Hamilton took a seat in the Jim Crow car of a Southern train, he was asked to move to the white section. In a small Southern town, Mr. Hamilton stopped for a milkshake at a segregated lunch counter. He was served his milkshake by the white waitress, but was recognized by the black short-order cook, who told him, "You don't belong here." (Many blacks claim that, with a kind of black radar, blacks can recognize other blacks whom white people accept unquestioningly as white.) "You go to hell," said Mr. Hamilton to the cook. The cook thereupon told the waitress that she was serving a Negro. The waitress, flustered, appeared not to know what to do about the situation. "So," says Mr. Hamilton, "I decided to take the horns by the bull, and said to the waitress, 'May I have a straw?' " He got his straw, drank his milkshake, and left the establishment without incident.

The Hamilton family also has deep roots in Atlanta, and a number of white relatives. Henry Cooke Hamilton's great grandfather was white, and his mother's grandmother was an Indian. He is descended also from Alexander Hampton, a white governor of South Carolina, and from Alexander Hamilton, the first United States Secretary of the Treasury. Henry Cooke Hamilton's father was Alexander Hamilton III. His older brother is Alexander Hamilton IV. *His* son is Alexander Hamilton V. And Henry Cooke Hamilton's

grandnephew is Alexander Hamilton VI. Of the original
Alexander Hamilton, who was killed in a duel with Aaron
Burr, Henry Cooke Hamilton — a man not without a sense
of humor — says, "We have always considered him the black
sheep of the family."

The Hamiltons live in a comfortable modern house hard
by the University of Atlanta campus, built on property adjoining the much larger house in which Grace Hamilton
grew up, and with a garden that presents a spectacular view
of the Atlanta skyline. It is typical of Atlanta's enlightened
mood — and indicative of the Hamiltons' position in the
community — that when two white workmen appeared at
Mrs. Hamilton's house to clear away some branches of trees
that were overhanging Mrs. Hamilton's garden and were
conferring with the lady of the house as to what should be
done, the white workmen were careful to call Mrs. Hamilton "Ma'am."

During segregation days, times for blacks in Atlanta were
humiliatingly bad, but old-line Atlanta blacks were dough-
tily proud. When the Atlanta streetcars became segregated,
Grace Hamilton's father, who was also an educator, simply
stopped riding the streetcars, and walked to work. Others
did the same. A lawyer friend of the family's, Mr. Peyton
Allen, whose office was on the other side of town, used a
bicycle to get to his office and, on one of his long bicycle
trips, he was struck by an automobile and killed. Children
of Mrs. Hamilton's generation were forbidden to ride the
streetcars, and were not allowed to go to movies in the Jim
Crow theatres — though Mrs. Hamilton confesses that she
and some of her young friends covertly sneaked off to the
movies whenever they could, where they met their beaux.
Blacks could not use the same drinking fountains as whites.
In department stores, where they were allowed to shop, they
could not ride on the elevators and — in the days before
escalators — had to use the stairs. A black mother, Mrs.

Hamilton recalls, who had to take a brood of children to Rich's for back-to-school clothes usually made a shopping day of it. But if one of the children wanted to go to the toilet, there were no black rest rooms in the store. The nearest were located blocks away, at the railroad station. There was no restaurant in downtown Atlanta where blacks could eat. "Still, we were very protected, all of us," Mrs. Hamilton says. "If we passed an ice cream counter, and wanted something to eat, the excuse was never 'We can't eat there because we're colored.' Mother would just say, 'Oh, let's wait till we get home — the food's better there, anyway.' "

Today, it is all quite different. Now blacks and whites dine comfortably together at the best restaurants, sit side by side at the symphony and theatre as well as on the bus, and wander in and out of the most expensive hotels. Led by the liberal Coca-Cola Company — Atlanta's leading industry — equal job opportunities for blacks exist on every level. (Atlanta blacks are very loyal to Coca-Cola and keep their refrigerators stocked with it; it is said, furthermore, that when Coca-Cola first appeared in Jacob's Drug Store on Peachtree Street it was made from a recipe developed by a black cook, who, of course, got no credit for her earthshaking invention.) In Atlanta today it is possible to believe that half a century of oppressive treatment to blacks never existed. The major area where discrimination still exists is in housing. Atlanta's whites still do not want black people living next door, no matter how affluent they may be. In northwest Atlanta a section called Collier Heights is somewhat unique in that it was developed by a black builder as an exclusive community of expensive homes for wealthy blacks. Large, sprawling houses on large lots dot the hillsides of Collier Heights, where the streets wind prettily through tall stands of Georgia pine. Many of the houses have backyard swimming pools, and there is little that one would call garish or tasteless here; Collier Heights is where "old black money" lives, and it has acquired the polish that Dr. Brown so admired. Because there was nothing but a forested wilderness there before, there was no problem when black families staked out Collier Heights as a place to live. But in southwest Atlanta, which has become a more recent enclave of black wealth, it was a somewhat different story. Southwest Atlanta was originally an upper-middle-class, largely Jewish, area, and, when black families began moving in, there was panic. Large houses were thrown on the market for a fraction of their worth as white people saw the neighborhood "going black." One black woman recalls with amusement how she bought a house worth easily $100,000 ten years ago from its fleeing white owner. She had watched the price tag on the house slip from $50,000 to $40,000 to $35,000. At the $35,000 level, she and her husband made the owner an offer. He explained that he had promised the house to another black, but that the man had not been able to raise the final $500 of the selling price. The prospective buyer had begged for time while he tried to borrow $500 from his father-in-law, but had telephoned to say that he had not yet been able to locate his father-in-law. As it happened, the woman knew exactly where the missing father-in-law was at that given moment. He was playing bridge with some friends of hers nearby, but she decided not to impart this information. She snapped up the house for $35,000 cash. At one point, as blacks were moving farther and farther into southwest Atlanta, the real estate panic reached such a fevered pitch that a barricade was erected across a road leading into an all-white section called Peyton Forest to prevent blacks from penetrating any deeper. The barricade soon came down. South*east* Atlanta, meanwhile, remains lily-white.

In addition to the Hamiltons, Townses, and Howards, the Atlanta Old Guard black families include the Ruckers (in real estate), the Caters, the Yateses (both families in the grocery business and there is a white C. R. Yates as well as a black C. R. Yates in Atlanta), the Miltons (banking), the Harpers, Trents, Hopkinses, Faulkners, Penns, Pittses, the Thomases, the Holmses, the Whites (the late educator, Walter White, was an Atlantan), the Martins, Murphys, Palmers, and Holloways. Holloway's Jewelry Store was where every proper black Atlanta girl picked out her engagement ring. The Cunninghams prospered in the real estate business, and one Atlanta woman recalls, "Mama liked Sam Cunningham's son, Ralph, and tried to pair us up together. I said to Mama, 'You know, that Ralph Cunningham's just not as nice as you *think*.' She said, 'Well, he ought to be. He's from a nice family.' " Old Mr. A. F. Herndon, who made a lot of money operating barbershops in downtown Atlanta for an all-white trade, in 1905 organized the Atlanta Life Insurance Company, which today is the fourth largest black-owned life insurance company in America. A. F. Herndon became Atlanta's first black millionaire, and his son, Norris Herndon, a bachelor, still lives in the huge Georgian Herndon mansion, just across the street from Grace and Henry Hamilton, and serves on the board of Atlanta Life. Originally, the businesses that made these men rich were all located on or just off Auburn Avenue, downtown, and the families that owned the businesses lived nearby. Mr. Herndon started his company in a one-room office in the Rucker Building on Auburn Avenue. Holloway's Jewelry Store was there, and so was the Rucker real estate office and Mr. Howard's funeral home. The merchants of Auburn Avenue prospered to such an extent that the street became a kind of symbol of black achievement — first to black Atlantans, and eventually to upwardly moving blacks everywhere. John Wesley Dobbs was a legendary Atlanta figure who headed the black Masonic Lodge. Though he was only a postal clerk, he managed to put all six of his daughters through college, and all of them became successful women — the most famous of whom is singer Mattiwilda Dobbs. Mr. Dobbs was a spellbinding speaker, and in his speeches he began extolling the glories of "Sweet Auburn Avenue." Maynard Jackson, Sr. — the father of Atlanta's present mayor, who was a clergyman and married to one of Mr. Dobbs's daughters — took up the phrase "Sweet Auburn Avenue" in his sermons, and eventually it made its way to Tin Pan Alley, where it became the title of a song. If a man could make it to Sweet Auburn Avenue, he could make it to the stars.

The families that prospered along Sweet Auburn Avenue, many light-skinned, were a proud and tight-knit group. Upper-class blacks often make a distinction between "friends" and "visiting friends." Friends are mere nodding acquaintances. Visiting friends are like family, and the Auburn Avenue families not only visited each other but called each other "Auntie" and "Uncle." Their children married each other. Most were members of the First Congregational Church, Atlanta's black "society" church (Friendship Methodist Church and the Baptist African Methodist Episcopal Church are also "nice" black churches, but exist farther down the social ladder). First Congregational became the fashionable church because of Atlanta University's early ties with Congregationalist missionaries, and it was at First Congregational that the National Medical Association was founded in 1895 when the American Medical Association would not admit black physicians to its ranks. A local joke has it that no one can join the First Congregational Church unless his skin is as light as the lightest faces in the stained glass windows.

Along Auburn Avenue, probity was stressed along with piety. "Education, Determination, Integrity" were the three themes emphasized by Auburn Avenue parents. A high moral tone was demanded of everyone because, after all, black people came from all over the country just to walk down Auburn Avenue to see the stores, business and professional offices, and fine homes of well-to-do black men and women who had managed to "get over" despite a segregated situation. Of course there were some people on Auburn Avenue who managed not quite to measure up to the high standards set. There was Mr. Ben Davis, for example, who was the head of the Oddfellows and who was considered a "questionable character." Ben, it was said, "had a lot of women on his string," and he "set them up in houses." Ben Davis's son was not permitted to call on nice black girls and, sure enough, the son later went to prison. So strongly did old Mr. Rucker feel about Ben Davis that he wouldn't let his daughters walk on the same side of the street as Ben Davis's establishment.

Auburn Avenue today is not as sweet as it once was, as black businesses have spread to other parts of the city and black families have scattered to the northwest and southwest suburbs. Atlanta Life is still there, along with a few black real estate, doctors', and lawyers' offices. But it is still, as a glorious memory, a powerful symbol to Atlanta's blacks. When the Citizens Trust bank, rated the seventh largest black bank in the United States, and the board chairman of which is old Mr. L. D. Milton, moved to its handsome new glass tower several years ago, it decided not to move *too* far away, and the new bank is just a couple of blocks off Auburn. It is also possible that Auburn Avenue, and the success it symbolized, is a major reason why Atlanta became integrated so quickly and easily: black wealth in the city had simply become too powerful a force to discriminate against. Cynics in Atlanta say that Atlanta's liberal treatment of blacks today is not due to intellectual enlightenment or to Christian tolerance. But when, in the 1950's, blacks began boycotting Atlanta stores and streetcars, the economic pinch that was felt was fierce. The city had to integrate or go under.

But why did integration come with such relative smoothness and ease to Atlanta, whereas other Southern cities, such as Shreveport, Louisiana — which is still considered the most segregated city in the United States — resisted it so belligerently? Perhaps it is because Atlanta is a new city. It even has a new name. It used to be called Terminus, Georgia, because East-West and North-South railroads terminated there. When it was renamed, poetically, Atlanta — with suggestions of a legendary sunken civilization risen from the depths — it seemed to take a whole new grasp of things and view of life. When General Sherman's troops marched through Atlanta, they left little standing. The city had to rebuild itself from scratch. Such Southern cities as Savannah and New Orleans seem still to be frozen in time, somewhere in the last century. But Atlanta had to renew itself, and did, and is now bursting with youth and vigor. "There's a feeling here that Atlanta is on the crest of the wave of the future," one man says. "The last thing an Atlantan wants to be accused of is not keeping up with — or even not being ahead of — the times." And so Atlanta became an oasis in the black South. During the period of Reconstruction and the era of segregation that followed, former slave-owners saw the wisdom of promoting their ex-slaves in business, and of helping them set up their grocery stores and chemists' shops along Sweet Auburn Avenue. The Atlanta *Constitution* also helped, by taking a moderate editorial tone toward black people. The many educators and clergymen were powerful go-betweens in race relations, and there was a strong moral tone carried from Protestant New England by missionaries of the Congregationalist Church. What had been a black bottom class became a kind of ruling class.

And yet, ironically enough, the very fact of segregation once helped certain black businesses to succeed in Atlanta. When black customers were not particularly welcomed at white banks, a black bank had to be the answer, and — consistent with Atlanta's spirit of enterprise and building — thus came into existence the Citizens Trust Bank. When white insurance companies were reluctant to issue policies to blacks, or were unwilling to pay black claims, a company such as Atlanta Life filled the need. Black funeral directors were in a unique position of power. In any Southern town during the segregation era, the two most powerful men were its white sheriff and the black funeral director. The two men usually worked in tandem. The sheriff had authority for obvious reasons, and it was wise to be on his good side. But when a black man or woman was killed in a Saturday night barroom brawl, and the sheriff was called, he brought the body to a black undertaking establishment. In return for this favor, he usually received a slight consideration and, furthermore, he could be reasonably sure that the undertaker would help him get votes in the black community at election time.

Ironically, too, integration has created problems for black businesses by diluting the power of black money. A black sheriff may find that it is more rewarding to deliver a black (or white, for that matter) corpse to a white funeral parlor. Today, though the Citizens Trust Bank, once one of Atlanta's proudest black institutions, boasts deposits of $27,683,000 and assets of $33,688,000, things are not quite as rosy as those figures would lead one to suppose, according to its new president. The bank was founded in 1922 by an insurance man named Herman Perry, and its presidency was later assumed by L. D. Milton, of a prestigious old-line family. The Milton family and the Yates family were partners in a drugstore business and, as an indication of how tightly knit Atlanta's black families can become, Mr. Milton is married to a Murphy, whose grandfather is a Howard. Mr. Milton, a graduate of Brown University, had been a schoolteacher and, though his lineage was of the finest, it did not seem to occur to anyone that his qualifications as a banker were somewhat slender. Still, all seemed to go well until Mr. Milton began approaching his twilight years. One of Mr. Milton's protégés was a young man named Joel Stokes, who was widely touted by Mr. Milton and his bank as a financial genius. A genius he may have been, but Stokes also managed to misuse and misplace certain funds, to use collateral put up for loans for his own private purposes, and to lose track of some $35,000 of the bank's funds. When his defalcations were discovered, Stokes was arrested, sent to trial, convicted, and sent to the penitentiary. At the time of the trial, Mr. Milton was declared too ill to testify, although, according to a friend, he seemed to recover from his illness shortly thereafter. Mr. Milton resigned his presidency in 1971, his wife took over his personal financial affairs — the bank made Mr. Milton very rich — and a new president was appointed.

He was a young man named Charles McKinley Reynolds, Jr. Mr. Reynolds held an economics degree from Morehouse College, had done additional study in business administration at Wayne State and Atlanta Universities, and also had a degree in mortuary science. But his tenure at Citizens Trust was short-lived, and Reynolds remained with the bank only four years before moving on to another post.

There were other problems. Heavy loans, coupled with a drop in deposits, had resulted in what the bank euphemistically described as "a capital deficiency." The 1974–1975 economic recession, of course, did not help matters. The bank had been a heavy lender in consumer credit and had been heavily into home mortgage loans. The bank had not dealt heavily in commercial credit, had made few business loans and, since most black businesses are small, these loans are small. But the recession made it more difficult for black businesses to compete with white businesses and with one another, and rising interest rates made it harder for the Citizens Trust to compete with other banks and deliver the same quality of service. In the recession, several black businesses that the bank had financed went under. Individual customers who had taken out mortgage or home improvement loans could not make their payments.

Also, the bank has lost the emotional power in the black community that it once held. During segregation years, a black bank could count on the black community to support it out of racial loyalty. Once the restrictions against blacks began to lift, this racial loyalty began to diminish. White banks are now actively competing for black customers, offering them better service than black banks can afford to give, and blacks are less willing to accept the poorer service of black banks.

To help itself out of a mare's nest of financial problems, and recapitalize itself, the bank has managed to raise $3,000,000 in new capital — by turning to the Ford Foundation for $1,000,000, to Atlanta Life for another $1,000,000, and the balance from a number of other small black banks in Georgia as well as from MINBANC, a federal agency that has guaranteed half of the sum borrowed in capital notes, and another half in stock. Since January, 1975, the bank has had a young and energetic new black president named I. Owen Funderburg, who is determined to do his best to turn the bank's fortunes around. A native of Monticello, Georgia, Mr. Funderburg graduated from Morehouse and from the business college of the University of Michigan. He has a solid banking background, having started as a teller at the Mechanics and Farmers Bank of Birmingham, where he rose to the position of cashier and a member of the board of directors. In 1966, he left Birmingham to become executive vice president and chief executive officer of the Gateway

National Bank in St. Louis, where he was also a member of
the board. One of the things Mr. Funderburg hopes to do is
to change Citizens Trust from a bank that dealt only with
black customers into a bank that will deal with the entire
community. "Blacks used to subscribe to the motto, 'Don't
put your money where you can't work,' but now that rally-
ing cry no longer works, since blacks can work anywhere,"
says Mr. Funderburg. If he can turn Citizens Trust into a
bank with a racially mixed clientele, he will have accomplished a considerable feat. Since Citizens Trust is universally known in Atlanta as "the black bank," one wonders
whether whites can really be persuaded to be depositors or
borrowers. But Mr. Funderburg insists that he knows Atlanta. Though he was not born there, he grew up in a small
town nearby, where his father was a country doctor, and he
visited the city often as a young man. In Atlanta, Funderburg has many friends and a number of relatives. On the
plus side, he points out that the bank's shiny new building
is now more than ninety-five percent rented, with a number
of prominent white tenants, including several government
agencies and the offices of the Atlanta Bell Telephone
Company.

And yet Owen Funderburg was distressed when, in the
summer of 1975, *Black Enterprise* — the monthly black answer to *Business Week* — published a list of the thirty-eight
largest black-owned banks in the country (led by George
Johnson's Independence Bank of Chicago), and Citizens
Trust did not make the list. Funderburg wrote a complain-
ing letter to the magazine's New York publisher, Earl
Graves, who printed a correction in the next issue of the
magazine, saying that with the bank's stated assets and deposits, it should have been listed in eighth place. Mr. Funderburg shows the correction to visitors.

And as news of the bank's woes has crept into the newspapers, more black depositors have begun pulling out. "I

wouldn't put my money in that bank," says a black Atlanta taxicab driver with emphasis. And there is a persistent rumor in Atlanta that, in the end, the Citizens Trust will be absorbed by the Citizens–Southern Trust Company — a white bank.

19

"King's Wigwam," and Other Unhappy Memories

THE SEGREGATION ERA LEFT DEEP PSYCHOLOGICAL SCARS ON the blacks of the South, and the old people remember it best. Mrs. Edward Miller is a tall, dignified lady in her early seventies, with fair skin and softly waved gray hair, who lives in a large brick house in southwest Atlanta not far from Peyton Forest. The wife of a prominent architect, who has designed a number of Atlanta's churches and university buildings, Mrs. Miller is a woman with a healthy distrust of taking things at face value. Though she agrees that blacks in Atlanta are infinitely better off than when she was growing up, she wonders how sincere white Atlantans really are when they say that they want black people to continue to advance. "People here say things that they don't really mean," she says.

She remembers, for example, when the last white family on her street sold their house and moved away. The man was a minister, and he repeatedly told his neighbors that he liked the street and was happy living there. He often told his black neighbors how proud he was to be in this lovely neighborhood, where black families took care of their houses, their spacious lawns, gardens, and boxwood hedges. He told them how happy he was so often, in fact, that some of his neighbors, including Mrs. Miller, became just a bit suspicious. When the minister's house went on the market, he gave the neighbors some excuse about having to move to California to care for an elderly sister. Nobody quite believed him.

And in the days when the Reverend Martin Luther King, Jr., was struggling to effect radical changes for blacks throughout the South, Mrs. Miller recalls that a white friend said to Dr. King, Sr. — whom most people in Atlanta call Daddy King — "I think your son is going too far." Dr. King replied, "Have you ever heard my son preach?" The man said, "No — I'm afraid he might convince me." "And that was a white man speaking," says Nina Miller.

Mrs. Miller's father was the late Cornelius King, another great patriarchal figure in Atlanta. Cornelius King was no relation to Martin Luther King and, in fact, there is an enormous social gap between the two King families of Atlanta. "We knew those Kings," Mrs. Miller says, "and in fact our house was a stone's throw from theirs, and I went to kindergarten with Mrs. King, senior. But we weren't visiting friends. After all, Daddy King was nothing but a little old Baptist preacher, and Ebenezer Baptist Church was *not* the sort of church that families like ours attended. Not in the same category at all. It wasn't until his son became so famous that anybody paid any attention to those Kings." Many in black Atlanta society feel that the Martin Luther Kings used their famous son to climb socially, and Mrs. Martin Luther King, Jr., has not made herself popular in the city. She is "too full of herself," they say, and blacks mock the way Coretta King has of speaking, theatrically, of *"Mah Husband."* Behind her back, Coretta King's nickname has become "Mah Husband."

"Everyone thought the sun rose and set on my Papa," says Nina King Miller. "He was a true aristocrat. He made something out of nothing." Cornelius King's father had been a slave, but his mother was a Cherokee Indian. One of his grandfathers, furthermore, was a white Irish missionary who had been sent West to convert the Indians. "And so what does that make me?" Mrs. Miller asks. "I'm part Irish, part Indian, and part Negro. I'm certainly *colored,* but I'm not black." Like many others of her generation and caste, Nina Miller dislikes and disapproves of the word "black," and looks forward to the day when it will go out of fashion. Cornelius King grew up in the Indian territory of Oklahoma, where his Indian mother owned some property. There he met the daughter of Bishop Henry McNeil Turner, who was traveling in the territory, and married her and moved to Atlanta. "Bishop Turner thought the world of Papa," Mrs. Miller says. "He regarded him more highly than he did his own two sons, both of whom were drunkards." Cornelius King's wife lived only a few years in Atlanta before she died. Then he married Mrs. Miller's mother, a Spelman-educated Warrington, Georgia, girl. "My grandmother was white, or at least you couldn't tell her from white. It was something we never talked about," Mrs. Miller says. "She may not have had much education, but she was a perfect lady. Even when she was very old and in a wheelchair, she wouldn't be wheeled out to the porch without her hat and gloves on, and the little black velvet ribbon tied around her throat."

For a while, Mr. King worked as a machinist. Then he worked for an Atlanta law firm, as a detective. From there, he moved to the Department of the Interior, and, in 1895, was a member of the Henry Dawes Commission on Indian Affairs, and went into Indian territory again as a liaison man. Mrs. Miller has a picture of him in his elaborate Indian headdress. There was a brand of tennis ball called "Indian King," and Mr. King, with his Indian looks and his Indian headdress, posed for the picture that became the company's trademark. Back in Atlanta, Mr. King worked for a number of years as the steward of the Atlanta Athletic Club, "where he got to know who was who in Atlanta. All the top white businessmen in Atlanta knew Papa. He was *eminently* well respected." He was so well respected, in fact, that white businessmen helped him establish his own real estate business on Auburn Avenue, where he prospered. Mrs. Miller's brother runs the family business now.

"Papa was a very good provider," Mrs. Miller says. "We always had the best of everything, and we were very protected. We lived in a big corner house on Auburn Avenue. I remember that when I was in the fifth grade we were the first family to have a furnace, and we were among the first to have electricity. We always had a laundress. My mother and Grace Hamilton's mother both worked for the Gate City Free Kindergarten, which was a charity school for less fortunate Negroes." Growing up in Atlanta in the early 1900's was a cozy and secure experience for little girls like Nina King, surrounded as she was by doting parents, grandparents, and family friends, and free from any real financial worries. On weekends, the family and visiting friends gathered in the Kings' parlor for tea and talk while the children were sent upstairs or into the yard to play. Everyone played the piano, and there were musical Sunday afternoons after church where everyone played and sang or listened to the old wind-up Edison gramophone. Birthday parties were great occasions, with homemade blueberry ice cream and cakes with candles, all manner of cookies and other sweets. Little girls dressed up in white dresses with crinoline underskirts, and tied pink satin sashes about their waists, and the boys wore suits with Eton collars and wore black patent-leather shoes with silver buckles. There were games — musical chairs, pin-the-tail-on-the-donkey, in-and-out-the-windows — and story-telling hours. At bedtime, children said their prayers and thanked Jesus for all the beautiful presents they had received that day.

As Cornelius King's real estate business continued to prosper, he purchased a summer home for his family in the country at Kennesaw, Georgia, and forty-five acres of surrounding land. Here in the piney hills the Kings began spending each summer, while Papa stayed in Atlanta during the week and joined his family in the country for weekends. On his land, Cornelius King built a spring-fed artificial lake and a tennis court. All the young people — Nina King had an older sister and two brothers — played tennis. Because the house was large, there were nearly always a number of weekend guests consisting, again, of family and friends — the Hamiltons, Yateses, Murphys, and Townses. In fact, the idyllic little retreat became so popular with the Kings' Atlanta friends that the real estate man in Cornelius King made him decide to put his summer place to a use that would turn a profit. He built a number of small summer cabins in the surrounding woods and glades and offered them for rent. Black Atlantans flocked out to Kennesaw in the summertime, taking Mr. King's cabins for a weekend or an entire month, and before he knew it he was operating a small, select black summer resort. He built an outdoor dance pavilion and hired a piano player to play for dancing on weekend evenings. He christened his place "King's Wigwam."

Then, all at once, a terrible thing happened. Bertram Hamilton, Henry Cooke Hamilton's brother, had come up to "King's Wigwam" to visit Nina King's brother. Both boys were tall and slender and were superb tennis players and, for an entire weekend, the two youths were hardly ever off the court. The Kings and their friends had always assumed that they got along well with their white neighbors in Kennesaw. There had been no friction, no unpleasantness of any sort. The Kings and their friends shopped at the white stores in town, and had always been scrupulously prompt about paying their bills. And so, when what happened happened, it seemed like a horrible dream, and Mrs. Miller's eyes still cloud over when she thinks about it. Bertram Hamilton was accused of raping a white girl in the village.

The sheriff came, and the Ku Klux Klan. Terrified, the family telephoned Cornelius King in Atlanta. He urged them to get out of Kennesaw as quickly as possible, and back to Atlanta. That night, Bertram Hamilton was smuggled out in the trunk of a car, and everyone made it safely home. That was over fifty years ago, but none of the family or their friends has ever gone back to Kennesaw. Cornelius King put "King's Wigwam" up for sale — the house, the land, the lake, and the little dance pavilion. It was sold at a great loss. Today, Nina King Miller is half convinced that the rape allegation was part of a plot on the part of the Kennesaw whites to get her father's property. She hopes this isn't true, but it might have been. Such things, in those days, happened often in the South and, if it was a plot, it succeeded. She tries not to be bitter, and to look upon what happened all those years ago in the most charitable light. "I know that it's hard, for people who have led hard lives, to see another person, particularly a colored person, have a little success," she says. "Perhaps that was it. It was a poor, sharecropping town. It may have been difficult for them to see us there, having such good times as we did. All people are not alike." Still, when she thinks about it, her eyes cloud over.

"Some of the myths about the South in segregation days were not true," says Donald Hollowell, a young Atlanta lawyer and regional director of the Equal Employment Opportunity Commission with a territory covering eight Southern states from Kentucky to Florida. "But some of the facts were more brutal than most people ever knew." Hollowell, who successfully defended Martin Luther King, Jr., when he was threatened with prison in 1960, has specialized in defending blacks accused of such crimes as rape and murder, and is credited with having saved a number of men from Georgia's infamous chain gang. Rape is the charge black men in the South dread the most. White women who have dallied with black men and who have the misfortune of becoming pregnant frequently charge "rape" in order to protect themselves in the eyes of their families and friends, and Southern judgments in these cases can be swift and harsh. In one such case, a fifteen-year-old boy was charged with rape on a Saturday and sentenced to die in the electric chair the following Wednesday. In four days' time, however, Hollowell managed to get the judge's decision reversed, and to save the boy.

Hollowell himself has been subjected to numerous indignities because of his race. A native of Wichita, Kansas, he was a high school dropout who later managed to earn his high school diploma through a correspondence course. He then completed three years at Lane College on a football scholarship and, in 1941, as a Regular Army reservist, he was ordered to report for military service at Fort Oglethorpe, Georgia. At Fort Oglethorpe, he discovered that he was the only black at the induction center. Segregation was just as strict in the United States Army as it was elsewhere in the South, and Private Hollowell was ordered to eat in the kitchen. He refused. He was then told that he could eat with the prisoners and this, it turned out, had certain advantages. "I had a table to myself, with a whole pitcher of milk, and a whole pound of butter," Hollowell recalls. "I was eating better than anyone else on the base." Still, he was barred from the day room and the post movie theatre and, to his amusement, was told that he could not play Ping-Pong. The latrines were another problem. At Fort Oglethorpe, a white base, there was no provision for a "colored" toilet. When Hollowell entered the latrine to shower and shave, he was confronted by a group of fifteen or twenty angry white recruits, brandishing razors and knives, who ordered him to leave. When Hollowell explained to the company commander that he would, if the commander wished, use the lawn in front of company headquarters as his toilet, he was given a private bathroom.

The idiocies and hatred of segregation went on and on, and yet Hollowell was able to emerge from the United States Army as a first lieutenant. He finished college on the G.I. Bill, and went on to Loyola University to obtain his law degree. He met and married an Atlanta girl, and decided to settle there. "There was culture and tradition among blacks of the South," he says, "that had not had a chance to develop among blacks in the Northern cities. Blacks here had been forced to do for themselves, and those who had done it had done well. There was a kind of survivalist elite here. I decided that if a black lawyer could do a good job he could make it here. I've fared as well as any other lawyer around, and I've been here for twenty-four years. It wasn't all easy. There were state laws that ran contrary to federal laws, and that I've helped change. There were judges who were unfair. There were some setbacks, but there was also some cooperation. There could have been chaos. But, as bad as it was, there was a resolution in the end."

While all this was going on, there were other Southern blacks among the "survivalist elite" who were quietly and purposefully working for reforms, and were doing so without slogans or marches or demonstrations — or much fanfare. When John Wesley Dobbs reorganized the socially, and politically, important Masonic Lodge, he made it a rule that no one could join the Masons of Atlanta unless he was a registered voter. When the men of a nearby county begged to be excepted from this rule — since county laws, in defiance of federal law, denied blacks the vote — Mr. Dobbs agreed to make an exception in their case. Word of this reached the newspapers, much to the embarrassment and ire of the white worthies of the offending county, who preferred to have their attitudes and practices kept out of the press. A sheriff from the county in question appeared at Mr. Dobbs's door one night with a summons. Alone, and at great personal risk, Mr. Dobbs drove out to the county courthouse to defend charges of creating unpleasant publicity for the county. He was, fortunately, given a scolding and a reminder to "keep in your place," and nothing more. Because he was aware that his life was in danger most of the time, Mr. Dobbs always carried a gun. At one point, he was arrested for carrying a weapon, even though he had a perfectly valid permit to do so. Similarly, Grace Hamilton's father, Mr. Towns, on his way to the Atlanta courthouse to pay the poll tax that was required in order to vote, spoke to each black person he met along the way and urged him to do the same. "Your ballot is your weapon," he used to say. When this unwelcome activity was noticed by the whites, he too was threatened. Still, he persisted, and survived.

Public pronouncements had to be made with great care. Bishop Turner, Cornelius King's father-in-law, who used to preach in favor of blacks returning to Africa, once declared, "The United States flag is just a dirty dishrag to the Negro." For this slur, he had to go into hiding for a while. In Mound Bayou, Mississippi, Dr. Theodore Roosevelt Mason Howard was the local surgeon and president of the Mound Bayou Mutual Life Insurance Company. Though there was no chapter of N.A.A.C.P. in Mound Bayou, Dr. Howard often spoke to fellow blacks about the value of voting, of education, and of achieving economic advancement. By 1955, segregation had been outlawed by the United States Supreme Court, but Mississippi was dragging its Deep Southern heels in terms of doing anything about it. Mississippi's governor, Hugh White, called a group of one hundred black leaders in the state together, and the theme of the meeting was to be "Mutuality of Interest." It was to the blacks' and the whites' mutual interest, the governor suggested, that the state proceed slowly toward compliance with the Supreme Court's directive. In fact, it might be to the mutual interest of all concerned if actual integration were to be postponed indefinitely. Some black leaders, more timorous about the effects of integration than others, tended to go along with Governor White and to say "We don't think it's quite time to end segregation." But the blacks elected Dr. Howard to be their spokesman, and Dr. Howard held a different view. In Jackson, Dr. Howard stood up before the governor and said, among other things, "Black boys are fighting and dying in Korea for liberty and democracy, but here in Mississippi we don't know what liberty and democracy mean."

Gently, the governor reproved him, saying, "Now look here. You know, and I know, that if we asked all the Negroes in this state how they felt about integration, ninety percent would be opposed to it. Don't you believe that?" Dr. Howard replied, "Governor, if I told you that ninety percent of the blacks in Mississippi didn't want to go to Heaven, would you believe that?" The newspapers seized the story, with headlines that screamed: "BLACK SURGEON CALLS GOVERNOR A LIAR!" In Mississippi, a bounty of a thousand dollars was immediately offered for Dr. Howard's head. He and his family made it out of Mississippi as rapidly as possible, sold their property, and have never returned. Dr. Howard settled in Chicago, where he reestablished his practice and, three years later, opened his Friendship Clinic, a full-service clinic offering medical, dental, and even psychiatric service, which made Dr. Howard a multimillionaire. It made Dr. Howard able to afford to become an avid big-game hunter in Africa and, with his many trophies, he turned the reception room of Friendship

Clinic into a taxidermal zoo, with the animals in natural poses surrounded by pools, waterfalls and a jungle of live tropical trees.

In retrospect — perhaps because he managed to become so successful elsewhere — he insisted that he was not bitter about the treatment he received in his former home, and that he harbored no hard feelings against white people in general. After all, he pointed out, his "salvation" came from the fact that his mother worked as a cook for a white Mississippi doctor named Robert Mason, after whom Dr. Howard was named. Dr. Mason took a paternal interest in his namesake, and put him through school, college, and medical school. As a result, he was the only member of his family since slavery to receive a higher education, and a half-brother in the South works as a manual laborer. "The whites of Mississippi and the blacks of the state were close," Dr. Howard said. "The plantation owners were good to their people, and I was respected by the whites in the state — as long as nobody tried to rock the boat. But the whites in Mississippi don't like to see things change. They take the attitude of 'We're not gonna have anybody tell our niggers anything different from what we've *always* told 'em.' When somebody tries to do that, that's when the feathers fly."

Donald Hollowell also maintains that he harbors no ill feelings toward whites, no bitterness because of the indignities he suffered during segregation days. "I've learned," he says, "that if you let rancor and bitterness seep in, you lose your *perspective* and your *effectiveness*. I've absorbed enough negatives to rend one's soul. But I've tried to maintain the Christian principle, and to forgive them their debts. There is always a day of reckoning. I couldn't have achieved such success as I have if I'd had rancor eating away at me. Rancor is just not practical."

Hollowell admits that many — and he goes so far as to say

"most" — blacks bitterly resent (and *hate* would not be too strong a word) white people. But those, he insists, are from the poor and the uneducated lower classes.

Perhaps an ability to forgive, and a refusal to be consumed by bitter feelings, and an ability to absorb insults and rise above rancor are, in themselves, among the hallmarks of an upper class.

~ 20 ~

"Interpositionullification"

AS MORE AND MORE PROUD BLACKS OF THE SOUTH BOYCOTTED the segregated streetcars and buses, and refused to trade at stores where they could neither work nor use the restrooms, segregation became, to all intents and purposes, no longer "practical." When not working quietly and peacefully toward an integrated society, blacks comforted each other with their own special sense of humor and bits of doggerel such as the one — at the time of the famous 1938 reencounter between a black fighter and a Nazi white supremacist — that went:

> *White folks, white folks, don't get mad —*
> *Joe Louis will whip Max Schmeling's ass!*

Still, the daily humiliations were difficult to endure. Dr. and Mrs. Asa Yancey, for example, live in a sprawling California ranch-style house in the Collier Heights suburb of Atlanta. Dr. Yancey, a surgeon, is Medical Director of Grady Memorial Hospital, associate dean of Emory School of Medicine, and a member of the Atlanta Board of Education, and there have been Yanceys in Atlanta for over seventy years. His wife, however, was a Dunbar from Detroit, the daughter of a wealthy lawyer and manager of a housing project, and was brought up according to strict democratic principles. Neither Mrs. Dunbar nor any of her children ever called a servant by his or her first name. "If one of Mama's maids was a Mrs. Smith, that was what we all called her," Marge Dunbar Yancey recalls. "No one was permitted to address her as 'Mary.' Of course Mama often became friends with some of the people who worked for her, and if that happened they *both* used first names, but the children never did. It wasn't because we were stiff and formal. It was because we respected human dignity." When Marge Yancey married and moved to Atlanta and had her first taste of life in a segregated Southern city, she found the experience "incredibly distressing." Like most young black mothers, she tried to protect her children from the more petty expressions of segregation. But neither Marge Yancey nor her husband will ever forget the time, nearly twenty years ago, when the children first felt segregation's effect.

The Yanceys and their four young children — the eldest was barely six years old — were returning from a family outing, and Asa Yancey pulled up to a Dairy Queen to buy ice cream for the children. He got out of the car, and went up to the window of the ice cream stand. The counter girl scrutinized him for a moment — Dr. Yancey was so fair that he, too, might pass for white — then motioned him away. When he returned to the car empty-handed, the children wanted to know what had happened. "The place wasn't clean," he told them. "There were flies buzzing around." Today he explains, "I didn't want to lie to them. But I felt that there probably *was* a fly or two in the place, and so it wasn't a real lie, just a half-truth." The family drove homeward in silence for a while, and then the six-year-old said suddenly, "*I* know why we didn't get our ice cream there. It's that *seg-reg-ation* Mom is always talking about on the phone!" The Yanceys were astonished that a child of that age could already have become so sensitive to the situation.

Dr. Yancey's father, Arthur Henry Yancey — always called "Aytch" for his first two initials — had been a carpenter by trade. His first job in Atlanta had been to build a flight of steps, which took him ten hours and earned him $2.50 — an amount, he realized, that was more than his father had ever earned in a day in his lifetime. His next job was bigger, and earned him more, and presently it began to seem to Aytch Yancey as though his future was secure. Presently, he was hired by a contractor to complete a house that another subcontractor had fallen through on, and the man was so pleased with Yancey's work that he subcontracted with him for a new house at rates that more experienced white builders were getting. Yancey took the job, finished it days ahead of schedule, and from then on was a general contractor, hiring subcontractors of his own. This was in the early 1900's, and Aytch Yancey was prospering — so much so that the white community began to notice his prosperity, and this, perhaps, was the beginning of his trouble.

He had signed a contract with a white man to build a small house, and the price agreed upon had been $650. During the building, the white man's wife seemed unusually friendly, even flirtatious — Aytch Yancey was a slender and handsome young man — and she hung around the construction site, chatting, joking and making suggestions. Yancey tolerated her intrusions politely. When the job was completed, Yancey presented his bill, and the owner asked him about building a small servants' wing on the house. Yancey said that he would be delighted to do this, and the cost would be an additional $125. "Oh, no," the man said. "I've paid you enough already. You just go ahead and build the wing." Yancey refused, and the case went to court. When the hearing convened, the white judge — who already appeared to know a good deal about the case — opened the proceedings with "Yancey, why don't you go ahead and build the servants' room like a good boy, and stop causing us trouble."

"Because it's not in the contract," Yancey replied, and offered to show the contract to His Honor.

"I don't care about contracts," said the judge, waving the document aside. "This lady says that you told her, in the presence of her husband, that you'd build the extra room, and so now you're just going to have to go ahead and do it." And so Mr. Yancey built the added room, as ordered. His legal fees for the case had come to $150 and, of course, he made no profit on the job. He was beginning to see where he stood as a Negro contractor in the South.

Later, under a carefully worded contract, Aytch Yancey agreed to build a house for a white policeman named E. O. Eddleman, and the price agreed upon was $883. When the building was finished to Mr. Eddleman's satisfaction, Mr. Yancey presented his bill. The policeman demurred, saying that he wanted first to be sure that Mr. Yancey had paid all *his* bills for lumber and building materials. So Yancey accompanied Eddleman down to Mr. J. J. West's lumberyard, where Eddleman was assured that Yancey owed only $81. Eddleman then wrote out a check to Mr. West for the $81 and, in the process, muttered something about "That nigger still has eight hundred dollars of my money." Overhearing this, Mr. West said, "Now, Eddleman, Yancey is a good boy and he always pays all his bills." Eddleman handed West the check and started to leave, whereupon Yancey reminded him that he had still not been paid. Still grumbling about "eight hundred dollars of my money," and "damn niggers," Eddleman wrote out a second check and tossed it to Yancey. It was for $800 — two dollars short of the contract price — but Yancey, who considered himself lucky to be paid at all, made no mention of the discrepancy. Eddleman stalked out the door, and immediately Mr. West said, "Beat that man to the bank, Yancey!" Getting the point, Aytch

Yancey leapt over the back fence of J. J. West's lumber company, ran through the D. R. Wilder Candy Company's plant, and all the way to the Atlanta National Bank, where he cashed his check. Later, the teller told him that Eddleman had appeared at the bank just moments afterward to try to stop payment on the check — too late.

Experiences like these made Aytch Yancey conclude that he could never succeed as a building contractor for whites and, of course, there were few building jobs for blacks. He took a job at the post office, as a letter carrier. The salary was only $600 a year, but at least the work was steady. And there was another advantage: no one knew the size of his paycheck, and there was no way for a white man to get his hands on it. Still, life for a black letter carrier was not without its vicissitudes. Early in his new career Aytch Yancey learned that the white housewives along his route presented a certain peril. Because he was a handsome, light-skinned man — like others, part Cherokee, part white, part Negro — women frequently invited him in and made seductive offers and advances. Aware of the terrible consequences of a charge of "rape," he was meticulously careful to resist these overtures. Once, on his route, he was talking with a patron when a woman across the street called to him to come over and pick up a letter she wanted to mail. When he did not immediately come, the woman cursed, threw the letter on the sidewalk, and went back into her house. Yancey did not cross the street or pick up the letter. A few days later, his postmaster received a complaint which read:

Dear Sir:
  I want to call your attention to the discourteous and almost insulting manner in which a certain nigger letter-carrier of your office treated my wife. I feel it is only necessary to report it to you in order to make him behave properly.

The letter was given to Yancey to reply. He wrote:

Dear Sir:
   This charge does not state the infraction. It merely states, *as a fact,* that it was a certain *nigger* letter-carrier. Perhaps it is there wherein lies the near insult. If so, the gentleman does not expect an apology from me.

Respectfully yours,
A. H. YANCEY

The letter had to be channeled through the postmaster for approval. He returned the letter to Yancey, and instructed him to apologize.

Though his pay was small, Aytch Yancey was a thrifty man and managed to save enough to buy a lot and build for his family, in the Georgia style, a large red-brick one-and-a-half-story house, which still stands near the Atlanta University campus. Much of the work on the house he did himself, but he hired a workman to whom — as he set out on his mail route in the morning — in a joking way Yancey said, "I'll bet I get more work done on this house between when I get home from work and nightfall than you'll get done all day." And he usually kept that promise. Aytch Yancey also managed to send all seven of his children through college. Three of his sons became physicians, and one of his daughters earned a master's degree. By the time he died several years ago, at the age of eighty-eight, he had established the Yancey family as members of the black aristocracy of Atlanta.

Though he lived to see segregation in restaurants, buses, housing, schools, elevators, and the Armed Services all outlawed, he still believed fiercely that blacks were unjustly treated in the South, that despite advances in civil rights, blacks were still regarded as second-class citizens. There was a word he coined — "interpositionullification." He sent the word to hundreds of educators and lexicographers, urging that "interpositionullification" be included in dictionaries. Though he never got the term into a dictionary, in 1959, at the age of eighty-four, he wrote and published a book with that as its jawbreaking title. Mr. Yancey defined "interpositionullification" to mean that when a state interposed itself between federal laws and the rights of its citizens the result was the nullification of the rights of black people, that the prejudiced person could nullify any just act. As an old man, A. H. Yancey liked to gather his children and grandchildren about him, and talk about interpositionullification, how they must fight and work against it and yet learn to expect its effects when they occurred.

Mr. Yancey lived to see one of his doctor sons killed when, working as an intern in an outdated black hospital in St. Louis, he was accidentally electrocuted by a faultily wired piece of X-ray equipment. It was impossible to sue the city, but the family was given a check for $1,500, which barely covered funeral expenses. A positive result of the accident, however, was the building of a much-needed new hospital, the Homer G. Philips, which became the finest black hospital in St. Louis.

Mr. Yancey liked to tell the children and the grandchildren about his own childhood, growing up in a two-room log cabin with a porch and lean-to in rural Georgia. Most of the Yanceys' neighbors were white and, because the Yanceys were hardworking and God-fearing, they were respected in the neighborhood. As a child, most of Aytch Yancey's friends and playmates were white children but, when they reached a "certain age," the childhood friends became distant and barely spoke. Mr. Yancey remembered when a black man could not call another black man "Mister" in front of a white without fear of reprisal. When he was six years old, Mr. Yancey remembered how he had assumed that he would be going off to school, and how he had been puzzled by the looks of deep distress that came over his parents' faces when-ever he mentioned school. He did not realize that, though there were black taxpayers in the town, there were no black schools. The nearest black school was miles away in another county. The white schoolmaster had offered "to put a few seats in the back of the room" just for the children of Green and Julia Yancey. But the Yanceys had declined this favor, fearing the reaction in both the white and the black com-munities if such an exception were made for their children and if even a small degree of integration were attempted. Two years later, however, Green Yancey succeeded in get-ting a one-room log cabin missionary school established for blacks of the area. Aytch Yancey did not start first grade until he was nearly nine years old.

One youthful memory remained indelible. It was late De-cember 1900, and Aytch Yancey, who was nine years old, and his brother Homer, eleven, were walking across the wooded hills with two young girls to a Christmas-tree party in a nearby hamlet called Frogtown. It was late afternoon, most of the trees were bare of leaves, and the air was cool and crisp, with a promise of frost by nightfall. The children had bundled up against the cold, but their spirits were high and happy, looking forward to lighted candles and gifts under the Christmas tree. Then, at a turn in the narrow woodpath, four white men suddenly appeared. The chil-dren recognized the men. They were the two Cox brothers and the two Edwards boys. The men arrayed themselves across the path, blocking it to the approaching children. One of the Edwards boys was carrying a shotgun.

As the children warily approached, the Edwards boy raised his shotgun, held it across their path, and demanded, "Where in hell you niggers gwine?" Aytch Yancey started to answer the question but, with that, the other Edwards boy walked around his brother's gun, stepped up to one of the little girls, opened her coat, reached under her dress, and seized her breast. She screamed, slapped him full in the face, and then spun past him and ran to safety in the underbrush. In the confusion of shouts and screams that followed, the other little girl managed to make her escape also, leaving Aytch and Homer Yancey faced with four men, one of them armed. The Cox brothers seized Homer and began pummeling him, while the Edwards boy held Aytch at gunpoint. Suddenly the four men had a new idea. They would force the Yancey boys back to their house at gunpoint, and then run after and catch the girls. Aytch Yancey was never certain of what happened next, but somehow, as the Edwards boy shifted his gun from his right arm to his left, he stepped backward and tripped over Aytch Yancey's foot. Aytch Yancey fell, and the Edwards boy stumbled over Aytch's body, did a backward somersault and also fell to the ground. In the process, the butt of the shotgun struck the other Edwards brother in the face, and a shot went off into the air, rendering the gun harmless for a few moments. Aytch and his brother ran off in the direction the girls had taken, with the Cox and Edwards brothers in howling pursuit. Soon the Yanceys managed to outdistance their pursuers, however, and they made their way to the cabin of friends, who took them in for the night. The last shouts the Yanceys heard were to the effect that they would be killed if they ever came back that way again.

Late that night, nine-year-old Aytch Yancey, with a borrowed Winchester rifle, set out through the woods toward home to tell his father what had happened. He arrived home without incident, and his father decided that he and Aytch should set out right away for the friend's cabin and collect the other children. They started off through the deeply wooded trails in the cold night, which was fortunately moonless. Father and son found the other children safe, and headed home with them. It was 1:30 in the morning when they approached their own cabin, but, as they neared it, they knew that something was wrong. The light that should have been burning in the window was not.

The Yanceys entered their darkened home and found the younger children sleeping peacefully in their beds. But Mrs. Yancey was missing. Aytch Yancey's father called, "Julia! Julia!" and then, from a darkened corner of the front room, heard soft moans. Here he found the figure of Julia Yancey, a tiny woman, crumpled and bleeding. Yancey carried his wife into the bedroom and placed her on the bed. Her face was a mass of blood. Aytch Yancey was dispatched to get a doctor because, among other fears, Mr. Yancey knew that his wife was four months pregnant. When Mrs. Yancey regained consciousness, she told her husband what had happened. It was the Cox and Edwards boys. They had come to her door at midnight, and forced their way into the house, demanding money. When Julia Yancey protested that she had none, they called her a liar and began beating her about the face and shoulders with the butt of their rifle. That was the last she remembered. Then the white men had ransacked the house and taken, among other things, $42, which was the childrens' Christmas money. The doctor treated Mrs. Yancey for multiple bruises and contusions, but he was not able to save her unborn child. She miscarried the following morning.

The Cox and Edwards boys were eventually brought to trial and, though their defense attorney attempted to imply that the incident was actually just a case of a black man "beating up on his wife" in a domestic quarrel, character witnesses came forward for both Mr. and Mrs. Yancey, and the four men were convicted by a judge named Gober and sentenced to the penitentiary. It might have seemed as though justice had prevailed, but the story actually had another, more ironic, ending. Some months after the trial, a white politician named Patterson was campaigning for Judge Gober's job, and he came to see Mrs. Yancey. He asked her to sign a petition asking that the sentences of the Cox and Edwards boys be commuted. In return, Patterson promised Julia Yancey that if he won she and her family would never be molested again and would have his "protection." Julia Yancey signed the petition. Patterson ran on a campaign that, among other things, promised that no white Georgia man would ever be sentenced to the chain gang and that used the Yancey case to brand Judge Gober a "nigger lover." Patterson won. At the time, Julia Yancey was severely admonished by the Negro community for signing Patterson's petition, which got the Cox and Edwards boys an early release from prison. But Julia Yancey had signed the petition out of fear and a desire to spare her family from any further trouble with the whites.

The trauma of seeing his mother beaten and brutalized by white hoodlums may account for what happened to Aytch Yancey's older brother Homer. His life turned out quite differently from Aytch's. Homer had been the fairest of the family, with blond hair and blue eyes. When he grew up he worked as a night engineer at the largest ice plant in Atlanta, and it was said that he could have had the job of chief engineer — he looked so white — but for the fact that "everyone knew" that Homer Yancey was a Negro. As a young man, Homer began to express deep shame, even hatred, of having black blood. He married a black girl, but he and his wife soon separated. He was sued for alimony, did not pay, and was thrown into jail. He was released when his first wife died, and he promptly married a girl who he insisted was a Puerto Rican, though his family was certain that she was as much a Negro as Homer was. Homer and his wife tried to invade Atlanta's white society, but were not successful; the fact that Homer was a Negro was too well known. He and his wife were divorced.

Then, in 1920, Homer Yancey decided to resign from the black race. He moved to Chicago, where he married a white girl and — because his origins were not known — successfully joined the whites. In Chicago, Homer Yancey became known for his virulently anti-Negro views. He denounced blacks at public gatherings, and fought against civil rights. He had become a true white supremacist, and preached against social, political, and economic equality for blacks. In Chicago, it was said that "the black man never had a worse enemy than Homer Yancey." At home in Georgia, Homer's picture was turned against the wall and his name was forever banished from family conversation.

Aytch Yancey never talked to the children and the grandchildren about his brother Homer.

VI

Where Are We?

~~ *21* ~~

Dollars and Cents

THE LARGEST BLACK-OWNED BUSINESS IN THE UNITED STATES today is Berry Gordy, Jr.'s, Motown Industries, Inc. Motown employs some 375 people, and has annual sales in the neighborhood of $45,000,000. Next to Motown, John Johnson's publishing company and George Johnson's cosmetics manufacturing firm run just about neck and neck in terms of size, with sales of about $40,000,000 a year each. In the entertainment industry, Motown is something of a phenomenon; it has been in business barely fifteen years. And its president and chairman of the board, Mr. Gordy, has come to be regarded as something of a mystery man. One of the mysteries is: How could a man with so little education and business experience create such a large business in so short a time?

Born about forty-five years ago — he dislikes revealing his age — on Detroit's Lower East Side, the son of a plasterer father and a mother who was an insurance agent, Berry Gordy dropped out of Detroit's Northeastern High School in the eleventh grade to become a featherweight boxer. Gordy is a small, compact man who still weighs a trim 140 pounds, and has a round, not unhandsome face with a nose that looks as though it had been pushed in in a fistfight. It was, several times. Between 1948 and 1951, Gordy fought fifteen Golden Gloves fights, knocking out seven of his opponents and beating five others. Then his boxing career was interrupted when he was drafted into the army and sent to Korea.

When he was discharged in 1953, Gordy returned to Detroit where, using what money he had saved in the army, his discharge pay, and $700 borrowed from his father, Gordy decided to go into the record-store business. "I loved jazz," Gordy says. "Stan Kenton, Thelonius Monk, Charlie Parker — and so I decided to concentrate on jazz. I wanted to let people know I was modern, so I called the place the Three-D Record Mart. But people started coming in and asking for things like Fats Domino. Pretty soon I was asking, 'Who is this Fats Domino? What is this rhythm-and-blues stuff?' I listened and ordered a few records by these people, and sold them. But all my capital was tied up in jazz, and jazz didn't have the facts, man, the beat." The 3-D Record Mart shortly went bankrupt.

For a while, Gordy became what is known as a "street hustler." He did odd jobs. For a while, he worked for his father. Then he took an $85-a-week job with the Ford Motor Company, where he worked on the assembly line, tacking on the upholstery of Lincoln cars. Working at this boring occupation, "to keep from going crazy," Berry Gordy began composing songs in his head. When he got home at night, he wrote them down. On weekend evenings, he roamed around Detroit's nightclubs and bars, trying to interest singing groups in performing his songs. A few did, and a few were placed on records. The results were not distinguished. Finally Gordy decided to try to produce records of his songs himself. He rented a small recording studio, hired some musicians, and put his songs on records, sometimes with himself as vocalist. Periodically, whenever he had enough money scraped together, he set off for New

York to try to persuade the big record companies to listen to his songs and, perhaps, to buy them. His first sale, to Decca, was a song called "Reet Peteet," which Gordy wrote with his sister Gwen. It earned him $1,000. His first real success was with a song called "Way Over There," in 1959. It sold 60,000 copies.

Berry Gordy's greatest talent, some people say, is an ability to listen to good advice when it is given to him. With the success of "Way Over There," a songwriter friend named William Robinson suggested that, instead of selling his titles to record companies from master cuts, Gordy should start mass-producing records under his own label. "Why work for the Man?" Robinson said. "Why not *you* be the Man?" Gordy agreed, and Motown — for "Motor Town," Detroit's nickname, was born. Another $700 — which seems to have been Gordy's favorite borrowing figure — was obtained from his father and, in 1960, "Shop Around" was the first song published under the new Motown label. The song had been written by Robinson, who was then only nineteen years old, and performed by his group, Smokey Robinson and the Miracles. Within a year, a million copies of "Shop Around" had been sold, and Motown was on its way.

But despite the success of "Shop Around," the young company had definite growing pains. Berry Gordy, it began to seem, might be a tough and able administrator of his new company and might possess an ear for hit songs. But he was not a particularly talented money manager. One of the problems in the beginning was that Gordy had relied on financially shaky independent distributors to place the record before the public. When the first record became a hit, a number of these overextended themselves in order to handle the sudden volume. It began to seem as though — though Motown was earning a lot of money on paper — there was going to be some difficulty collecting the money owed the company in cash. The distributors, who had borrowed heavily to handle the unexpected volume, could not pay their own bills and could not pay Motown. Incredibly, it also began to seem as though the cost of a hit might be another bankruptcy for Gordy. But at that point Gordy's sister stepped in, took over the collection of the money that was owed, and managed to raise enough cash to keep the company going.

Gordy, meanwhile, busied himself by rounding up bright young songwriters and performers. He plucked the Supremes — Diana Ross and her friends Florence Ballard and Mary Wilson — right out of high school. (Miss Ross had already earned a certain reputation locally for her singing in a Detroit Baptist church.) Along the way, he also found Marvin Gaye, the Four Tops, Martha and the Vandellas, Stevie Wonder, and the Temptations. Gordy wanted to develop what he called "the Motown sound," a style he describes as "a combination of rats, roaches, dirty dishes, and soul, but that's really a ghetto sound. It could happen in Harlem, Chicago, or anyplace else." He divided his company into three divisions — Hitsville, U.S.A., which controls the company's recording studios; the Jobete Music Company — an acronym from the first names of Gordy's three children, Hazel Joy, Berry, and Terry — which holds and markets the copyrights on songs written by Gordy himself; and the division called International Talent Management, Inc., a "finishing school" for Motown's performing artists.

International Talent Management was an unusual operation in many ways. Since Motown's artists were for the most part young blacks who had grown up in the ghetto or on the streets and who lacked any degree of sophistication, Gordy decided that it was important that they learn to present themselves properly and attractively to the public. In his school, performers were taught how to speak, walk, shake hands — "a firm grip is most important" — how to sit, smile, pose for a photographer, and how to hop up onto a piano.

Performers were given lessons in makeup, grooming — "a bath at least once a day is most important" — and stage choreography. Sometimes it took as long as six months for a performer to complete the course to Gordy's satisfaction. Even more valuable lessons were given in money management and how to avoid the temptation of high living and compulsive spending that often overtakes people who suddenly, and with no preparation, find themselves with large amounts of money in their hands. A singer's professional life — like an athlete's — is often brief, and Motown's young performers were reminded that poorhouses are full of old performers who, once upon a time, made thousands. At Gordy's "school," performers were instructed in the difference between a checking account and a savings account, the difference between a stock and a bond. They were taught about tax shelters and investments, and were reminded of something many of the young performers had never heard of — the existence of the Internal Revenue Service.

In his record-publishing business, Gordy decided to go after hits rather than volume. He held down the weekly output to one or two titles, less than half the production of other record companies. To get the quality of sound he wanted for a hit song, Gordy sometimes insisted on dozens of retakes on a recording before he was satisfied. With this tactic, Gordy soon managed to boast that three out of every four Motown songs were hits — an unusually high average in the record industry. Motown's most successful group, in all likelihood, was Diana Ross and the Supremes, and Gordy likes to say that he "made" the Supremes. It is probably equally true that the Supremes made Berry Gordy. In any case, by 1967 Motown was grossing $30,000,000 a year in record sales.

At the same time, Gordy and his financially savvy sister were keeping Motown's overhead low, operating out of eight ramshackle houses on both sides of Detroit's West

Grand Boulevard. In 1970, however, Gordy decided that, despite Motown, Detroit would never be an entertainment capital, and that he should move his company to the heart of things: Hollywood. The company now operates out of the tenth and penthouse floors of an eleven-story building on Sunset Boulevard.

On the West Coast, Motown continued to expand. To-day, as chairman of the board and president of Motown Industries, Inc., Berry Gordy controls not only the Motown Record Corporation (which still maintains offices and re-cording studios in Detroit) but other subsidiary companies, including Jobete Music, Stone Diamond Music Corporation, Stein & Van Stock, Inc. (all music publishing firms), Motown, Inc. (a New York production office), Motown-Weston-Furre Productions — which was formed to produce the movie *Lady Sings the Blues* — and Multimedia Management, which evolved from Gordy's International Talent Management Corporation. Gordy likes to say that his business was built on "love and character." He does not claim much business acumen, and for the last several years his chief business mentor has been a white New Yorker named Michael Roskind. Roskind is credited with Motown's expansion into motion pictures, television, and Broadway theatre. There have also been rumors of "other interests moving in" to Motown. These Gordy hotly denies.

Berry Gordy usually refers to himself grandly in the third person as "the company president," and he is a cheerful believer in wholesale nepotism. His mother, father, brothers, sisters, and in-laws are all on the company president's payroll. Gordy's life-style is expansive, not to say extravagant. He is a ferocious golfer, often travels with his personal golf pro, and becomes even more ferocious when he loses a match, breaking expensive golf clubs across his knee five at a time. Clearly, the rules of thrift and prudence that his company tries to impress upon its artists do not apply to Berry Gordy, Jr. He loves to gamble, and frequently jets to Las Vegas, where he always sports a large bankroll. His collection of silk and velvet suits in every color of the rainbow is legendary, as is his collection of huge, floppy pocket scarves and neckties. He owns more monogrammed silk shirts than a Jay Gatsby could have wished for in his wildest dreams. Berry Gordy loves parties and pretty girls — he has been married and divorced twice — and for some time his relationship with Diana Ross was so well publicized that it was assumed the two would marry. At the time Gordy commented, "We haven't chosen to be married for several reasons." Then he laughed and added that he had "tried to marry her a couple of times. But why should she marry me when she's got me already? She's free, rich, and talented. Get married for what?" Shortly thereafter, Diana Ross married a white publicist named Robert Ellis — apparently to Gordy's distinct surprise. A Motown official commented, "The whole company is surprised and hurt by it."

In manner, the company president is autocratic and aloof — and often rude. When, at the suggestion of his financial advisor, Mr. Roskind, Gordy put money into the Broadway musical *Pippin,* he was invited to the customary backers' audition. Gordy yawned and fidgeted all through the first act, and then wanted to leave. The show's producer, Stuart Ostrow, said to him, "You can't do that, Mr. Gordy. It would be an insult to the director and the entire cast and company." So Gordy remained for the second act, looking bored. Now that *Pippin* has paid back Gordy's original investment of $135,000 at a ratio of five to one, with more money still to come, Gordy has taken to calling himself "The producer of *Pippin,*" which amuses the actual producer, Mr. Ostrow. "He wasn't even a major backer," Ostrow says.

In Beverly Hills, Gordy bought the ranch-style mansion

of comedian Tommy Smothers and decorated it in a lavish style that almost, but not quite, defeats his personal style. "Give me a drop-dead house," he told his decorator, and the decorator complied. "In that house, little Berry almost gets lost in all the mirrors, silver brocade, and gold lamé," one friend says. The house is the scene of Mr. Gordy's most opulent parties, and its most arresting feature is perhaps the life-size portrait of the diminutive president of Motown that hangs in the dining room. It depicts a bearded Berry Gordy dressed in full imperial regalia, posing as Napoleon.

Another friend says of Gordy, "He flashes money like an old-time street person. He's basically still a street hustler from Detroit."

There are some thoughtful blacks who think that there may be a kind of conspiracy — perhaps an unwitting one — among the media, including such publications as *Ebony* and the *Amsterdam News,* to overemphasize and overpublicize black money success as a means to keep blacks from advancing farther. "There's so much printed about successful blacks and 'black millionaires,' " one man says, "that pretty soon, when we try to get even closer to equality with whites in the business world, white folks are gonna say, '*What?* They want *more?* Haven't those niggers got enough already?' " It is true that black business success must be kept in perspective and that, compared with white wealth, black wealth is still very small. Berry Gordy's Motown is pint-sized compared with Columbia Records. George Johnson's entire cosmetics company may do a business of $40,000,000 a year, but Revlon has annual sales at that figure for a single feminine deodorant spray. All the black-owned banks in the United States combined would not have assets equal to those of a single branch of the Bank of America or the Chase Manhattan. With his annual check of $5,000 to the Urban

League, John Johnson is one of the League's most important individual philanthropic sources. He could never ap-
proach the largesse of a John Davison Rockefeller, who, in
his lifetime, gave away more than $600,000,000. In every
American black success story, it is important to remember
that these men have been successful not as Americans, but *as
blacks*. The share of black money is still painfully, and
disproportionately, tiny.

It is clear that blacks have been most successful in business in the largest cities. Of the one hundred largest and
richest black-owned companies in the United States, eighteen are in the greater New York area. Twelve are in Chicago, and eight are in or around Los Angeles. Five are in
Detroit, and five are in Philadelphia. Four are in Washington, D. C. It is interesting to note in which business areas
blacks have been the most successful. Of the hundred top
firms, nineteen are either supermarkets or food distributors
or processors. Eighteen are automobile dealerships, led by
the Al Johnson Cadillac agency of Chicago — Mr. Johnson
was the first black to be granted a dealership by General
Motors — or dealers in automotive accessories. Seventeen
are construction firms or building contractors. Eleven are
publishers of music, newspapers, or magazines, and four are
beer or liquor dealers. There are a handful of manufacturers — one of plastics, one of electronics, one of chocolate,
and one of sausage. It is also worth noting that, of the top
one hundred businesses, only fifteen can boast sales of
$10,000,000 a year or more. Sixty have sales of $5,000,000 a
year or less. The smallest, a plate glass company in Yonkers,
New York, has an annual business of just over $2,000,000,
clearly no threat to Owens-Corning-Fiberglas, nor do black
businesses control a significant share of the American
economy.

Blacks have tended to do well in business areas that involve sales and services — particularly services to other blacks. They have done less well in manufacturing, with the exception of companies that manufacture black cosmetics. One woman who has been particularly successful in the area of services is Mrs. Freddye Scarborough Henderson of Atlanta, who, in the early 1950's, organized her Henderson Travel Service, the first fully appointed black travel agency in the United States — "fully appointed" meaning that Henderson Travel is licensed to handle domestic, international, and steamship travel. Freddye Henderson, a vivacious brown-skinned lady, got into the travel business almost by accident. She had studied fashion design at New York University and, when she had her degree — the first black woman to earn a degree in fashion merchandising — she went to Europe to look behind the scenes of such houses as Dior, Fontana, and Hardy Amies. She was impressed with the way the tour was handled and decided to try the tour business for herself. She picked Atlanta because it was a center of black money and because black Atlantans have a tradition of culture.

"Blacks, even those with money, used to feel insecure about travel," Mrs. Henderson says. "You didn't know where you'd be welcome, or where you'd be kicked around. The attitude used to be, 'Heck, I can get kicked around at home for free — why travel?' But those attitudes have changed." Mrs. Henderson's company has achieved a number of firsts in the travel business. It was the first to organize tours to Africa for culture and not just to look at animals. It was the first agency, black or white, to put together group tours to Ghana, beginning in 1957, when Ghana gained its independence, and it was through Mrs. Henderson that Pan-American inaugurated regular flights to Accra. (On a Henderson tour, a Ghana visitor can have the dubious pleasure of visiting an old slave castle and seeing other grim reminders of the slave trade.) Hers was the first black firm to receive the Africa Trophy — in 1972 for excellence in African tour production and operation. She was also the first black agent to reach a million dollars in yearly volume.

Mrs. Henderson does a lively business in tours from church and professional groups — not only to Africa but to other parts of the world. Winter cruises to the West Indies and the South Pacific are also popular. She has devised innovative tours, such as a trip to Japan with a way stop in the Holy Land. "I try to sell the idea to blacks that travel is prestige," she says. "Blacks want prestige. Often, they would rather spend money on a trip to Europe or a West Indies cruise than on a house. And when black people travel, they don't want the bottom line. They want first class." Mrs. Henderson thinks rather little of Professor Frazier's criticism of blacks' conspicuous spending on luxury travel and expensive wardrobes to go with it. "Blacks have always been good-time-oriented," she says. "Why, when they have the money, shouldn't they spend some of it on good times — travel, nice luggage, nice clothes? Isn't that more fun than spending it on some dreary stocks or bonds?"

Apparently Mrs. Henderson's philosophy is paying off. She has one client, a black Atlanta lawyer, who spends $25,000 a year on travel through her agency. Another black couple takes their four grandchildren on a different grand tour of Europe every year. Her volume has already reached $2,000,000 a year. Considering the fact that the average *white* travel agency does about $1,000,000 a year, Henderson Travel is doing double the average. Freddye Henderson's son Jacob has joined her in the business, where, he says airily, "My main ambition in life is to become a capitalist."

With a twinkle in her eye, Freddye Henderson — who does all the right things to get to know the leaders of the black community, such as serving as president of the Atlanta

Links — says, "Black travel in this country is potentially a *billion dollar* business."

In recent years, a number of blacks have been given positions of responsibility in white businesses, where, their white co-workers notice, they often seem ill at ease, faintly hostile, even somewhat rude (the black bank teller, for example, who, though beautifully dressed and groomed, chews gum as he works). When blacks work alongside whites, there is nearly always a touch of racial tension in the air. At Saks Fifth Avenue not long ago, a black salesgirl was waiting on a customer who absentmindedly walked off without her change. The girl called after the customer, who returned, thanked her, and accepted her change. A fellow salesgirl, white, said jokingly to the black girl, "I'll bet you wish she hadn't heard you." The black girl was furious, thinking it a racial slur. Most blacks admit that they are still most comfortable in all-black situations. (At schools and colleges, as well as at West Point, Annapolis, and the Air Force Academy, it is noticed that black students stick together.) White people, too, still feel most comfortable with other whites. "It's a funny thing," says one white man. "I don't feel that I'm a prejudiced person. But there are some blacks I can talk to and, after a minute or two, I completely forget they're black. But there are others whom I talk to, and the whole time — whether it's their looks, their speech, or something in their eyes — I'm self-consciously aware that they're black and I'm white. It's a kind of chemistry. I don't understand it."

It is a chemistry based on color of skin, and fear. A white visitor to a black doctor's office on Harlem's Strivers' Row asked nervously, at the end of the visit, "Will I have trouble finding a taxi?" A black patient, sensing the white man's uneasiness, offered to walk with him to Seventh Avenue, and waited with him until a taxi appeared — for which the white man was most grateful.

On Washington's Fourteenth Street, a white boy, with a camera slung around his neck, was waiting for a bus. He was approached by a black youth, who said something to him that he didn't understand. "I beg your pardon?" the white boy said. The black youth repeated the remark, which the white boy still could not understand. What the black was saying was "Gimme that camera." But the white boy kept repeating, "I beg your pardon? I beg your pardon?" And this innocent tactic worked. The black youth finally shrugged, and walked away.

Of course the blacks reply, "This could have happened to a black child too — if he was out of his own neighborhood."

What, in the end, is the solution to fear? How can such a powerful and yet helpless emotion as fear be dealt with — whites' fear of blacks, blacks' fear of whites, and blacks' fear of other blacks? Fear is at the heart of every busing controversy, every housing dispute, and fear, unfortunately, is something no government can legislate against. It is fear that makes the white executive feel, anxiously, that he should have more blacks on his payroll if only for the appearance of things, and that makes the black employee suspicious of his white employer when he is hired. It is fear that makes the white college professor give a black student a passing grade when, perhaps, he has not quite earned it, and that makes a black student scornful of a teacher who would give him such a grade. Fear causes a black patient to prefer a white doctor when he can afford one. Fear is what has kept George Johnson, already so successful in black cosmetics, unwilling to move on into products for whites, even though he is perfectly equipped to do so. All these fears, of course, are self-defeating.

These fears are rather like the self-closing doors that

Charlotte Hawkins Brown warned about. "Take a firm hold on the knob," she advised, "turn it gently, pull the door open at least two-thirds of the way so as not to touch either the door or door jamb, pause for just a second to recognize the person who may be looking your way. . . ."

Doors can be frightening things. "Do not make the mistake of letting a self-closing door push you into the room," she wrote. Or push you out of it, she might have added.

22

Heroes

THE OLD GUARD, OF COURSE, IS LESS BUSINESS-ORIENTED, LESS impressed with the money success of the newer-arrived entrepreneurs. "After all," says one woman, "Negroes have also made money in prostitution, gambling, the numbers racket, and drug peddling. A lot of these new 'millionaires,' I suspect, have rather shady pasts. I know a lot of rich doctors, for example, who, before they were legal, made pots of money performing illegal abortions on poor black women for huge fees. Most of these rich men made their money by exploiting their own race." The Old Guard tends to look, instead, to the past for its heroes — to men and women like Booker T. Washington, William E. B. DuBois, Mary Church Terrell, Charlotte Hawkins Brown, Frederick Douglass, Mary McLeod Bethune — who worked to gain cooperation with the whites in order to win a series of quiet victories for the Negro race.

The trouble is, no two members of the Old Guard can quite agree on who the greatest black hero of history was. Some champion Frederick Douglass, the great Abolitionist, who was recently honored by having his likeness placed on a United States postage stamp. But others disparage Douglass for having taken, as his second wife, a white woman who took him into the purlieus of white society in Washington, where he seemed to take on rather grand and patronizing airs. Dr. William Edward Burkhardt DuBois and Dr. Booker Taliaferro Washington — the former from New England and the latter from the South, and both with imposingly long names — never did see eye to eye on anything. Many of the Old Guard subscribe to the theories of Dr. DuBois, who wanted to create an aristocracy out of "the talented tenth" of the black population by giving them the kind of education offered at Harvard. But Dr. DuBois's theories are questioned by some because, in later life, DuBois got his views all mixed up with Marxian socialism. Others lean toward the beliefs of Booker T. Washington, who preached a gospel of advancement through hard work, thrift, and industrial education. Those who side with Booker T. Washington insist that, if the philosophy he laid down during his lifetime had been carried on and forward at Tuskegee after his death, Tuskegee today would be as great an institution as M.I.T.

Washington's detractors say that his reputation and success were based on a conciliatory and accommodating attitude toward the white community, that he demeaned himself before whites, that he was guilty of obsequiousness and bootlicking, that he was an original Uncle Tom. And yet Booker T. Washington had to work within the framework of the white social power structure that existed in the South at the time. Had he not been able to ingratiate himself a bit with the white community, to make compromises with it and concessions to it, it is doubtful that the Sage of Tuskegee would have ever been able to create his college at all. One must often "accommodate" in order to survive. Washington placed economic solutions to blacks' problems above political solutions, and at least one black historian, Lerone Bennett, Jr., accuses Washington of "a fatal misunderstanding of the connection between politics and economics and an equally fatal misunderstanding of the forces of the age." Mr. Bennett also downgrades Booker T. Washington by saying that he was "only one of several voices of the embryonic middle class [and] . . . was challenged in his lifetime by several men, notably John Hope and W. E. B. DuBois." Clearly, Mr. Bennett is a DuBois man.

But Booker T. Washington himself was one of the great forces of the age. A former teacher at Tuskegee recalls the "almost mystical" power of his presence and his words, and says, "We were all so instilled with his philosophy that everything he said was like the word of God Himself." His faculty and staff worshipped him. He rode around the Tuskegee campus on horseback, a majestic figure, inspecting everything. He was obsessed with tidiness and cleanliness and, dismounting from his horse during his tours of inspection, he ran his white handkerchief over desktops and bookshelves, checking for dust. He inspected the dormitories and the libraries, the laboratories and the lavatories. In one washroom, fitted out with a washbowl, soap, water pitcher, and towels, he lifted the water pitcher and found it empty. "How," he asked, "is one expected to wash one's hands without water?" He often dropped in, unannounced, on Tuskegee classrooms, just to see how his teachers were doing. One former teacher, who worked in Tuskegee's kindergarten department, remembers how Dr. Washington visited her classroom one autumn morning. He entered the room quietly, as usual, and took a seat at the back of the room. The teacher, as was customary, made no acknowledgment of his arrival, and continued with her class. She had drawn with colored chalks on the blackboard a frond of goldenrod, and she then read to her children a little poem about the pretty goldenrod and how it grew. After a few minutes, Dr. Washington rose and just as quietly departed. But he returned a few moments later with a stalk of live goldenrod in his hand. Gently, he asked the teacher, "Why go to the trouble of drawing a goldenrod on the blackboard, when the real thing is growing right outside the door?"

He was a spellbinding speaker, with a gift for vivid metaphor. In one memorable speech before a black audience he held up his hand, spread his fingers wide, and said, "In all things social, we can be as separate as the fingers on a hand. But, as the palm of the hand, we must be as one when it comes to the good of the country." But he was not pompous, and had a wry sense of humor. He once commented, "Whenever you see a Negro who's not a Baptist or a Methodist, you know some white man has been messin' with his religion." Booker T. Washington's detractors often point out that while he may have been a great orator and teacher, none of his children amounted to much. The children of Franklin D. Roosevelt and Winston Churchill did not amount to much either.

But Booker T. Washington died over sixty years ago. All the great charismatic leaders — DuBois, Douglass, Garvey, and the three named ladies, Mary McLeod Bethune, Mary Church Terrell, Charlotte Hawkins Brown — have gone. So has Martin Luther King, Jr. The closest thing to a black leader in recent times has been Elijah Muhammad, but he too has died, and his son, Wallace, who has succeeded his father as head of the Nation of Islam, possesses only a shadow of his father's electrifying personality and power. There is no single, unifying leader in black America today (to which blacks counter that neither is there a great white leader) . Though Berry Gordy heads the leading black business in America, no one would call him America's greatest black business leader. John Johnson's magazines influence many black people, but John Johnson himself could not be called a leading force in black American life. It has been suggested that, with the power of his publications behind him, John Johnson could run for President. But Johnson expresses no interest in politics, and his aloof and enigmatic personality make him seem unsuited to it. Who is the Great Black Hope today? If he exists, no one knows his name, or hers.

Instead of leaders, there are factions, and factions within factions. The Old Guard looks askance at the newer-rich, and the "visiting friends" just visit one another. The newer-rich ridicule the Old Guard. The blacks in the South think little of the blacks in the North, and vice versa. The educators and professional people disdain the businessmen. The Episcopalians and Congregationalists think little of the Methodists and Baptists. The rich dislike and distrust the poor, and the poor hate the rich. Well-to-do blacks often despair of the poor. In New York, Guichard Parris, a long-time Urban League official, says, "There are children growing up in Harlem today whose parents have never done a day's work in their lives. Their grandparents have never worked, and their *great*-grandparents have never worked. You have families who, for five generations, have survived on one form of charity or another. How can you talk about a 'work ethic' to people who don't know what work is?" The talk, in this fractured world, of "Brotherhood" and "Sisterhood" has no real meaning, and these are terms that describe a situation that does not exist. A black traveler, returning from abroad, will not stand in a line that has a black customs inspector; he knows that his luggage will be more thoroughly ransacked for possible costly contraband than that of white travelers. Black entertainers and athletes exist in a social limbo of their own. Their success is assumed to have been based not on education or business acumen, but merely on good looks or muscle. Instead of racial unity there is disunity.

Blacks cannot agree on what to call themselves — black, Negro, colored, or something else. Guichard Parris uses the terms "black" and "Negro" interchangeably, but his wife, who is fairer-skinned, refuses to use either term and the Parrises have been at an impasse over this throughout their marriage of nearly fifty years. Blacks cannot agree on what white motives really are, whether whites really want to help the Negro race or hold it back. Some successful black men — like Chicago's late Dr. T. R. M. Howard — have given full credit to white benefactors for their achievements. Others, like George Johnson, say they had to fight a white Establishment all the way. At an integrated party at the penthouse apartment of Dr. William Clarke, another prominent black Chicago physician, a discussion started on the subject of whether a white person "could ever really understand what it is like to be black." The discussion quickly turned into a rout, with blacks shouting profanities at each other, and the white guests fleeing through the kitchen door.

Dr. Clarke's three slender, handsome, college-age sons, meanwhile, are models of good manners and decorum — full of bows, handshakes, "sirs," and "thank yous." Dr. Clarke drills his boys with the authority of a Marine sergeant; whenever they appear, he peppers them with questions about their studies, about current affairs, about politics, science, and the Bible. To be sure, he gambles with them, and once, when one of his sons had won quite a bit of money from his father at cards, Clarke would not let the boy leave the game until he had won the money back. Like parents everywhere, successful blacks worry about their children: What will become of the next generation? John Johnson's son, a high school dropout, got married at nineteen, and he and his wife live in his parents' vast apartment. John Johnson, Jr., is interested in motorcycles, fast cars, airplanes — "anything fast, man," he says. The Johnsons' daughter, Linda, grumbles when the chauffeur is not available to take her where she wants to go. At a family luncheon party at the Johnsons', guests wondered why the young people, who were at home at the time, did not join the family at the table; they took their lunch on trays in their rooms.

Barbara Proctor's only son is a withdrawn, introspective, studious teenager. The Eugene Dibbles' children, on the other hand, are lively, outgoing, family-proud — having worked together to draw up the massive family tree connecting their family with their cousins in Africa — proud of their continuing connection with the Mount Hermon school in Massachusetts, each child firmly set on a future career: one to be a doctor, one already with his own car-washing business (the boy offers visitors his printed business card). In other words, successful blacks probably have the same degree of success — and failure — with their children as successful whites.

Blacks cannot agree on whether black businesses should employ blacks or whites. John Johnson's staff is almost a hundred percent black. Barbara Proctor, on the other hand, in her Chicago advertising agency, prefers to hire bright young whites right out of college for her copywriters. Blacks cannot agree on issues-of-the-moment such as busing and integrated schools. Most of the Old Guard are opposed to busing, and consider it an absurd crusade conducted by misguided whites and lower-class blacks. They point to the distinguished and successful men and women who have come out of all-black schools like Palmer and Dunbar High School, and out of black colleges like Lincoln and Howard Universities. Guichard Parris says, "I just won't buy the idea that a Negro can't get a decent education unless he's in an integrated situation. If you say that, it's the same as saying there's no chance for anyone in black Africa." Parris, however, a New Yorker since 1916, who went to Amherst — where he was one of nine blacks, six of them from Dunbar High School — never knew that there were black colleges in the South until he learned of them from his fellow blacks at Amherst. If there is one thing that there is some agreement on, it is that "we've got to change the system." But no one is exactly sure what "the system" is.

Is it housing patterns? Is it discrimination within the labor unions? Housing patterns have been breaking down — albeit slowly — in many cities, and so has discrimination in the unions. Is it the "system" that prevents George Johnson from expanding his business into manufacturing cosmetics for white people? In fact, George Johnson's products could be sold to whites right now. It is a myth that skins of different colors require different cosmetics. A shade of mascara or face-powder tint will work equally well on a white face and on a black, and black hair-straightening products will straighten white curly hair also. All that Johnson would have to do, he admits, would be to start advertising his Ultra-Sheen line to whites and, if that didn't work — if the "black" connotations proved too strong to make Ultra-Sheen acceptable to whites — he could issue the same products under a different label. And yet he is timid. The system seems not quite ready for that, and besides, he is happy with the success he already has.

No one seems to agree on what success is, or how it is best attained. Is success money and possessions, as *Ebony* seems to say? Is it a good education, followed by a useful professional life, as Mary Gibson Hundley would insist? Is success achieved by dogged hard work and perseverance, as it was in the case of John and George Johnson, neither of whom went to college? Is it achieved by sheer luck, as seems to have been the case with Berry Gordy, who happened to have some lucky hits? For Barbara Proctor, success has alienated her from her mother and sister, neither of whom understands what she does or approves of it, since she leaves her son at home with sitters. There is one thing, however, that nearly all blacks agree on: a great deal, in the end, depends upon the color of your skin, and the shape of your facial features. It is as the Jews often say: "If you have a cute nose, you smell like a rose." Blacks agree that if you have light skin and white features — or, in the current vernacular, "keen" features — you have a better chance in business. Features are even more important than color of skin. People with *black* skin and keen features also have an advantage in the business world, and in the world of entertainment. Most blacks believe that it is best to have "a nice brown color in between," minimized Negro features, and that the person with black skin and Negro features, or even light skin and Negro features, is at a disadvantage. Such a person should not attempt a career in business or show business, and should compromise by going into one of the professions, the clergy, or the civil service. The rule could almost be stated as a mathematical formula: fair skin plus white features equals money, social acceptance, integration. The unspoken corollary of this rule, of course, is that it is better to have white ancestors.

If having "Negro features" is still at least a psychological handicap for a black man or woman, it might be supposed that there would be a heavy demand for cosmetic surgery among these people, just as Jewish children born with prominent noses routinely have them bobbed at a certain age. There is no shortage of skilled black surgeons; in fact, some white doctors claim that blacks make particularly good surgeons because they have especially deft and agile hands. But the fact is that people with black skin have a tendency, for some reason, to develop keloids — white, welt-like scar tissue — as a result of surgery. The lighter the skin, the less chance there is of keloids developing. And so, ironically, the blacks most willing to take the risk of facial surgery are those with the least need for it. Light-skinned, white-featured Doris Zollar says that she would certainly consider having her face lifted "if and when the time comes." A black-skinned friend would not. Many blacks, meanwhile, correct protruding teeth with orthodonture.

And yet why do some blacks achieve success while others, with similar background, equal intelligence, equal opportunities, and similar appearances, do not? In many cases, a kind of achievement drive seems to have been instilled in individuals by certain families for generations. Wade H. McCree, Jr., for example, is a United States circuit judge from Detroit who has honorary doctorate of laws degrees from seven different universities, from Tuskegee to Harvard. He was the first black placed on Harvard's Board of Overseers. When Thurgood Marshall became the first black appointee to the United States Supreme Court, many people thought that Wade McCree was better qualified than Marshall and should have been the one appointed. (Was it because Mr. Justice Marshall has "whiter looks" than Judge McCree?) Achievement, a sense of justice, and a sense of history have been an integral part of the McCree family's life for a long time (a distant McCree ancestor is said to be Robert E. Lee). Wade McCree's mother graduated from Fisk and taught in the South for a while with Mary McLeod Bethune. At one point, McCree's mother and another teacher purchased a ticket for a black sharecropper who was being pursued for not paying a debt, and helped him escape north to Pittsburgh. At the time, Mary Bethune criticized the two women for "not being consistent with the system."

Wade McCree's paternal grandfather escaped from slavery in the Carolinas by swimming the Ohio River near Evansville and made his way to Illinois, where he joined Thomas's army, and fought in the Battle of Franklin and Nashville. McCree's father had been a dining car porter, and, on his trips across the country, he fell in love with the State of Iowa and decided to settle there. With the help of a black doctor in Des Moines, the senior McCree attended pharmaceutical school and opened the first black drugstore in Des Moines. During World War I, a black Officer Candidate School was opened at Fort Des Moines, and Mr. Mc-

Cree operated what amounted to a black U.S.O. from a big room that was available above his store. His sister, Wade McCree's Aunt Mary Ellen, knew all the local girls and so, as McCree says, "There isn't a black officer from World War One who doesn't know my family."

After the war, however, there were business reverses, and the family moved back to Massachusetts, where McCree's mother had many relatives. In Boston, where Wade McCree attended Boston Latin School, where admission was by competitive examination only, McCree's father worked as a federal narcotics inspector, a job he disliked. With his training, he felt, he should have been made a supervisor, but instead he was moved here and there about the country on assignments, and kept in his place. Mr. McCree wanted to institute a narcotics education program; it was turned down by his superior. At one point he inspected a drugstore, found some discrepancies, and reported them. A Boston Congressman wanted him to change his report. He refused and, for this, his son recalls, "He was given a lot of dirty jobs."

Still, growing up in Boston was pleasant. The McCrees lived in a comfortable house in an integrated neighborhood — Leonard Bernstein was one of Wade McCree's boyhood neighbors — and Mrs. McCree conducted what amounted to a salon. Young black students and educators who came to Boston made the McCree house their headquarters in the days when blacks could not stay in hotels. Roland Hayes, the tenor, was a frequent visitor, as were Wade McCree's favorite aunt and uncle, Aunt Laura and Uncle Julius. Aunt Laura ran a beauty parlor in Northampton, Massachusetts, where she dressed the hair of all the Smith College girls, and she was definitely an intellectual. Uncle Julius, an erudite man, had a vast library. Wade McCree grew up in an atmosphere of music, scholarship, and literature. Good conversation was encouraged, and reading. As a boy, Wade McCree fed himself avidly on a diet of Shakespeare, Byron,

Keats, Hawthorne, and Thackeray. He read the old *Compton Encyclopedia* in its entirety, and devoured Redpath's *Universal History*.

He loved to listen to the stories Grandpa Harper, his mother's father, told. Grandpa Harper *talked* history. He talked of all the heroes — black and white — of the past, of Booker T. Washington and Abraham Lincoln, of Frederick Douglass and General Stonewall Jackson. Heroes were his theme. Though Grandpa Harper did not have a heroic occupation — he was a janitor at the Boston State House on Beacon Hill — he was always sure to make his grandchildren aware of visiting heroes when they came to Boston. When Charles Lindbergh came to Boston on his tour after his heroic flight, Grandpa Harper saw to it that his grandchildren got a spot front and center on the State House steps, where he could lift them up and give them a good view of Lindbergh's face.

When Grandpa Harper had had a drink or two, he would tell the children about how Stonewall Jackson had been killed by his own troops. Grandpa Harper's father, Great-Grandpa Harper, had been a sexton at the church where Stonewall Jackson worshipped, and when the Confederate general was killed in 1863, it had been Great-Grandpa Harper's job to dig Stonewall Jackson's grave. When the grave was finished, Great-Grandpa Harper lifted his young son into the grave and said, "Now you can tell your grandchildren that you were in Stonewall Jackson's grave before he was." It is a story that has been told in the McCree family for over a hundred years, and through six generations. Wade McCree now tells *his* grandchildren, "Your Great-Great-Grandpa Harper was in Stonewall Jackson's grave before he was."

Booker T. Washington was the hero and inspiration for Mary McLeod Bethune and her Daytona Institute, which later became Bethune-Cookman College. When she was a young woman, Booker T. Washington appeared to Mary Bethune in a dream. In the dream, she was sitting forlornly at the bank of a broad river when a man on horseback came riding up to her. He was wearing a uniform and perspiring from a hard ride and, as he drew near her, he dropped his horse's reins and the horse stood still in front of her.

"Who are you?" the man asked.

"I am Mary McLeod Bethune."

"Why are you sitting there, and why do you look so sad?"

"I am trying to think how I am going to build my school," she replied.

The man on the horse said, "I am Booker T. Washington," and he pulled from his pocket a handkerchief as though to wipe his brow. But as he opened the handkerchief Mary Bethune saw that within it was wrapped a large and glittering diamond. "This is for you with which to build your school," he said, and handed her the stone. Then he rode away. When Mary Bethune awoke, the vivid dream and the vision of the shining stone stayed with her.

Mary Bethune did not actually meet Booker T. Washington until several years later. By then, her school — helped not by diamonds but by philanthropies of such people as James M. Gamble (of Procter & Gamble, who supplied her not only with money but also with cases of Crisco and Ivory Soap), John D. Rockefeller, Jr., Madame C. J. Walker, and the Carnegie Foundation — had already opened.

Like Booker T. Washington, Mary Bethune believed that Negroes should learn useful skills, and her Daytona women students were taught home economics, cooking, and housekeeping. Her greatest appeal was therefore to the blacker group, and to women who were less well off. These, as she used to say, were "my black girls" — not the fair-skinned daughters of doctors and lawyers and clergymen who went to Palmer. It was easy for the fair-skinned group to laugh at Mary Bethune. She took herself, and what she saw as her great mission in life, with such terrible seriousness. Though intimates called her "Mama Bethune," and those less intimate referred to her, almost worshipfully, as "Mother Bethune," she loved the thunder-roll sound of her full name, "Mary McLeod Bethune" and to hear herself presented at the speaker's dais with, "Ladies and gentlemen, I present — *Mary McLeod Bethune!"*

She was the first of seventeen children of a slave family to be born to freedom, and for this fact alone she considered herself "different" and special, even Heaven-sent. She liked to tell of how, when she was born, her mother held her up to show to her father and said, "She is a child of prayer, Samuel! I asked the master to send us a child who would show us the way out!" And how, at the time, her old grandmother, sitting in her rocking chair and puffing her corncob pipe, cried out "Thank you, Master, for another grandchild! This is a different one. Thank you, Lord!"

Mary Bethune was a heavy woman, but she carried her weight with dignity, even majesty, and with what some people thought a bit of pomposity. But to watch Mary Bethune come into a room was like watching the entrance of a reigning monarch. Mary Bethune's critics also say that she made too much of her "close friendship" with Mrs. Eleanor Roosevelt, whom Mary Bethune met when she became president of the National Association of Colored Women, that she used her White House connections for publicity purposes, and that she "tried to ride on Mrs. Roosevelt's coattails."

Mary Bethune thought of herself as the most important Negro woman of the twentieth century, if not of all time, and probably as the most important Negro *person.* Surely this was one reason for the break-up of her marriage to Albertus Bethune after barely ten years. He went home to

North Carolina, where he died of tuberculosis in 1919, while she went on to greater and greater things. Her sense of her own importance was, to some people, ludicrous. Grace Hamilton of Atlanta recalls telephoning Mrs. Bethune at one point to ask her support on some program Mrs. Hamilton was then involved in, and Mrs. Bethune's reply: "My dear, you have nothing to worry about. *I* am at the helm!" Mrs. Hamilton says drolly, "It turned out that the program had already gone down the drain."

Mary Bethune was a brilliant fund-raiser, unexcelled at ringing the doorbells of wealthy men she barely knew and coming away with bequests of hundreds of thousands of dollars for her school. She had tremendous presence, and an enormous sense of theatre. She would sweep regally, head held high, to the speaker's platform, face her audience for a moment, and then say, "Ladies and gentlemen . . ." and there would follow a long, pregnant, dramatic pause. Then she would say, "I stand before you in all humility. . . ." The audience would gasp.

She also, no doubt, had an enormous ego. She once told a friend how she handled speaking engagements at racially mixed gatherings in the South. She always came up to the speakers' table last, so as not to create any embarrassment about where she should be seated. She would then deliver her address. "Then," she said, "I leave the auditorium during the standing ovation."

Mary McLeod Bethune was deeply conscious of her own blue-black color — almost obsessive about it. Though she insisted that she thought her color was "beautiful," she repeated this theme so often that some suspected that, deep down, she had secret doubts. Still, she used her color as a symbol of the purity of her race and, by transference, to the purity of her purpose. She did not have a great sense of humor on the subject of color, or on any other subject, but she did have an ability to deliver pithy comments — some of them, surprisingly, almost antiblack. "Negroes," she once said, "are not very smart. But they're very *wise*."

She could also express herself in a way that was quite poetic. Charles Turner is a young Atlanta white who directs the United Board for College Development, a facility that develops a variety of programs to aid traditionally black colleges. As a young boy, Turner met the legendary Mrs. Bethune, who died in 1955, and she apparently was taken with him, as he was with her, and he was particularly struck with something she said to him. It was a remark intended for him, as a white, but it might also be taken to heart by blacks — Old Guard and new-rich, fair-skinned and dark — as they struggle for achievement, status, recognition, for parity with whites and for some sort of racial unity in America in the late 1970's. It might even have been an item included in Charlotte Hawkins Brown's little etiquette book.

Mary Bethune had just come back from a trip to Switzerland, where she had been struck by the beauty of the rose gardens that bloomed along the south-facing shore of Lake Leman. "There were roses of all colors," she told young Turner. "There were white roses, pink roses, yellow roses, and red roses. There was one variety of rose that was of so deep a shade that it was almost black. And I realized that all roses bloom if you give each variety an equal amount of sunlight." Looking at him with her arrestingly deep brown eyes, she said, "You're a young man. You've got a long life to live, and a lot of sunlight to shed. Make sure that your sunlight shines on all the roses."

23

Peeking Ahead

"ONE THING THAT CAN BE SAID FOR THE BLACK UPPER CLASS,"
says one black woman with more than a touch of pride, "is
that we're always nice to our servants." This comment,
with its curious echo of the classic statement of the gentle-
woman of the Old South ("We were always good to our
slaves") is an indication of the growing emphasis placed, by
middle- and upper-class blacks, on *niceness*. In addition to
a nice house in a nice neighborhood, with nice things to
go in it, with nice schools for the children, and nice places
to go on holidays, today's black elite wants nice manners,
nice speech, and to be regarded as nice people.

Under the Kennedy and Johnson administrations, which
created federal educational programs, extended loans to
small businesses, initiated such notions as Head Start, thousands of poor blacks were helped out of ghettos, into colleges and graduate schools, and into the mainstream of the
American middle class. In the Nixon years and following,
these programs have gradually begun to go out the window,
but their accomplishments remain and what they did cannot be destroyed. In the decade between 1960 and 1970, the
number of blacks employed in technical and professional
occupations increased by 131 percent, and the number of

black clerical workers increased by 121 percent. There have been qualitative as well as quantitative changes. There is decidedly a new maturity among the black middle class, and a new sophistication. They have left militancy behind them, have relaxed their guardedness, dropped at least many of the chips from their shoulders in favor of becoming nice, middle-class Americans. Nowhere was the new quality of black life exemplified better than at a recent staff meeting of a large Midwestern hospital, when someone casually mentioned having bought a pair of Gucci loafers. None of the white doctors or social workers in the group had ever heard of Gucci. But a pretty young black nurse had. "Gucci makes a wonderful shoe," she said.

To be sure, many white professionals — notably doctors and lawyers — complain that the federally funded programs put many blacks through colleges, universities, and graduate schools who were not qualified, and that blacks, in too many cases, were given passing grades and, eventually, degrees that they did not deserve simply because it was the easy way to avoid a racial hassle. This may be true, but it is not the point. The point is that *they got their degrees*. Now a sifting-out process will take place, and the truly talented will separate themselves from the less talented, the cream rising to the top. From this cream will certainly emerge the black upper class of tomorrow.

As part of the increased maturity and sophistication of this emerging class, other changes are taking place. Black speech is changing, for one thing. As recently as fifteen years ago, for example, it was almost always possible to tell whether the person one was speaking to on the other end of the telephone line was white or black simply by tone of voice or inflection of speech. Today, differentiating between white and black voices is much less easy. The colleges have done this. The new college-educated blacks are also more interested in integrationist conversation than in the African nationalist "rap" of a few years back. Though the mothers and grandmothers of this generation may have preoccupied themselves with such matters as whether one had "good hair" or "bad hair," today's educated blacks talk freely and easily about the advantages and drawbacks of black hair texture, even with their white friends and acquaintances. The colleges have also undoubtedly eased the young blacks' suspicions about whites and whites' motives and have also caused whites to be less distrustful of blacks. The intangible "differences" between the races, at least on the educated level, have begun to seem much less apparent. Already, in most parts of the country, there is much more social integration and intermingling between the races, and this will doubtless increase even further. As this happens, interracial marriages will probably also increase — slowly, but perceptibly.

The black Old Guard — particularly the older people among the Old Guard — may continue to prefer their quiet, conservative lives, their old neighborhoods, and to content themselves with their small circle of "visiting friends." But the new middle class of educated blacks is already beginning to eclipse this smaller group in economic importance, and to push forward toward business and political success in an important way rather than to view success in terms of the security, honesty, and probity exemplified by the Pullman porter or the government clerk. As the new middle class moves into the new upper class, improving, as it goes, its style, speech, tastes, and niceness, it will not so much expand as solidify, taking on more and more values and attitudes that will seem almost indistinguishable from those of middle- or upper-class whites. This is beginning to happen already, as blacks moving upward are eschewing Cadillacs in favor of compacts and station wagons. In the future, no doubt, there will be a proliferation of black country clubs.

As blacks grow more secure with their new status, black

society will cohere and become less divisive and competitive. But stratification within the group will result, as it always has in any upwardly mobile society, and there will always be "certain people" at the top of the social pecking order. And as more and more blacks become successful, the more they will be resented by the less successful and, inevitably, the gap between the educated and successful blacks at the top and the ill-educated poor at the bottom will seem wider and more unbridgeable.

In America, social class has always been defined by money more than anything else. Once money comes, manners and social "polish" follow, as a rule, in time. The newly rich of any color or ethnic group are always quick to surround themselves with costly possessions, things, the flashy trappings of wealth — whether they are the late Mrs. Horace Dodge, a former schoolteacher, who bought herself a huge yacht and a necklace of pearls the size of pigeons' eggs, or John H. Johnson, covering the walls of his closets with fake fur. You get back, as the saying goes, with what you get — though to an older moneyed class this attitude might seem a bit vulgar. As money in families ages, it becomes boring. One grows tired of one's yacht and lets it sink, as Mrs. Dodge did, into the mud of Lake St. Clair. One begins to underplay one's possessions, and to distance oneself from one's wealth, and to cultivate other areas. While the haves try to get away from their money, the have-nots are doing just the opposite. As more blacks become haves, and become accustomed to their situation, they, too, will become more reluctant to flaunt what they have got, and probably take on the quiet ways one associates with the American gentry. In a way, this is too bad because, as a corollary to this, they will also lose what is currently their special vitality, their brash charm, their distinctiveness — that wonderful raffishness — just as the German Jews did when they turned from scrappy peddlers into stolid city burghers with top hats and town houses.

George Johnson has said, "If a black has enough money today, he can live anywhere he wants." This is without a doubt true, and Johnson proved it by moving peacefully into an otherwise expensive, all-white suburb. But what Johnson overlooks is the fact that his is not the *most* expensive neighborhood on Chicago's North Shore. What was a peaceful move to Glencoe might be a somewhat less peaceful move to, let us say, Lake Forest. In matters of real estate, tremors of fear are still felt in white breasts when a rumor circulates that a black family wants to buy a house in an all-white part of town — not fear of violence, but simply a fear that valuable investments will be lost if an area "begins to go black." Whites have seen too many neighborhoods go downhill when blacks moved in, and have heard too many lurid, often exaggerated, tales of others. What they have not heard are the many less interesting stories of white neighborhoods that have become integrated and remained stable. At the same time, blacks themselves who live on pleasant, integrated streets feel the same sort of fear when a neighborhood is threatened with becoming "too black." Not long ago, a prosperous young black couple from Mississippi moved into a house on such a pleasant and integrated street in Cleveland where a prominent black surgeon and his wife also lived. The doctor's wife paid her new neighbor the customary housewifely call, bringing a cake she had baked as a welcoming gift. But in the course of her visit, the surgeon's wife said, a trifle tersely, "This has always been such a nice neighborhood. I do hope you're going to keep it that way." The message was quite clear, and as more and more blacks move to "nice" streets, more and more pressure will be put upon them to keep the streets nice — by their fellow blacks.

To avoid this pressure, it seems likely that as a new black upper class emerges there will be more and more elegant, well-manicured all-black suburbs like Collier Heights on the face of our land. Of course, government efforts to enforce integration, in matters such as busing, will stem this process — which is why so many upper-class blacks oppose busing.

Not long ago, in Cincinnati, Oscar Robertson and his wife were considering buying a house on Grandin Road. Grandin Road is perhaps Cincinnati's most prestigious address. With the grounds of the Cincinnati Country Club on one side, and the curving Ohio River on the other, the street is lined with imposing hillside mansions with sweeping river views. With the news that the Robertsons might become the first black family on Grandin Road came waves of anxiety and doubt. There was no question that the Robertsons were exceptional people and would make splendid neighbors. Voted the National Basketball Association's Most Valuable Player, a former co-captain of the United States Olympic Gold Medal team, a former guard with the Cincinnati Royals and, later, the Milwaukee Bucks, Oscar Robertson was not only eminently respectable, a gentleman, but also a national celebrity. One should be proud to have him in one's midst. But still, it was Grandin Road. The Robertsons were black. Cincinnati likes to think of itself as a bustling, up-to-date, Eastern town, not a Middle Western backwater, but it still carries a bit of the flavor of the antebellum South. There was a great deal of agonized soul-searching on Grandin Road. People took sides. Hackles rose. Some neighbors stopped talking to other neighbors. People who did not live on Grandin Road called the Grandin Road people bigots and snobs. Grandin Road bitterly denied these allegations. And so it went.

In the end, the problem resolved itself when Robertson decided against the Grandin Road property and bought a house in another part of town. Grandin Road was much relieved. A showdown had been avoided, at least for a while.

Oscar Robertson's new house is in a fine, affluent neighborhood. But it is not quite as fine and affluent a neighborhood as Grandin Road. For Oscar Robertson, the choice of second-best seemed the most sensible, the most peaceable solution for his family — at least in 1976.

And so the black and white races move tentatively but steadily together, like confluent streams moving slowly from disparate sources toward a delta meeting in the future. Everyone knows that the meeting must take place. Not yet, perhaps. But soon . . . but soon. From her pink — or black — cloud, Charlotte Hawkins Brown, looking down on the progress of the converging streams since her departure from this earth, must in all likelihood be pleased with what she sees. As an educator, she was a fervent believer in education and its power to "lead out." As an authority on etiquette and manners, she was an ardent believer in taking things slowly, easily, tactfully. Though many of her views strike blacks today as hopelessly old-fashioned, she was in a sense, a forerunner and an advocate of much of what is happening today. Much could be accomplished, she knew — given patience, politeness, and time. "Keep at it," she might caution. "But remember that you're black, and different — a rose of another color, as dear Mary might say — and be smart."

Name Index